Glasgow: Tales of the City

GLASGOW
TALES OF THE CITY

JOHN BURROWES

MAINSTREAM
PUBLISHING

EDINBURGH AND LONDON

First published in Great Britain in 2001 by
MAINSTREAM PUBLISHING COMPANY
(EDINBURGH) LTD
7 Albany Street
Edinburgh EH1 3UG

ISBN 1 84018 462 0

A catalogue record for this book is available
from the British Library

Typeset in Sabon
Printed and bound in Great Britain by
Mackays of Chatham

This is my city.
A Billy or a Dan
or an old tin can.
Hail Glasgow, stern and wild,
fit nurse for an aggressive child!
from Tom Wright's 'This is My City'

Contents

Foreword

Rarely has a book series been so self-generating as *Great Glasgow Stories*. When I first started this project a number of years ago, I thought that one book would surely suffice, but, during the course of my research, I uncovered so many other fascinating stories that I ended up writing another volume entirely – *Great Glasgow Stories II*. And now, here I am on a third collection which has required as much reluctant selection as the previous two of the amazing people and incredible events that have made up the fabric of this great city of ours over the past century or so.

My research has uncovered everything from the mundane to the truly bizarre. For instance, when I was trying to get a feel for life in the city during the nineteenth century by studying the newspaper advertisements of the era, I discovered the strangest newspaper advert. It had been placed in the hands of the newspaper's advertising department by a Glasgow-based bank – which happened to be the biggest bank in Scotland at the time – informing its customers that it would not be opening for business on that particular day. The reason – it had gone broke! Can you imagine the panic that must have caused – not just in Glasgow but throughout the country. I knew previously about the fall of the great City of Glasgow Bank, but hadn't realised the full extent of the ramifications it had throughout the United Kingdom – the heartache and suffering it caused to those who had been investors, bringing penury and the poorhouse to many former shareholders and creating severe unemployment throughout the country as scores of firms were forced out of business, having lost their money.

Like many, I had always known that Glasgow-born Jim Mollison was one of the greatest pilots Scotland had ever produced. I often passed the tenement house in Pollokshields where he grew up, reading the plaque outside his close, dedicated to Glasgow's greatest flier. It wasn't until I researched his story further that I realised quite how remarkable this character was. Here was a real-life Indiana Jones; a man who flew his little Gypsy Moth solo all the way from Australia to England, landing at night in the darkest of jungles and by day in remote Arabian deserts. Mollison crossed vast oceans and, deprived of sleep for most of the journey, went on to break the Australia–England record in what is regarded as one of the greatest feats in aviation history. He made many more record-breaking flights including solo trips across the North and South Atlantic Oceans, and became a household name in America to such an extent that in New York they gave him a ticker-tape reception and Hollywood begged him to become their next big star.

Robert E. Kingsley is widely recognised as the founding father of modern sportswriting. Better known by his nom de plume – Rex – he reported for several decades on every major sporting event in Scotland and his writing still stands the test of time today. In his day he was a real star, walking the streets of Hollywood and Broadway, rubbing shoulders with some of the great legends of American sport and showbusiness, even being introduced to the President.

This collection also includes the moving account of a dying man in a small council flat in an eastern suburb of Glasgow who was somehow, miraculously, given another chance to live. The story of John Fagan, the man from Queenslie, is a compelling testament to the faith and dedication of one family and their religious beliefs. The full story of two of Glasgow's more memorable characters – the comedian Lex McLean and the actor Mark McManus, Scotland's favourite TV policeman – are also included in this third volume of tales from Scotland's great metropolis.

Acknowledgements

Books such as this are only possible with the help and advice of a great many people. Among those who so willingly contributed their services in the making of *Glasgow: Tales of the City* and to whom I am so greatly indebted are the writers and journalists Sandra Ratcliffe, Phil Davies, Alex Cameron and John Millar; veteran showbusiness writer Gordon Irving; former BBC producer Ian Christie; Bob Main of the Scottish Music Hall Society; for their great knowledge of boxing and boxing officialdom, Tommy Gilmour and Gerry Woolard; Helen Vincent, Faculty of Law, Glasgow University; Norrie and Pat Kingsley of Clarkston; the late Monsignor Tom Connelly; Paddy and Kathleen at the Catholic Media Office, Glasgow; Father Alan Chambers and Father Gerry Prior, of Livingston; May and Joe Smart, of Livingston; John Conway, of Livingston; Colin MacMillan and the staff of the *Daily Record* library; and all those who so dutifully serve and help at the Glasgow Room of the Mitchell Library.

Chapter One

Legendary Lex

Like a rare and special breed, the traditional Glasgow music hall comedian is a dying species. From that long and legendary line of Scots comics came a character remembered as one of the most outstanding of his time. He had a long nose, a whine in his voice and prided himself on being ordinary looking in his trademark bunnet and horn-rimmed specs – he was more like a meter reader than a crowd pleaser. But few were more memorable than Lex McLean. Although he was enjoyed all over Scotland, Glasgow was closest to his heart, so much so that he used the 'I Belong to Glasgow' tag for his souvenir programmes.

Lex McLean packed out the punters' own Pavilion theatre for years, and Glasgow audiences loved him. Accepting the mantle of King of Mirth left behind by the great Tommy Morgan, McLean topped his predecessor's record attendance at the theatre and so established himself as one of the truly great entertainers in a city that saw some of the best – Tommy Lorne, Jack Anthony, Jack Radcliffe, Dave Willis, Sammy Murray, the Logans, the Droys, and many more in a tradition that goes back to the last century and the very beginnings of the music hall.

The introduction of suggestive material into his comedy

routines – a daring move in the 1950s and '60s – earned him the nickname 'Sexy Lexy'. Compared to comics of today and to material that appears to begin in the sewer and head down that way, McLean's own brand of humour was probably more saintly than sexy but at the time it was risqué in the extreme. He didn't swear and wasn't overtly salacious, but he was a master of the *double entendre*, leaving it to his audience to decipher. And it didn't take much decoding: 'Did you hear about the lady barrister who made a fortune with no briefs?'; 'Diana Dors is in hospital. She was badly crushed trying to play the accordion'; 'Bus driver becomes father for the eighteenth time. That's the trouble with bus drivers, they don't know when to stop'; 'There's a women's meeting in London for equal rights and one forceful speaker gets up and says, "As long as we are split the way we are, man will always be on top"'; 'Did you hear about the call girl who had an educated mother? She was two streets ahead of her.' On and on the gags would come – political correctness something in the distant future – with jokes and material that would have horrified the PC luvvies of today.

It was the same with the football team he supported. No diplomacy or eggshell-treading there. McLean was a Bluenose, with a capital B. A proud and lifelong season-ticket holder at Ibrox, he never refrained from letting everyone know it. 'I am a Bluenose and I've never tried to disguise the fact. I'm a Rangers fan, but I'm not a bigot, or anything like that.' And, of course, there would always be a mention of one or the other of the two principal Glasgow teams in his stage routines: 'My favourite football team? Shush . . . you know who'; 'My favourite smoke? The Celtic cigarette – you cannae get a draw out of them'; 'So Jock Stein arrived at Celtic Park, and when he rapped the door he heard Bob Kelly singing "The Sash My Father Wore".' Just as he wasn't politically correct, neither was he sportingly correct, as those typical gags show. But this vociferous and oft-proclaimed Rangers' support did nothing to deter legions of Celtic supporters from his audiences and he didn't hesitate to make the

Rangers team the butt of his gags if they were off form and playing badly: 'Do you know any good jokes?' a punter asks Lex. 'Aye, there's 11 of them playing at Ibrox'; 'A burglar stole the trophies from Ibrox and Parkhead and got £2,000 more for the Rangers cups because they were antiques'; 'There was a fire at Ibrox and Davie White ran about shouting "Save the cups!" and everyone rushed to the tearoom.'

Lex was the old-fashioned, professional jokester. He didn't have the funny face or the infectious grin like Bob Hope, Frank Carson, Eric Morecambe or Tommy Cooper, faces that made you laugh out loud just by looking at them. Neither was he a Billy Connolly, poking fun at life itself. Nor did he need the props or the cross-dressing of Baxter or Emery. Lex, instead, had the prime ingredient for his brand of funnyman – a computer-like memory that could continuously download megabytes of humour from one-liners to funny stories to comedy situations and more. As soon as he had an audience in front of him, Lex went 'on-line': the memory bank processing the required material for a normal show's duration – around two and a half hours – during which he would entertain with his endless quips, cracks, put-downs, spoofs, gibes, japes and gags.

He wasn't really inherently funny, being a somewhat sombre, shy loner in his private life. It wasn't that he was an unhappy man, it was more just that he seemed that way. A real Jekyll and Hyde whose metamorphosis occurred as soon as he walked on stage. It's been said that he suffered the same kind of syndrome as the great clown Grimaldi – so mirthful on stage, so melancholic off it. As the story goes, Grimaldi went to see his doctor during one of his famous bouts of depression. When he described his symptoms, the physician, not knowing who his patient was, suggested that he needed cheering-up and that he should try going to the theatre and seeing Grimaldi in his show! Likewise, perhaps a night watching Lex McLean in action might have similarly cheered up the Scottish comedian.

Telling jokes for him was a business, not a pastime. Talk to the likes of Billy Connolly or the late Chic Murray and a whole host of other funny stage performers and they'll have you in stitches because they simply can't stop being funny. It's their way. It wasn't Lex's. He wrote and collected funny jokes and situations then regurgitated them to earn a living. And just like any other tradesman, when the day's shift was over, the shutters would come down and he would leave his workplace for another day. His unique take on humour set him apart – Lex McLean had few rivals.

Lex McLean was born Alexander McLean Cameron in Clydebank in 1908. The younger of two sons, his was a typical working-class Clydeside family – his father was employed as a moulder in the town's huge Singer factory. Lex's older brother emigrated to the United States when he was just 18 and never returned to Scotland. He died on the other side of the Atlantic.

Lex attended Radnor Primary and then Clydebank High where he was good enough to be made captain of the school football team and not much else, by his own confession. He was a wayward child and not academically minded, his only ambition was to be a soccer player. Unruly and ill-disciplined, he was a habitual truant, and was eventually expelled from school. Aged just 14 he went to work instead. His first job was in a local butcher's shop, but things didn't work out so he joined scores of other young Clydesiders on the shipyards, where he worked at John Brown's. Here again are similarities with Billy Connolly who used to base much of his early material on the life and times of the shipyards; the funny men and their 'crack' shared with colleagues. But this was not the case with young Alexander McLean Cameron. He never settled to yard work and culture: you had to be up and ready to begin a hard day's graft by 6.15 a.m. with the gates slammed shut precisely seven minutes later – stragglers beyond that time were barred from starting work until lunch break, losing half a day's precious wages. The closing and the opening of the gates were orchestrated by the work's sirens, grimly reminiscent of the assembly-line drudgery in Charlie Chaplin's classic film satire *Modern Times*. McLean found little joy in his days as a shipyard apprentice, saying it made him feel like he was in prison: 'You went in and came out like cattle. It preyed on my mind a lot and I thought it must be hellish to go through life like this.' He never stopped searching for an escape route.

Next to sport, McLean's other great love was going to the theatre – no rare activity in those pre-TV days. Every Greater Glasgow locality had its own live entertainment venues – Clydebank had four vibrant theatres. There was the New Gaiety on Elgin Street at the corner of Glasgow Road with seating for 1,400; the Empire on Glasgow Road boasted 'all-electric lighting' for the comfort of its 1,300 audience; the Cinema Varieties on Graham Street had its own tearoom and featured films as well as live entertainment; and the Pavilion on Kilbowie Road was the biggest of them all – built just after the First World War, it housed an audience of 2,000 on handsome oak seats made by disabled soldiers. Such variety in theatre and entertainment was typical at the time of numerous small towns throughout Scotland which supported a vigorous and buoyant showbusiness industry, employing hundreds of entertainers and support crews.

The entertainers themselves were as diverse as the theatres and locales in which they gigged. A typical bill playing at the Clydebank Empire on Glasgow Road, from around the time when Lex was a young man, would show Elroy, 'the armless wonder whose feet perform the actions usually delegated to the hands'; Cora Corina, a 'quick-change artiste'; Ernesto, a 'comedy and musical equilibrist' (a comical tightrope walker!); G.W. Fyvie, the Irish comedian and expert dancer; and the Lavaines, 'in patter and harmony at the piano'. The best nights for Lex were Fridays at the New Gaiety when they conducted amateur contests. The theatre issued a standing invitation to anyone who considered they had talent – 'comic and sentimental singers, clog dancers, Highland dancers, cake-walkers (performers of a modern dance with intricate steps), musicians, Irish and Scottish comedians, song and dance couples and tug-o-war teams'. A bizarre and eclectic mix that goes a long way to rival so-called state-of-the-art entertainment these days. When he could afford it, Lex would also attend other nights at the theatre, the non-amateur nights when touring revues would be featured. He was greatly impressed by those performers and more so by the lifestyle that they led, or at least, the kind of lifestyle he imagined they led. To Lex they looked great up there on stage, happy and relaxed. They were always so clean and colourful too, not like the grime and sepia of the shipyards.

The reality, of course, of the life of a stage performer was an entirely different story. Behind the make-up and the colourful costumes was a similar kind of hard-working life, where wages in the main would be on a par with those of the men in the shipyards and life was lived out of a suitcase on endless tours around the country. When you weren't travelling or entertaining, your time would be spent in dingy boarding houses – 'digs' as they were called – insalubrious places like Clydebank or Coatbridge, Airdrie or Alloa. None of this, however, deterred the young Alex Cameron who remained as determined as ever to join the world of showbusiness. He would meet and chat as often as he could with these itinerant performers, soaking up their hair-raising stories of some of their Friday and Saturday night audiences. 'I'm telling you, lad,' they would say, 'if you can survive the night without getting a rotten tomato in the face, then you can consider yourself either lucky or that they liked you, or else they were too busy fighting among themselves to be caring.' But that was the way of it in those days for the troupers who danced and sang, joked and tumbled and juggled their way around the scores of small theatres and halls throughout the country. They had to win bookings in the small coalfield towns of Fife and Lanarkshire before getting a chance to appear in the more prestigious theatres of Kirkcaldy or Lanark or Dumfries, and they had to like you there if you had any chance of hitting the big-time in places like Perth, Ayr, Inverness or Aberdeen. The hallowed halls of Glasgow and Edinburgh were a chance of a lifetime and the only staging-post that really confirmed you were going places.

Although they could barely afford it, Lex's parents scraped together enough every week in order to send their younger son to piano lessons. Those lessons were to lay the foundations of a better life for Alex, but not by the route which his parents had intended. Lex often mentioned to his mother his interest in going into showbusiness and it had horrified her to the extent that she expressly forbade him to even think about it. While his teacher introduced him to the intricacies of the classics, the small clubs in his home town opened him up to jazz. For Lex, ragtime and boogie were much more appealing than Rachmaninoff or Bach, and by the age of 16 he became a popular performer of the honky-tonk scene in and around Clydebank. And just as audiences adored him, the young Lex quickly learned to love the appreciation of an audience – perhaps there was something magical about showbusiness after all.

His mother by now had learned about these clandestine appearances with the local jazz group, and was bitterly disappointed when he told her he was seriously considering quitting his apprenticeship at John Brown's to look for work on the stage. She refused to speak about it and when he left home to start his new career – with a new name, Alex Cameron becoming Lex McLean – all she would say to acquaintances was, 'He's travelling', implying he was employed as a company rep.

Lex's proficiency on the piano earned him an audition as pianist for a summer revue called The Pierrots and he was overjoyed when the show's producer gave him the nod and the job was his. Lex was in showbusiness – real showbusiness. It didn't matter that the venue was Girvan and that it was an open-air event on the sea front, or that the wages were £3.50 a week, from which he had to pay for his digs – usually about £1 a week – and for food. He had never been so happy and was gaining experience of facing really sizeable audiences for the first time, occasionally leaving the piano behind and accompanying some of the other performers with his accordion. When it came to the end of the season, however, he was confronted with the perennial problem entertainers used to face year in, year out. Where do you go when the show is over?

It was early autumn, just after the September weekend, when all the summer shows around the country closed for winter and hundreds of entertainers would find themselves out of work. They never confessed to being unemployed, of course. No one in showbusiness ever does. 'Resting' is the word. McLean couldn't face up to the prospect of returning home and admitting he was out of work thereby fulfilling his mother's worst fears about his chosen profession. So, instead of heading north for Glasgow, he went south for Stranraer and took the ferry to Belfast. All he had were his last wage packet from Pierrots, his accordion, and an unflinching optimism that something would eventuate. He would do what many out-of-work entertainers did back in Glasgow – earn a living from busking to the nightly queues at the cinema theatres. As luck would have it, however, he didn't have to busk for long, as a man approached him on one of his first nights and offered him the chance to join his show. His production was about to take off on a tour round Ireland and, with half a crown signing-on fee in his hand, Lex willingly accepted the deal.

The show, as it turned out, was unlike any other he had ever witnessed before and made the one he had just left in Girvan feel like it had been Broadway. The Irish show consisted of just four people: a yodeller, a singer, Lex with his accordion, and the wheeler-dealer who had recruited Lex in the first place. His operation consisted of hiring venues in small country towns, then acting as master of ceremonies, introducing his cast of three acts with a build-up that Elvis would have been proud of. After each had done their turn, back they would all troop on stage for one final performance, at the end of which their effusive MC would appear – and conduct a raffle! Like the show, the raffle was an anything-goes affair, the prizes being a weird collection of items he had picked up somewhere on the road – a set of false teeth, a few cheap dishes, maybe even some second-hand clothes he had collected at the market in the previous town. It all added flavour to the evening and after the raffle was over and his 'stars' had done their turns, the audience would then be asked to stack their chairs for the rest of the evening's entertainment – a dance. And the orchestra? Lex and the other two performers, of course. Such was showbusiness in the late '20s but it was to prove a tremendous learning experience for the ingénue performer Lex McLean.

Eventually, at one of these small venues, Lex was asked to stay on as the permanent accordionist for the village dances and, with more money on offer, was able to leave the touring production. The new job saw him through to the following spring when work in the business back in Scotland was more readily available, the entertainment season beginning to crank up again. By this time he was considerably improved as a musician, having mastered a few other instruments, including the concertina, saxophone and the bagpipes! Because of his versatility, it made work easier to obtain and within days of returning he secured work in a touring revue followed by a variety of jobs in cinema pit orchestras – each theatre would hire its own musicians as backing for the silent films and as an accompaniment to the live performers who would make up half the show.

Just as Highlanders in those days would meet on Argyle Street, under the bridge they were to call their Umbrella, showbusiness folk at that time would gather outside Lauder's bar, down Renfield Street from the Pavilion, at the corner with Sauchiehall Street. At weekends crowds of them would stand around the four corners of the intersection gossiping and chatting about the entertainment world in Scotland – who was dating who, who was booking who, who was doing well, who was doing badly, who was heading for stardom and who wasn't, which acts were starting up, which ones were breaking up. Lex would be there regularly, picking up what information he could about likely spots for himself. And so he learned about a new act just formed which involved 'blacking up' – or, in other words, appearing as a black man. It was a popular stage transformation in those non-p.c. days and set out to mimic the rhythm and blues of American Negroes. Lex's act was called The Five Duskies!

Playing sax, accordion and piano, Lex and his four dusky stage mates were a big success and got bookings one after another in a succession of theatres throughout Scotland. On his next tour Lex substituted the black make-up for tartan. One old picture has him dressed from head to toe in tartan and looking like the real Hielan' Laddie. Appropriately, the show was called The Imperial Scots and was a big success – touring not only round Scotland, but across England and Ireland as well. Lex remembers this show as 'a very posh effort'. They were, in fact, an all-tartan concert party which went under the full title of Jock Downes's Imperial Scots. Jock acted as the master of ceremonies for a show which consisted mainly of various musicians and singers, including Jock's sister, a soprano. According to Lex, the show made Downes a fortune, its tour seemingly endless and pulling in expatriate Scots for a big part of its audiences wherever it went. But perhaps he remembered it more than other shows because it was the first one in which he played a comedy part. Among his other roles, Jock Downes was the show's humourist, but after a while he started to include Lex in his routines, who took to his new role more than admirably so much so that Downes started to feel threatened by Lex's talent and would often be heard saying: 'Keep it down, Lex.' But that's showbiz!

When his long tour with the Imperial Scots was over, instead of heading for Lauder's corner, Lex had other ideas and decided to take matters into his own hands. He got in touch with two contemporary performers whose work he respected, Roy Allan and Jack Radcliffe – the latter going on to become one of the star comedians of his day in Scotland – and together with some others they set out on a tour similar to that of the Imperial Scots. There was no comparison between the two shows – Lex and his friends put together a highly professional troupe. They would often joke together about how amateurish Imperial Scots were, with Jock Downes standing out front performing his nightly routine which never varied. As Lex would describe it, 'There he was, in a dinner suit, his hands clasped in front of him, and supposed to be a funnyman.' They would do much better, they assured each other, before taking off on a tour round Ireland. The Imperial Scots got the last laugh, however. Amateurish or not, their show continued its successful tours whereas Lex and his friends ran for just nine weeks, during eight of which they actually lost money. It was only on return to Stranraer from Ireland that they finally got a full house, highlighting the uncertainty of their profession to Lex and his partners.

In later years, when Lex had become an established top-of-the-bill act, he would remember fondly those difficult and unpredictable days: the various acts in which he appeared, the many other musicians from those small pit orchestras who became his workmates, and some his lifelong friends, the different theatres with managements as varied as their audiences and the anticipation and excitement of those meetings outside Lauder's and what might accrue from them. 'It was a struggle, of course,' he was to tell a showbiz correspondent in the 1980s, 'but far more fun than showbusiness is now. Today it is purely the survival of the fittest. It had something exciting about it then and when you went on tour, it wasn't just for a few weeks, it could be a year or more, and that was just to do the rounds in Scotland. Showbusiness back in those days really got a grip of you and made you feel that you were really doing something to entertain people. It kept you going on tours when sometimes you didn't think there was going to be a tomorrow.'

Undeterred by the disastrous Irish tour, Lex, Allan and Radcliffe formed yet another revue troupe, this time called The Meltonians. Maybe it was the name. More likely it was the cast – all solid and seasoned performers. Whatever the reason, their new show was a smash hit. They toured continuously for the next four years – from church halls, to village halls, to town halls, to big tents if necessary. Sometimes it was like the days of the old 'gaffs' – the touring circuses who would bring and erect their own marquees on location. At Crieff the venue provided for the show was a marquee, but it was Lex and The Meltonians themselves who were left to erect it. The old 'gaffs' had experienced joiners to do such things, all the Meltonians had were experienced jokesters. 'We hadn't a clue how to put it up,' remembered Lex. They had arrived at Crieff on the Sunday and collected all the material for putting together the big tent. Late on the Monday afternoon they were still hard at it, but at least they had the canvas big top in shape and the stage assembled. With the tent erected, the team turned to the few remaining jobs still to be done, like putting all the seats in place, the piano on stage and, as the show didn't start till eight o'clock in the evening, arrange the lighting. It was then they discovered they had neither piano nor lighting. Someone came up with a solution about a piano saying that their landlady had one she was willing to lend them. But how were they to move it? Someone suggested the old, faithful, universal form of transport usually reserved for occasions like this – particularly if you were short of cash and in an emergency – a coal lorry. A horse-drawn one, that is. The landlady was so horrified at the prospect of her good piano going anywhere near the old coal cart that had arrived outside her door that she doggedly refused to let it be touched. But, as they always say, the show must go on. And it did, with neither piano nor lights, in the gloom of an unlit tent, with music provided by Lex and his accordion. But, surprisingly, it didn't deter the following night's audience and they had another packed house. Only this time they had some lighting, having borrowed a collection of old Tilley paraffin lamps, which kept the staff occupied between acts running around and regularly pumping the pressure burners to keep the tent illuminated.

Just like Crieff, other towns provided similar surprises for the touring Meltonians. At Aberlour one winter none of them could find accommodation. It seemed showbusiness people had an unsavoury reputation locally and it was only after Lex made an appeal from the stage at the end of their first performance that they were able to get fixed up.

The cast shared the takings from the show, on a percentage basis of course – Lex, Roy Allan and Jack Radcliffe as organisers taking the biggest share. But with audiences being the inconstant commodity they were, the share out could often be more than disappointing. At the Beach Pavilion in Saltcoats they were an enormous success, taking in nearly £300 for the week, something of a record for the venue. Yet just down the road a little, at Irvine, the total takings on their opening night came to less than £1, to be shared between 12 of them. The following Saturday, however, they cleared more than £35 – again to be shared – but enough to stay on in the town for another week of performances.

The uncertainty of the cashflow was eventually to prove too much for Jack Radcliffe, who told his partners that he wanted a wage rather than a share. And the wage he wanted was £25 a week. Accommodation at the time was still only around £1 a week, so Jack's demands were a little optimistic and eventually he left the show.

Jack, from Bellshill, had started life as a performer in the most sober of circumstances – as a member of the Bellshill Baptist Church Male Voice Choir. From chorister he had graduated to regular appearances on the Friday talent nights in his local theatre, the Airdrie Hippodrome (it was on Hallcraig Street) in which he called himself 'Airdrie's Own Komik'. Having survived that, his progression through the industry pretty much paralleled that of Lex McLean. Perhaps it was having known the hard times that they did which made them more fiscal minded than most. And in Radcliffe's case, money was a determining factor for him as he demonstrated later on in his career when he put shekels before scruples. In the late 1950s Radcliffe accepted an advertising offer from an oil company in Australia for which he was paid a small fortune. The role he had to play was that of the archetypal 'och aye the noo' tartan Scot who was billed as 'the meanest man in the world'. Part of the deal included having his own cabin on the flight to and from Australia, the best hotels and a chauffeur-driven car everywhere he went and him promoting frugality.

After his split with McLean and Allan, Radcliffe had gone on to some considerable success as a solo performer, billing himself at one time as 'Scotland's Greatest Comedian'. Radcliffe is perhaps best remembered as starring alongside Jimmy Logan in the sophisticated and long-running *Half Past Eight Show* at the Theatre Royal and Alhambra. Radcliffe was replaced by a comedian from Fife called Tommy Loman, and the show carried on as before.

Only after the Second World War did comedy start to play a bigger role in the stage career of Lex McLean. By then he had been in the business for more than a quarter of a century, but principally as a musician and show administrator-cum-organiser and, as he so often said himself, he treated the business strictly as a trade. At that time stage comedians had assistance with their routine – the feeds as they called them – and Lex found himself getting more and more work on that basis, progressing through the ranks till he was giving the come-on lines to some of the top comedians of the day, including men like George West. West was another of the great Glasgow characters who made his name in one of the most animated theatres of that time – the Grand in Cowcaddens. The Grand was one of those places which, to be kind, you would describe as 'lively'. A more honest summation would be that they took no prisoners. An old vendor would stand by the main entrance selling clay pipes, four for a penny. They were easily broken into small bits and hurled in the direction of the stage at acts the audience didn't like. Their amateur nights on Saturdays were infamous. George West survived them and regularly earned his four penny fee for having done so. But the story goes that George fled the audience at the Grand when they started throwing potatoes.

As well as feeding lines to West, Lex began working with the Logan family, as assistant to Jack Short, or Pa Logan, the father of Jimmy Logan. Lex was to credit the Logan patriarch with having taught him the comic's trade the hard way. He would say that anytime he asked Pa what his routine would be for the next sketch, the reply would invariably be: 'Just come on stage and see what happens.' Which was certainly one way of learning improvisation. After the Logans there was similar work with a variety of other comedians doing everything from stand-up comedy routines to knockabout sketches, which were always popular with theatre audiences. Playing the funnyman was a new departure for McLean and he quickly won a reputation for his slick timing and delivery. The funnyman who really wasn't a funny man was enjoying his new role, particularly when it came to counting his wages on a Friday.

By now he was represented by the famous Galt's theatrical agency who arranged his performances and eventually urged McLean to do his own comedy work on the basis that he was now getting more laughs than the stars with whom he was working. They booked him into a pantomime at the Palladium – the one in Edinburgh, that is – giving Lex his first big solo spot as a comedian. His agents again noted his popularity and as a result they secured him a slot in the variety show, again at the Palladium. This show was the making of Lex and confirmed his agents' instincts – in his first season at the theatre the box office achieved record levels of ticket sales. Ironically, it was Edinburgh that first fell in love with the man whose reputation was always linked with Glasgow. The record run at the Palladium convinced theatrical agents that Scotland had a new comedy star on their hands but, despite his success, Lex's mother never did see him on stage, his choice of profession remaining a bitter disappointment to her right till her death.

For Lex it was the big theatres in the big cities from now on – no more changing into costume in some village hall's broom cupboard with a sticker on the door saying 'dressing-room', or trudging round small country town streets cajoling suspicious boarding-house landladies, convincing them that showbusiness folk really were honest and respectable people, or battling against the elements to erect a stage in a marquee that had no lights.

During his time spent as a top comedian at the Palladium, Lex proposed to Grace Dryburgh, from Leven in Fife. Grace was a dancer with the Burntisland Entertainers, star attractions at the Beach Pavilion, and they had first met when he was the pianist of the show in which her dance troupe appeared. They had known each other for about 11 years when Lex proposed, this time when they appeared in the same show at Arbroath. With his future more secure than it ever had been, marriage was the next logical step, and in June 1950, in the presence of a few showbusiness friends, they became man and wife in a civil ceremony at the Martha Street registrar's office in Glasgow. After more than 25 years of a suitcase existence, Lex was also able to buy the first house he ever owned, a flat at the King's Theatre end of Bath Street, in Glasgow.

By now there were offers from Glasgow's Metropole and Empress theatres, and the management at the Edinburgh Palladium assured the Galt's agency that he could come back anytime. After some 25 years in the business, the good days were starting to roll for Lex McLean. It was goodbye to tents and Tilley lamps.

Perhaps it was his success at the Empress in Glasgow that first won over the city's audience in a big way. The Empress at St George's Cross, established in 1913, had a reputation among comedians as being a 'difficult' theatre to work. When Charlie Kemble, one of the great music hall veterans, went there after a highly successful provincial tour, he had to bolster his show with another comedian in order to keep the audience happy. Lex had no such problems there and not for the first time he found himself the talk of Lauder's at that Sauchiehall and Renfield Street junction.

By the mid-'50s the career of the legendary Tommy Morgan was coming to an end. He wasn't by any means an old man, but was plagued with ill-health and retirement loomed. For years Morgan had dominated the comedy scene in Glasgow, an incomparable giant in that brand of humour unique to the city. Morgan was the punter's punter, big and gallus, and there was nothing assumed about that Brig'ton bravado and humour, he really was from there. He packed them out in pantos at the Metropole and the Alhambra and for some 19 successive summer seasons – a record for any single performer in Britain – he was the star performer at the Pavilion, generating more money for the theatre than any act preceding him. The takings generated by McLean at the Empress and Palladium were noted by his agent and the theatre's owners and he was booked for his first season as the main act in the Pavilion show. He never looked back and audiences took to him and his own special brand of humour every bit as much as they had to Morgan.

Always the pragmatist, McLean realised that he couldn't simply copy the style of Morgan. Certainly there would have to be a concentration of what Glasgow liked best – the laughs that came with a 'half and a half' – but it was important to him to set his own precedent. 'I had seen years ago that the cycle of comedy was changing,' he said. 'What's important in this business is that comics must watch trends. What was okay years ago would die a death today. I listened for instance to a Harry Lauder record on the radio the other day and I almost fell off my chair groaning. He belonged to an era without radio or television.' Nowadays, he would add, Lauder couldn't raise a smirk at a church social.

A completely new character evolved: a touch of the cheeky Max Miller at times, a flavour of the sentimental Bud Flanagan at others, two legends he greatly admired. His brand of comedy was more suggestive than salacious, more risqué than rude, hence his nickname 'Sexy Lexy', a misnomer dismissed by McLean as 'rubbish'. Similarly, he resented being called a 'dirty' comic. 'One newspaper writer said I needed an X-certificate and then went on to say in another story that the show *Hair*, with its frontal nudity and four-letter words, was something not to be missed. That doesn't make sense to me. I don't use four-letter words and I'm not dirty. I leave things to the imagination, but you do need a broad sense of humour at my show.'

McLean's 'broad sense of humour', however, did occasionally land him in trouble. When he played to a packed house at the new, state-of-the-art municipal theatre in Motherwell the theatre's director at the time considered Lex's jokes so blue that he had second thoughts about inviting the show back again. In his report on Lex to the town council halls committee, he said the Glasgow comedian's jokes had been 'nothing less than crude' and that he had been greatly disappointed with McLean's 'over-spiced material'. He did add, however, that the show as a whole had been good variety and well done and that 'the audience loved it'. When asked for his comment, another committee man, the town's provost, said that while he hadn't seen the performance, if blue material had been used, 'then I would not approve'.

Lex was unperturbed by the Motherwell frowns: 'I'm a robust comic who tells robust jokes. But I'm not blue. If I was, surely my audiences wouldn't roll with laughter the way they do. I go in for adult comedy. You must move with the times. If your comedy is tame, you won't last. If you cater for the kids you'll end up in the gutter. The world is more cynical now. People just won't pay to listen to the soft stuff.' Examples of McLean's material from this time include: 'The Brush family have just had a little bristle. Of course, they swept together'; 'I was at a party and this girl said to me, "Let's play hide and seek. If you find me you can have anything you like. If you can't find me, I'll be in the bedroom."'; 'Teenagers have terrible problems in this day and age. I heard one the other day saying "Hey, maw, can I wear a bra?" and the mother replied, "Certainly not, George."'; 'I said to the wife one night, "Don't undress at the window. The neighbours will think I married you for your money."'

By today's standards, Lex's take on comedy was tame by

comparison and he always knew where to draw the line. 'I wish people would stop telling me dirty stories,' he would say. 'Just because I go in for this adult comedy, some people think that I'll enjoy listening to dirty stories. I can't stand them. I try to be polite, but I get away from people like that as quickly as possible.'

As McLean himself put it, he hated being known as a Blue comic. His preference was to be known as a Light Blue one – his love of Rangers Football Club featuring prominently in his routines.

When asked his opinion of the Celtic–Rangers saga, Lex declared: 'I'll make no bones about it, not being an osteopath [he loved that gag!], I am a Bluenose and I've never tried to disguise the fact. I'm a Rangers' fan and also a Protestant, but I'm not a bigot, or anything like that. I joke about the Rangers on the stage because the people who come to see the Lex McLean Show are a sporting crowd. They expect gags about sporting personalities and – note the word – personalities. I crack about big Frank Haffey [a Celtic goalkeeper] because he is a personality, just as I gag about Baxter or McMillan [Rangers stars] because they're personalities. I sometimes say "I'm tired, or I tire easily – like McMillan in the second half!" People might say I'm a Celtic fan because of that. I'm not, of course, I've got a season ticket at Ibrox and, if I can, I go to every home game when I'm in Glasgow.' He goes on to add that, 'Although I'm a Protestant, I wouldn't say I'm a churchgoer. I'm not in the Lodge, and I'm not interested in what religions people have. For instance, I'd say almost half the cast of my show just now are Catholics. I don't mind that! If they are good and talented, they could be Jehovah's Witnesses, Mohammedans, The Nameless Ones, or Arabs. I'm not interested in that side of it. All I'm looking for is talent, not religious maniacs, and believe me, I'm not one.' Despite being the most fervent of supporters, McLean never shirked from praising the occasional Celtic player. 'Even with all the larking about Rangers,' he said, 'Celtic players come and see me and my show regularly. Pat Crerand was in the night he was married. Billy McNeill is there often. And Charlie Tully came here just after he had joined Celtic and had roasted – and I mean roasted – Rangers at Parkhead. I made a speech about that, pointed to Tully, and said, "That man on Saturday turned on the greatest display of football I have ever seen in my life." Does that sound as if I'm biased against Celtic?' Nor was he ever slow to take a swipe at Rangers when he considered they needed it. Rangers officials and directors would often come under fire from him. And so too did their Protestants-only policy of that time: 'I've made a lot of jokes about Rangers but the one I like best is about the seal who is signed on at Ibrox and scores 50 goals in a game by nodding them in. Then he's sacked. Why? Because Scot Symon [Rangers manager] found out he was eating fish on a Friday.'

When Jim Baxter, one of the club's legendary players, had a wages dispute with Rangers' management, McLean made a public outburst on his behalf.

> I think Baxter is right in his stand against Rangers, wanting more money than the others. Why shouldn't he get more than them? He's better than the others. He's an attraction, a crowd puller, call him what you want. But he pulls in fans to Ibrox. Without being big-headed, he is in the same position as I am. I get more money than the rest of the acts in my show because people come to see me. The other acts are paid according to what I think they are worth. The same should apply to footballers. They are entertainers whether the directors like that or not. Baxter is an entertainer. They should differentiate with him, just as Rangers or any club would differentiate when they come to transferring players.
>
> You've got to think of entertainment and what the people want. If they don't want apples even if they're green, you've got to give them oranges. Baxter, for instance, would fetch more than the others who are not

quite in his class. The argument, as I see it, is unanswerable. It's time that the people who run Rangers understood that.

The fact that he was never at any time invited by any of the Rangers directors to watch a game with them proved something of an irritant to him. And he would constantly remind the Ibrox bosses of it. In one of his outbursts he declared: 'As I say, I'm not bigoted. I just like the 'Gers and don't care who they beat. Not that I get any privileges from the Rangers people. I'm just an ordinary fan of the Rangers. I go to their rallies and I've often said some hard things about the fact that few, if any, directors of the club ever turn up at the supporters' rallies. I suppose that hasn't done me any good with the directors. I couldn't care less. I still think I'm right anyway. If the Celtic directors turn up at their supporters' rallies, why can't the Rangers directors do the same thing? If I go to games in Edinburgh, or in Dundee or Aberdeen, I get the red-carpet treatment from the clubs there. I don't from Rangers. I don't look for it, even although I've been a fan all my life, ever since I played football for Old Kilpatrick and captained Clydebank High School.'

One of the biggest upsets he had with the club was when Rangers FC was going through one of its less successful periods, a regular blight which seems to affect both the Glasgow clubs. Lex had made a succession of cracks about the Rangers' performances as well as making manager Davie White the butt of a series of jokes – 'Davie White is raising the sinks at Ibrox by two inches – to keep the boys on their toes'; 'A Pakistani was walking past Ibrox last night and was heard making the comment, "I'm glad I'm no' white".' The jokes obviously got to them and White hit back in a Sunday newspaper advising Lex to 'lay off Rangers and not poke fun at the club or their players'. Referring to the fact that McLean was forever boasting about being a Rangers' fan, White added: 'He must be joking. If Lex is one of our supporters, then all I can say is who needs the opposition?' McLean was unrepentant, his retort to White being that he had been a lifelong fan of the club and topical jokes like the ones he had been making were the sort of thing his audiences appreciated. 'I've given Rangers more publicity than anyone. They're my team and will continue to be my team. I'll cheer them when they do well and crack jokes about them to the best of my ability.'

During his first appearance on stage after White's outburst the irrepressible Lex made a special point of cracking more jokes about them to an eagerly waiting audience. Within minutes of stepping on stage he told them: 'I've only got five jokes. It would have been 11 if the manager hadn't been so nasty.' The audience roared and Lex warmed to the subject. 'I'm here tonight because Davie White threw me out of Ibrox'; 'Did you hear about the people who were complaining about their rates. One man paid £56 a week but his neighbour only paid £7. But he had an excuse. His windows overlook Ibrox.' Following the show, he told reporters that he would not be changing his routine because of criticism by White. 'I wouldn't last long telling jokes about Ayr United, would I?' Perhaps the whole soccer scenario was just one big joke to McLean. One of his favourite gags certainly saw the funny side of it all: 'Do you know how football all started? It all happened in a mental home when the patients got a paper ball together and started to kick it about. The warders watched from the sidelines and then took the ball from the inmates and played themselves. The loonies have been watching it ever since.'

Accepted and established in the late '50s as the successor to Morgan at the Pavilion, Lex remained there for the next 15 years, smashing every box-office record the theatre had. They valued him so much that once, when they had taken him seriously over a remark about doing his shows from the nearby Empire Theatre, he was threatened with a court interdict to stop him. In 1966 he signed a unique showbusiness deal with the management, virtually guaranteeing him a contract for life with the theatre. His regular shows there were to continue until 1972, playing twice nightly, six days a week, six months a year. A programme cost 3p, the best circle seats 43p and the cheapest berth in the balcony 13p, 15p on a Saturday.

And how they loved him! Even the most critical of press reviewers would have had to admit his shows were the best variety productions in the country. He couldn't have got more favourable newspaper coverage had he been paying for it. Some headings for the 1963 season read: There's No Stopping Lex's Laughter . . . 'The Greatest' Says Lex – And He Is! . . . Lex Is Back With A Bang . . . Lex Is King Of Comics . . . Gales Of Laughter . . . Lex Is A Riot . . . The Best Lex Yet! . . . Bawdy But Still Scotland's Best. Archie McCulloch, the veteran *Evening Citizen* showbusiness writer of the day, was obviously a big fan of Lex. His review for that 1963 season read: 'The McLean show opening was a rip-roaring success and I enjoyed every minute of it. The man with the toughest job is the fellow with the scissors who must cut the show down to a twice nightly size. Better he than me. There is no doubt that Lex knows exactly what his public wants and gives them it.'

A whole range of performers at that time appeared with him, including the Alexander Brothers, the Humblebums folk trio, which included Billy Connolly and Gerry Rafferty, Andy Stewart, Roy Castle, Stan Stennett, Walter Carr, Helen Randell, Margo Bentley, May Bentley, Donna Douglas, the Kool Kats, Don Dale and the Melody Makers, Moxon Young Girls, Colin Stuart, Johnny Victory, Bobby Vincent, Charlie Sim, the Glen Dale Trio, Aileen Manson, the Parnells, the Barrie Brothers, Graham and Shack, Chris Lamb and the Universals, and many more. A rare collection of the fabled, the famous – and the forgotten. The shows themselves were the classical mix of the traditional variety fare, featuring acts with singers, others with dancers, some with both, music from solo accordionists and folk trios, impressionists and jugglers. All, of course, interspersed with the man himself, sometimes doing it solo, at other times with a feed, or with three or four others in a sketch, and now and then with the entire cast.

Being the star, Lex would feature more than the others, often taking part in up to eight of the 17 separate acts. As he said himself often enough, it was him they came to see. And he was right. Perhaps they loved him most in the comedy sketches, which encompassed a variety of scenarios, often enacted with a manic tempo and as much subtlety as a pantomime lampoon. You know the sort of stuff. Husband comes home from work early. The milkman boyfriend hasn't left the house yet. He hides beneath the bed. The rest you can imagine, with much shouting, running and jumping. Each sketch came with its own title – generally a good indication of what was to follow. Among the more memorable of those from his time at the Pavilion were 'What the Butler Saw', 'Medical Muddle', 'Scream-agers', 'Pools Winner', 'The Launderette', 'Pub Crawl', 'The Lollipop Man' and 'The Gossipers'.

McLean was also a shrewd businessman and had learned over the years, particularly from his touring days, that the more authority the star has over a show, the more autonomy it gives them in every aspect of the performance. He always assumed complete control over his Pavilion productions, picking and choosing his regular cast members, including Margo Bentley, Ronnie Dale and the comedy couple Carr and Vonnie, as well as selecting his guest artists. He sometimes made the wrong decision. For example there was one young group he used on his show who, after a few performances, he told should forget showbusiness and go and look for regular jobs. 'You'll never make a success as singers,' he advised them. A year later they were one of the best-known acts in the country, being billed as the Bachelors! When he heard about their success, Lex, unfazed, was to comment: 'For my show I thought they were just three "neuchs". They just didn't register.' He advised another performer one night after the show that he better be up early the following morning. When asked why, he retorted: 'So you can make it in time for the broo.' It was his way of telling the man he was sacked.

As well as control over the casting, his financial backers gave him autonomy over all the takings, including a share of the bar and programme takings, a deal that made him the highest-paid entertainer in Scotland, with all the trappings that brings. The flat he shared with his wife Grace on Bath Street became a luxurious villa called 'Loch View' on the seafront at Rhu, with its own private tennis court. From its bay windows he could look out to the marina where his cabin cruiser bobbed in the Clyde estuary. In the driveway was the special Mercedes Benz, a rare sight in those days, and the couple would holiday on the Costa del Sol, an exclusive and wealthy resort in the 1960s.

Despite all the lush trimmings, Lex always had his feet on the ground. The bright lights and late nights were not his scene. He might play at the Villa Marina at Douglas on the Isle of Man, earning one of the biggest fees in the history of seaside entertainment, but when the show was over, it was a fish and chip supper from the corner shop and home to bed. Towards the end of every show at the Pavilion he would regularly be heard asking the time. He had a train to catch, you see! It was all part of his 'this-is-just-a-job' syndrome. It didn't matter that he scaled the heights of showbusiness in Scotland, earning more than any of his predecessors, what he did, in his view, was just a job. You memorised your lines, learned your routine, you went on stage and performed, and when it was over, you went home. Lex McLean would briskly walk from the theatre down Renfield Street for Queen Street station to catch the 11.15 p.m., the last Blue train for Helensburgh. He would even take his final bow dressed in a smart business suit, collar and tie, so that within minutes of the curtain coming down, the expensive Burberry would be on and he would be striding out of the theatre door almost before the first of the stalls patrons had reached the exits. Once on the train, his broadsheet newspaper unfolded, there was absolutely nothing to mark Lex out from any other professional working man, be it lawyer, bank manager or stockbroker.

Ian Christie was a close associate of Lex's back in those days at the Pavilion. Ian, who went on to become a BBC TV producer/director, was working at the time as a writer for the theatre performers' paper *The Stage*. This involved going backstage at the various theatres and, at the Pavilion, punters would congregate just outside the No. 1 dressing-room. Two women came there every night and set up a canteen for the cast and it was certainly the place to be in order to get interviews and all the latest showbiz gossip. Lex too would come for his regular cuppa. Ian remembers the many occasions he would be in Lex's dressing-room when the stage manager would come in for a drink, and fill him in on the evening's performance – how much the takings were for the night etc. And on Friday nights it would be Lex himself who would go round the cast giving them their pay packets for the week. 'Although there was this distance about him,' says Ian, 'the real truth was that he was really quite shy, the opposite to what he came over on the stage where there was a confidence about him verging on arrogance.' This natural hesitancy perhaps explained his desire for complete control over his shows. As he explained to Ian, 'You see, Ian, being in charge of everything like I am, then there is only myself to blame if a show is not a success. I'm not like the others who are told what to do by theatre owners and producers and the like, and that's the way I like it.'

It wasn't until much later in his long showbusiness career that Lex was introduced to TV audiences. He had been shy of the medium, in all probability more than a little nervous of it. However, by the late '60s, Ian Christie changed all this. Ian was now working in television as a producer/director at the BBC and had been involved in such highly successful productions as The Stanley Baxter Show. It was after completing one of the Baxter series that the BBC in Glasgow were casting around for new shows. It was the style of things then that producers like Christie would be given a small budget, something in the region of £100, with the challenge not only to come up with an idea for a programme but to make a pilot film to show senior management.

Ian had wanted to make a situation comedy, which was something of a challenge on such a budget, requiring as it did getting a cast together, hiring a small hall somewhere to do rehearsals and, of course, finding someone to star in the programme – all for that £100!

Despite the fact that, by this time, Lex was the biggest name in showbiz in Scotland, he had so far shunned television, preserving his professionalism as a stage performer. He also knew that even highly successful entertainers like himself could die a very quick death on the medium.

Having got as close as anyone could in those days with McLean through those regular meetings at the Pavilion – and not many did – Christie put the idea to him about the possibility of a TV sit-com series. They would have to convince the bosses at the BBC, however, with a pilot show. McLean was intrigued with the possibility and accepted the conditions, which included rehearsing from Monday to Friday in a Byres Road church hall, then filming on the Saturday and Sunday, all for his share of the £100 budget which in real terms amounted to a fee of around £10.

'As it turned out, he was to be a delight to work with,' remembers Christie. 'There were straight actors supporting him, all with their scripts. This was something completely new for him – the scripts and remembering all the movements which were required. But when Lex came along for rehearsals, he had no script. He had remembered every line and was word perfect.'

The rehearsals went well and so too did the filming. Only one thing was missing – an audience. The budget hadn't allowed for that. And situation comedy, as you can imagine, falls flat if it doesn't have the accompanying laughter. It's gin without the tonic, lemonade without the fizz, Ernie without Eric. But it was Stanley Baxter who was to come to the rescue. That same day he had been recording one of his shows before a live audience at the BBC and when it was over, Christie had asked him if he would mind if his audience stayed on to watch the pilot film of Lex's show. 'I could name some who would have refused such a request, but not Stanley, who was marvellous and told us to go ahead.' Baxter's audience lapped up what they saw of the 15-minute film they watched and, to Ian Christie's delight, the BBC controllers' reaction was similarly favourable, extending an invitation to Lex to be the star of a new sit-com series. There were more than a few raised eyebrows, both inside and outside the BBC, about the senior controllers' approval of such broadly accented material, social gulfs being much wider in those days. One producer revealed that none of the BBC management had ever heard of Lex before Christie's film, the Pavilion was very much a punters' palace. They had even disposed of the likeable and cheery Cliff Hanley's morning radio programme because the popular writer's accent, which was by no means glottal, seemed to be more East End than West End. How things have changed!

Lex himself was just as surprised at the reaction, commenting that 'these BBC types, with their beards and sweaters, are different from the folk I usually work with. And the BBC canteen at Queen Margaret Drive – it's a' mince and mini-skirts!' Lex agreed to the series deal, produced and directed by Ian Christie, and, after the success of the 1968 show, two further series were commissioned right up to his last show in the early 1970s.

Shortly before that last TV show, however, ill-health struck McLean and in August 1971, at the age of 63, he collapsed at the wheel of his Mercedes en route to the King's in Edinburgh to perform in the last week of his summer show. He was rushed to the Western General Hospital where a double brain tumour was diagnosed and for a while it seemed Lex would never joke his way back on stage again. There was a major operation and a long convalescence for the man they were now describing as 'the last great music-hall comedian in Britain'. During his time resting at home in Rhu he continued to plan future performances, putting together a routine for a pantomime he had been booked for that Christmas in Dundee. When his doctor learned about that, however, the advice was to call it off, which he duly did.

While his Lex McLean Show went on without him at the Glasgow Pavilion, Lex persevered with ideas for other shows in 1972.

It wasn't until the spring of the following year that he was fit enough to return to work – one of his first appearances being as a guest with Grace on a TV panel show called The Generation Gap, a precursor of The Generation Game. When he got to the studios, he was asked if he would like to do a warm-up for the audience. And like the old trouper he was, McLean had suspected such an invite and had already prepared a routine. Ian Christie witnessed that performance and has said that after coming through what McLean had, that evening was something special. 'When I looked over at his wife Grace, I'm telling you the tears from both of us just flowed.'

Lex went on to do his fourth TV series, the only one recorded in colour. And he performed the occasional stage show too, which friends said was his way of showing he could still do it. But ill-health plagued him and in 1973, while performing at one of these shows, he collapsed once more and was rushed to hospital. His succession of illnesses had taken their toll and he was to be rarely seen in public again. Just two years later, in March 1975, Lex McLean died at his home in Rhu at the age of 67. Hundreds attended his funeral at Clydebank crematorium, North Dalnottar. Among the mourners were several directors of Rangers Football Club. Only speculation can provide the joke Lex would have cracked about that.

Chapter Two

The Miracle Man

One of Glasgow's most inexplicable and remarkable events took place in the top-floor flat of a council tenement in the Queenslie housing estate one morning in late winter, 1967. A man lay dying in the living-room of the house. He had been suffering from stomach cancer for the previous 18 months. His condition had deteriorated considerably and the cancer was now at a terminal stage. The family doctor had left him the previous evening, rightly concluding that, in medical terms, all hope for him was gone – he would be dead before the new dawn, if he even lasted that long.

Surgeons, too, at the hospital, had reached similar conclusions having discharged the man believing the abdominal cancer to be too advanced for any beneficial intervention. The only medical procedure left was what they termed 'symptomatic treatment', that is, treatment designed to alleviate the man's discomfort in the weeks, possibly days, he had left. His wife was advised on terminal care and the man himself was anointed by a local priest with the last rites of the Catholic Church.

Dawn on Monday, 6 March 1967, witnessed the beginning of a phenomenon which in due course became headline news – a story which would consume the fascination and interest of people throughout the world and which eventually became the subject of medical inquiries in an attempt to ascertain just what happened to that dying man. While interpretations and explanations vary widely, one thing is certain, whatever metamorphosis occurred inside the diseased and withering body of John Fagan that morning in March 1967 can only be described as miraculous.

As his wife Mary looked, John's pain-racked body, which had been convulsing throughout the night, suddenly went still. No breathing could be discerned. Even when she laid her head on his chest there was silence, the deathliest of silences. Faithful Mary's hope for her stricken husband finally vanished. But incredibly, inexplicably and only minutes after his lifeless slump, John Fagan re-emerged into consciousness. He was alert and aware as he hadn't been for weeks and he even requested food. John went on to make a full recovery and lived a fit and healthy life for more than a quarter of a century to come. When Dr Archibald Macdonald, the family doctor, called by the house just after daybreak, fully prepared to make out a death certificate for the patient who had been all but dead the night before, he was instead greeted with the incredible news that John had asked for something to eat. 'Good God!' the doctor exclaimed, 'I don't understand this. That man should be dead. I saw his stomach breaking up. I've seen a miracle.' He added, 'Mary, I'm not the same religion as you, but if you told me that you had taken John to Lourdes, I would have said definitely that it was a miracle.' The simple fact was that Dr Macdonald had no other explanation for what had happened that night, nor was it ever adequately explained medically and John Fagan of Queenslie, Glasgow, became known as the Miracle Man.

Fagan was the very epitome of the average Glasgow man. He was hard working and dignified, as honest a man as he was modest. He worked as a docker. He supported his football team, Celtic. He enjoyed his Friday night Guinness as much as he enjoyed the cigarettes he so expertly rolled himself with his favourite Golden Virginia tobacco shag. He loved nothing more than his big family. He was a good neighbour. He was a Catholic, but perhaps his attitude to religion was more passive than it was passionate. The Fagans initially lived in Anderston, one of Glasgow's first suburbs. In the late '30s, when John and his wife were starting a family, the area still had a community feel about it which did much to overcome the old and crumbling housing. Their first house, albeit just one room, or single-end as they were known, was in an aged and blackened tenement on Whitehall Street. Childhood sweethearts, they had both been born and raised on Whitehall Street and the area was very much their home.

Their environment was one of pulsating forges and pungent horse stables, engineering works and whisky bonds, places that made bread and biscuits, assembled ships' engines and carved ships' furniture, and all sorts of other works and factories whose forest of tall chimney stacks belched hideous brown and black fumes. The loud horns of the many cargo ships on the River Clyde would compete with the shrieking whistles of the surrounding works signalling the beginning and end of each shift. Old Anderston was never a quiet and peaceful place, but it had life and vitality.

When the Second World War came, John went off to serve in the Royal Scots and later the Armoured Corps and an anti-aircraft unit in the Italian campaign. Just two years previously, at the age of 23, he had married his girlfriend Mary, who was four years younger than him. After the war he returned to work in the bustling docks once more, and prudently moved his growing family to bigger and better houses in Anderston – to Lancefield Street and then to a two-room and kitchen with that rare amenity, an inside toilet, in nearby Dover Street. Though they didn't know it at the time, one of the wee boys who lived near them on Dover Street and who joined in all the street games was a certain Billy Connolly.

They continued to live with their six children in Anderston until the early '60s when the first major new Glasgow Corporation housing schemes were being completed. The Fagans qualified for a new four-apartment in Penston Road, Queenslie, one of the sprawl of estates built in the furthest eastern suburbs of the city. The family loved their new house – from the grimy streets of Anderston to a home that looked onto fields and open countryside. It was a whole new life for them, remembers May, the Fagans' eldest daughter. They had been at Penston Road for just over three years when John, aged around 50, experienced the first symptoms of the long illness that afflicted him. He had never been the most robust of men and, at half a century, like so many men of his day, was showing the ill-effects of long years of hard graft at the docks coupled with a life in crowded tenements. His illness began with a general feeling of being unwell and he started losing weight. It was in the spring of 1965 that Mary first became aware of him looking more gaunt than before and when she mentioned it to him, it was only then that he revealed he hadn't been feeling the best for some considerable time.

In the weeks to come his appetite diminished to the point where he was eating very little, some days hardly consuming a thing. Then he began to experience nausea at the very sight of food and began suffering epigastric pains in the upper middle abdomen. At first a stomach ulcer was suspected, some medicine was recommended by the family doctor and an appointment made for a hospital examination. However, about a fortnight later and before the appointment date, he was rushed to the infirmary after vomiting blood. There he was given a blood transfusion and his illness was diagnosed as a peptic ulcer.

Unfortunately, it soon emerged that matters were much worse than originally anticipated. The doctors had ordered a barium meal examination which revealed that John was suffering from cancer of the stomach. He was allowed home from hospital while waiting for a date for the operation which, hopefully, would remove the growth. Eight days later he was readmitted and on

Wednesday, 26 May 1965, the operation was performed. John remained for a further two months in hospital recovering from the operation and undergoing further tests. On 10 July he was finally discharged and as he was preparing to leave the consultant took Mrs Fagan aside for a word. 'It's about the cancer,' he said. He then went on to explain that they had located the disease between John's bowels and stomach. It had also invaded his colon and they had established a colostomy. But during the operation they discovered it had spread so much that they couldn't cut away all the affected parts. 'If we had gone any further with the knife, we would have killed him,' said the surgeon. Then he told her the worst of the news – that there was nothing further they could do. The cancer was entrenched in his body, and spreading. 'He has about six months to a year at the most,' said the consultant. He described how John's condition would deteriorate in that time. 'It might be that he would go through a stage where he would appear to be recovering,' said the surgeon. 'But that would be merely an illusion for after that he would start to go downhill again. And then it would continue that way . . . until the end.' Mrs Fagan was advised to seek advice on terminal care in order to make life as comfortable as possible for her dying husband. In those days doctor–patient relationships were different and John was not told of his condition. So Mary had to face the future alone in the knowledge that her husband had only months to live. For the rest of that year, and for most of the following year, John's progress followed a predictable course. He did appear to be recovering for a while, but as the consultant had suggested, this was just an illusion. At this stage he had already outlived that original forecast of six months. Mary anxiously counted the weeks and wondered if the apparent reprieve would last. During this time John attended the outpatients' department of the hospital for treatment. In November of 1966 he suffered a relapse, his condition taking a sudden turn for the worse with further abdominal pain and serious vomiting, necessitating his readmission to hospital. The only option left was the continuation of symptomatic treatment, that is drugs, including morphine, which would alleviate his pain. It was also the suggestion of the family doctor, Archibald Macdonald, that John be admitted to a hospice to die, suggesting to Mary that no one would be expected to cope with what her husband would go through in the days and weeks ahead, should he last that long. Mary couldn't bear the prospect, however. His presence in the family home was her last ray of hope and nothing would make her surrender that.

For the duration of Christmas 1966, the home on Penston Road was a hive of activity. Their eldest son Joe, who had emigrated to Australia, returned home on hearing the news, as did John's brother Jim, in Sligo, Ireland, where the Fagan ancestors had originated. A bed was made up for John in the living-room where the coal fire was permanently stoked. Cheer and comfort and the proximity of his family were all they now could offer, and they did so in abundance. Visiting relatives and friends were there every day and Mary, with four children still to look after, was never off her feet, confessing that throughout that time she had found herself 'going around in a daze'.

The festive season and the new year had come and gone and in those first few months of 1967 Dr Macdonald called regularly to administer the vital morphine injections and to note the normal regression in the state of his patient, who was following the inevitable route of someone with his condition, someone who was beyond any form of curative medicine, someone who was beyond all hope, except that of his devoted wife. John was now unable to eat, having consumed virtually no food since the beginning of the year. He had weighed 11 stone in good health but by now he was down to around five stone. By Saturday, 4 March, John's condition had deteriorated to what is termed a 'moribund state', that is virtually without life, and Dr Macdonald pronounced that death 'wasn't far away'.

Perspectives as to what happened to John Fagan subsequently depend considerably on one's beliefs. The dying man confounded medical specialists in that not only did he make a full recovery, but he went on to live a fit and healthy life for some two and a half decades after. For those of the Catholic persuasion, the answer is simple, a miracle did indeed occur, and one which is irrevocably entwined with the story of 'Blessed John Ogilvie', a Catholic martyr who died at Glasgow Cross more than 300 years previously.

The Fagans were practising Catholics and members of their local chapel, the Church of the Blessed John Ogilvie, the only church in the country to carry that name. Ogilvie is a revered Glasgow Catholic martyr and every year, together with hundreds of others, the Fagans would take part in the annual commemorative walk. It is strongly believed that it was the intervention of Blessed John Ogilvie that allowed John Fagan a second chance at life.

In 1615 John Ogilvie was executed for his beliefs. In those days Christianity in Scotland was at its brutal worst and, depending on the sectarian leaning of the ruling monarch, hundreds of innocent people were slaughtered for belonging to the 'wrong' denomination. In the case of John Ogilvie his death was down to his defiance of the authorities in early seventeenth-century Scotland by spreading the word of the Catholic faith and refusing to acknowledge the supremacy of the Protestant King James in spiritual matters.

The story of John Ogilvie begins much further north than Glasgow. He was born in Drum, near Keith, Banffshire, the son of a wealthy Calvinist family who raised him in their faith. His grandfather had been treasurer to Mary Queen of Scots, and his father, Sir Walter Ogilvie, had the grand if fearsome title of Commissioner for the Discovery and Capture of Itinerant Jesuits. Among his present-day descendants are the Earl of Airlie and Angus Ogilvy, husband of Princess Alexandra. Despite his spiritual upbringing, the young John Ogilvie became fascinated with the Roman Catholic Church. Even as a boy of 13 he demonstrated an acute interest in the Catholic faith, going as far as travelling to the continent with a tutor to pursue his studies. He was just 14 when he knocked on the door of the College of Douai, in Louvain, Belgium, declaring that he wished to become a Catholic. He stayed there for the next two years, before transferring to the Scots Benedictine College at Ratisbon, in Bavaria. His professors there felt that as a Benedictine monk he would find ample scope in his vocation. However, his true vocation was to become a missionary in his own land. So, from Bavaria he went on to study at the Jesuit College at Olmutz, in Czechoslovakia, proving himself an excellent student and winning a coveted Pope's bursary.

From Olmutz he went on to other colleges in Germany for further theological studies, spending a year in Vienna where he taught grammar. Following this spell as a teacher he continued his studies in France and in Paris in 1613 he was finally ordained as a priest, shortly thereafter he begged his superiors to be allowed to return to Scotland as a missionary. Due to the dangers involved – two of the last priests having recently been expelled – they advised against it but eventually relented after an appeal from the Earl of Angus to the Jesuit Superior asking for missionaries to be sent 'before the Catholic Church in Scotland is completely erased'. At the same time, the Scottish Earl was to warn of the perils such missionaries would face. 'The need for priests is extremely urgent, but I entreat Your Reverence to send none but such as both desire and are able to bear with a courageous heart the burdens and the heat of the day; for persecution increases and those who receive the missionaries are in exceeding danger. It is the law that whoever receives a priest, hears a mass or celebrates one, is liable to be arraigned for High Treason.'

Disguised as a retired soldier now dealing in horses and with the assumed name of Captain Watson, Ogilvie eventually returned to his native land in 1613 after an absence of some 21 years. It was just over a year later that his missionary work was discovered and he was detained by the authorities. When other priests had been arrested previously, they had been routinely deported with a warning not to return. But Ogilvie had committed a much greater sin – not only was he acting as a Catholic missionary, but he had openly refused to acknowledge the supremacy of King James VI in spiritual matters. And that, insisted his prosecutors, was high treason and was a crime worthy of the death penalty.

The trial of Ogilvie was set for the Bishop's Castle, at the top of the High Street in Glasgow on a site now occupied by the Royal Infirmary. It is an area rich in historical detail. Sir William Wallace himself fought one of his famous battles not many yards away on the steepest part of the High Street known as the Bell o' the Brae: an English garrison was stationed at the Bishop's Castle and when they came out to challenge Wallace, they were routed after a fierce clash on the slope of what we now call the High Street.

The initial stages of Ogilvie's trial were something of a *cause célèbre*. While no verdict would be reached at these pre-trial proceedings, the event itself, in today's terms, would have been similar to the O.J. Simpson trial. Thirty prominent officials were chosen as judges, the principal inquisitor being John Spottiswoode, the Archbishop of Glasgow. Appreciating the interest the king had shown in Ogilvie's arrest, Spottiswoode set out to handle the trial with all the skill he could muster, determined to discredit the accused Ogilvie as much as the Church to which he belonged. At the same time he was also determined that the proceedings be conducted with full recourse to the legal rules of the day so that he wouldn't stand accused of having given the Jesuit an unfair trial. Spottiswoode was fully aware too of the importance of the trial to the king's own long-running dispute with the Church in Scotland, then the Presbyterian Church. King James had been determined to devolve the power of the Church which claimed absolute authority in its own affairs, without justification to the king. A similar stance was taken by the Catholic Church. With the Union of the Crowns in 1603, King James found the State and the Church south of the border far more structured and it was his desire to introduce a similar subservience in the Scottish Church. Now he was faced with the trial of the Scottish Jesuit John Ogilvie blatantly undermining his authority by recourse to a higher power again – the Pope. And that, in Ogilvie's case, was a far more serious offence than missionary work or conducting Mass. Hence the king's wish to be informed of every development in the trial.

On the first day of the trial, one cool and windy morning in early October 1614, the Great Hall of the Bishop's Castle was packed to capacity, the enormous brazier fire at one end of the hall blazing fiercely in an effort to bring some warmth to the freezing structure. People had come from every part of the city and from outlying villages and hamlets; those who couldn't get into the building stood outside and picked up scraps of information from those standing at the rear of the Great Hall. They expected the accused – especially as he was considered by many to be a traitor – to have the furtive appearance of a criminal, and were surprised by the sight of an erect and muscularly built man who looked directly at the judges and answered their questions without hesitation in a distinctly Scottish accent. They asked him if he was of noble birth, to which he answered that he was, as were his parents in Banffshire. He was more cautious with subsequent questions. Anxious not to betray those who had sheltered him during the months he had been wandering in Scotland, he did not directly answer as to whether or not he had delivered Mass since his return. 'If to do so is a crime, it should be proved not by the oath of the accused but by witnesses,' he replied. The Archbishop Spottiswoode had a more ready answer for those assembled, informing the court that they had also detained 14 other Catholics along with Ogilvie and that there would be no difficulty in obtaining this information from them.

Ogilvie handled further interrogation with similarly oblique answers, explaining that he would only respond to questions he considered appropriate. He said he was not obliged to answer all the court's demands and he would avoid doing so rather than sin. His challenging attitude infuriated a member of the audience, a man of servant class and very obviously a supporter of the prosecution who, in an outburst, threatened to throw the accused into the fire warming the hall. Ogilvie incensed the man further by replying that now was as good a time as any as he was all but frozen with the cold. Order was called to the court and the judges continued with their questioning, persisting with the demand about whether or not he had conducted Mass. This time he replied that such examination of him did not belong to the king's jurisdiction and therefore he was not bound to give them an answer. This exchange of questions and answers between prosecutor and accused continued for some time and, with all the skill of seasoned counsel, hushed the court into rapt attention. When Ogilvie had replied that the authority for his actions came from the Pope whose own command went back to Christ himself, Archbishop Spottiswoode retaliated with the accusation that this was treachery. 'It is treason to assert that the Pope has any spiritual authority in the king's dominions,' he retorted angrily.

But Ogilvie was unflinching in his response, 'It is of faith to hold that he has.'

Upon which reply the judges demanded to know whether he would sign a declaration to that effect.

'With my heart's blood, if need be,' came the immediate riposte.

The packed audience in the castle's Great Hall were mesmerised by the drama unfolding before them. The stilled crowd watched the flurry of activity among the clerks surrounding Spottiswoode and the judges as a piece of parchment was prepared with the declaration written boldly on it. The document clearly stated that the Pope and not the king had spiritual jurisdiction in Scotland. Now, would John Ogilvie sign such an incriminating document such as that, knowing that his own life would most certainly depend on it? One of the clerks summoned an usher to hand it over to Ogilvie who carefully read the penned statement then, as a quilled pen dripping with ink was passed to him, he leaned over in the accused's dock and signed the document.

Court procedures in sixteenth- and seventeenth-century Scotland bear little resemblance to modern-day hearings – no verdict is handed down upon hearing evidence. First of all, the king would have to be informed of what had transpired at the inquiry and while this testimony was being prepared for him from the notes taken by the clerks, Ogilvie was detained in custody, spending the ensuing weeks in the dungeons of the Bishop's Castle. After being held there for more than two months, it was decreed that the prosecution should proceed to the next stage and that Ogilvie be transported to Edinburgh to give more evidence, this time before Royal Commissioners.

Once more he refused to answer directly, becoming involved in a long and acrimonious exchange with the commissioners regarding who had the authority to rule on religious matters. Ogilvie persisted he had committed no crime. The king, he said, had no authority to decree that Mass should not be said. Christ himself had instituted the Mass, therefore the king could not condemn it. That final statement exasperated the royal panel so much that one of the commissioners warned him he could face being tortured. It proved no idle threat – Ogilvie was returned to his cell in Edinburgh Castle and suffered great physical and mental abuse. They slashed him with daggers, put needles between his nails and fingers and pulled the hair from his head, but he remained defiant, taunting them, if they dared, to use the torture known as the 'boot'. The 'boot' was one of the Scottish authorities more specialised forms of torture – as dreaded as the rack, the apparatus used in England to stretch and tear bodies apart. The 'boot' consisted of four stout wooden splits tightly pulled together and when they were clamped around the victim's limb, an iron wedge, like an oversized chisel, was inserted between the splints resting on the leg of the victim. It was then sledgehammered through the limb, causing the most hideous amount of pain as it shattered the leg's muscles, arteries and bones.

After two weeks in the cells at Edinburgh, the broken body of John Ogilvie was returned to Glasgow on a bitterly cold winter morning of 28 February 1615, for the final part of the proceedings – the actual trial itself, conducted in the old Town Hall, immediately next door to the main jail and on a site adjacent to the present Tolbooth Steeple at Glasgow Cross. There was little doubt as to the verdict and workmen busily prepared the gallows for yet another execution before the first question had been asked in the courtroom.

There was little formality, even less procedure about the trial. It was all over by one o'clock and the sentence of death was passed down with instructions that it should be carried out immediately. Within the hour, John Ogilvie was dead and a new Catholic martyr was emerging.

Fourteen years after his execution at Glasgow Cross, supporters of John Ogilvie began the long process of having him declared a saint for his bravery – not an easy status to attain within the Catholic Church, the first stage of the procedure, which took nearly 350 years to complete, was to officially declare Ogilvie 'venerable'. Thereafter Ogilvie's life was investigated in full by a team of church officers. This lengthy process occupied much of the next three centuries, one group passing down their inquiries to the next until the papal authorities were satisfied that Ogilvie was indeed worthy of 'beatification' – the formal declaration by the Pope that a deceased person had showed a heroic degree of holiness in his or her life and was therefore worthy of public veneration. Ogilvie achieved beatification and was endowed with the title of 'Blessed', a sort of Catholic knighthood. His supporters were still determined that the Blessed John be elevated to sainthood and so they proceeded to the next stage of the long process, as laid down by a Pope in the seventeenth century. This involved the substantiation of the proposed saint having given favours in answer to prayers – the requested favours being of the most solemn nature.

As John Fagan lay desperately ill and unlikely to make it through the night, his parish priest, Father Thomas Reilly, in one of his regular visits to the Fagans' home, had suggested they seek the intercession of the Blessed John Ogilvie, whose name was also that of their local church. 'It's going to take a miracle to save John,' the priest had said to Mary Fagan. 'So why don't we ask for one?' Speaking about it afterwards, Mary told how, at the priest's suggestion, she had taken home one of the Blessed John's medals from the church and had pinned it to her husband's pyjamas. 'And every night before we went to bed the children and I prayed and on Sunday in church the whole congregation did likewise for John's life to be spared.'

Still his condition deteriorated to the point whereby on the Sunday morning, 5 March, when Dr Macdonald had called to the house, John was being violently ill. Despite not having eaten for weeks and therefore having no food in his stomach, he had nevertheless been vomiting. This, concluded the doctor after examination, had been as a result of the disintegration of his stomach. He had by now sunk so low, it was not just merely a case of how many days his patient might have left, but how many hours. And Dr Macdonald made Mary aware of just how little time was left by telling her that his next visit the following morning would, in all probability, be to sign the death certificate.

But Mary persevered, as usual, with her prayers that night, noting that very day that there would be the annual march in Glasgow in commemoration of the Blessed John Ogilvie. It was only hours after the end of the march that John Fagan opened his eyes to tell his wife of the dream he had had about a long-dead aunt and then, to her sheer astonishment, he asked for food. The truly miraculous had happened. John Fagan had been brought back from the dead.

Mary recalled in vivid detail the events of that momentous

night. 'When the doctor told me the reasons for John having vomited had been his stomach breaking up, then I thought that was it, especially when he said he would be back in the morning to sign the death certificate. That night John was still breathing, but faintly. I went into the room where he was sleeping. I had left the light off so as not to disturb him but the street lamp outside the window lit the room enough for me to see him clearly. I sat in the chair beside the bed, dozing and waking through the night. John was tossing in pain, and I tried to ease him into a more comfortable position. Then a strange and very frightening thing happened. He began to talk about his Aunt Annie. He had been very fond of her, but she had been dead for ten years. "I thought I saw her," he whispered to me. "She wanted me to go with her."'

Mary was terrified at that moment, terrified that his long battle was over. She stretched out her hand to put on the light by the bed and as she pressed the switch there was a sharp noise and she was blinded for a second by the flash of the light bulb blowing up. Joe, her eldest son, on hearing the noise, came into the room but Mary asked him to leave her alone with his father. 'I wanted the last moments with John to myself.' She kept her solitary vigil for the next four hours, dozing off from time to time as she sat by the bedside. It was about six o'clock in the morning when she awakened from one of these slumbers and noticed that John was breathing in a laboured fashion. He was still – deathly still. Mary moved closer to his side, hardly daring to breathe herself so that she could better hear her husband's respirations. But there was nothing to be heard, neither was there any movement from him. She held her breath once more and listened intently to the silence. She moved even closer to John, laying her head on his chest, but still there was neither movement nor sound. She moved back to the chair again and buried her face in her hands, sobbing for the only man she had ever loved, the dedicated husband whose children she had borne. Never once had she given up hope, but at that moment in that little room in Queenslie, her world seemed to end.

She continued to sit in the chair, alone with her thoughts, when after some time she heard the unbelievable. It was the sound of John's voice. 'Mary,' he said. 'Mary . . . I'm hungry.' Mary Fagan didn't believe what she was hearing. At first she thought the voice must be coming from some other part of the room. But it was his. And it was firmer than the pathetically thin, laboured and whispering voice she had been hearing for weeks. Hugging him tightly and crying in exhilaration, she confessed to him that she thought he had died.

John was not only alive, but was fully aware of what he had been through in those hours immediately previous. 'I had reconciled myself to death,' he told Mary quietly, at the same time recounting his dream about his Aunt Annie. 'But it's so strange now. I've wakened feeling quite different. I feel I can live now. I would even like some food.' Her tears were still flowing when she returned to the room with a boiled egg and some toast, one of his favourite light meals. He was unable to eat it but reassured Mary that everything was different and, though he couldn't manage that meal, the feeling remained that he wanted to eat. Perhaps not now, but the feeling was there of a returning appetite and that's what was different – for the past seven weeks the mere thought of food had nauseated him. That had now gone.

After Dr Macdonald's visit later that morning and his comments about having seen a miracle, Father Reilly then called. He also told Mary it had been a miracle, that the hand of God had been at work in the house.

The world of saints and miracles to those outside the Roman Catholic Church is sometimes difficult to comprehend and all too easy to dismiss. But such is the esteem in which they are held that it is widely believed that even beyond the grave saints have the power to work miracles, that power being passed on to them directly by God Himself as a proven sign of their significance and reputation. As we have seen, the ritual of declaring someone a saint is a long protracted process. At that time John Ogilvie was just one step away from sainthood, having been made venerable, then beatified, the latter bestowing on him the title of Blessed. The Fagans' local priest, Father Reilly, was determined that Ogilvie should receive his final acclaim, that he had been invested, through God, with the power to heal John Fagan; that it was solely through the intervention of Blessed John Ogilvie that the man from Queenslie went on to make a full recovery. At Father Reilly's request, the Catholic Church investigated the matter in a procedure that was to take the next nine years.

The first five years immediately following the incident were designated as 'waiting time', in other words, a period of observing whether the miracle had indeed worked. Had John Fagan experienced a relapse of any sort during those five years, then all the formalities and investigation would have ceased. Never the most robust of men, John's health was nevertheless restored to a condition similar to that prior to developing the tumour. Approximately one year after that incredible night in March 1967, he was back working in the docks again. Two years later, however, he was made redundant, but being an industrious man he was soon back in work, this time as a bread wrapper in one of the city's major bakeries.

As the end of the five-year waiting period drew to a close, Father Reilly, acting as one of the principal promoters for the canonisation of Blessed John, set about the formation of a panel of medical specialists to examine the case of John Fagan and to determine the nature of the mystery cure. The panel consisted of neutral doctors, that is, those not previously connected with his case. It was also important that they were not all Roman Catholics. There was a panel of three, headed by Dr Andrew Curran, senior lecturer in community medicine at Glasgow University, together with Dr Aloysius Dunn and Dr John Fitzsimmons, and they were empowered to investigate and analyse every aspect of John Fagan's illness, treatment and recovery. They were also advised to seek whatever help or advice they needed from the eminent specialists in the field, including Dr

James P.A. McManus, Professor of Medicine at Laval University, Quebec, and a former lecturer in gastro-enterology, and Dr James Shaba, senior pathologist and lecturer at Glasgow Royal Infirmary.

In his report, Dr McManus recorded that following a partial gastroectomy (surgical removal of part of the stomach) on John Fagan for a large gastric tumour, the prognosis could only be considered as poor. Among the several medical reasons he went on to list for this were that the large gastric tumour had ulcerated through to the transverse colon . . . that while the lymph glands did not show evidence of tumour, the lymphatic channels had been invaded . . . and that there were direct tumour invasions of the colon. These had been independently confirmed by microscopic studies made by two other specialists, one from Glasgow University, the other from Edinburgh University. In his summary, Dr McManus reported that John Fagan did indeed have stomach cancer and that after surgery no further anti-tumour therapy was attempted. 'The subsequent history of the patient's illness is entirely consistent with residual malignant disease until March 1967, when he developed a dramatic, abrupt and uninterrupted improvement with return to full health.' He concluded: 'After six years there is no clinical or radiological evidence of residual disease. I can offer no satisfactory explanation for this chain of events. Furthermore, discussion of the case history with other experienced medical and surgical colleagues substantiate this opinion.'

When the panel of doctors handed over their findings to Father Reilly, their consensus was: 'the final verdict was clear. There was no natural explanation.'

Other prominent medical specialists also aired their views: Professor Kenneth Calman, in charge of the Department of Oncology – the study of tumours – at Glasgow University, summarised his position with a statement to the effect that there had been about 250 well-documented cases throughout the world in the previous half-century where cancer victims, pronounced incurable by the medical profession, had somehow recovered. But that had to be weighed against the hundreds and thousands of other people in a similar situation who had died. He agreed that there seemed to be no rational explanation as to John Fagan's recovery. Professor William Duncan, of Edinburgh University, concluded that, although he was not himself a Catholic, he did believe that faith in spiritual power can have some effect.

Dr Gerard Crean, consultant physician at Glasgow Southern General Hospital gastro-intestinal centre, suggested that the mass discovered in John Fagan's stomach could well have been an abscess and not cancer. If this was the case, it could have discharged itself spontaneously, allowing Mr Fagan to recover.

All these various points of view were dispatched to Rome for further scrutiny by two medical experts, including Livio Capocaccia, Professor of Gastro-enterology at the University of Rome, secretary of the Vatican Medical Tribunal and who was often consulted on alleged miracle cures. The two experts concluded that the case should be referred to the next stage again – an examination by a commission of nine doctors, of varying nationalities, appointed for the occasion. Their specific task was to sift through the evidence on presentation in the hope of finding some rational medical reason for Fagan's remarkable recovery. After several months they had found none.

The commission's report was then submitted to the Promoter General for the Faith at the Vatican office – much better known as the Devil's Advocate – at the time an Augustinian priest called Father Rafael Percy. He was the final hurdle in the somewhat lengthy and arduous process. His specific job is to find some avenue of enquiry which will justify renouncing the claim. But he too found nothing and the Blessed John Ogilvie, the man they had hanged at Glasgow Cross all those years ago, entered sainthood on the basis of the inexplicable recovery of John Fagan from Queenslie.

The news from Rome was announced at a press conference in

Glasgow on Thursday, 11 March 1976, the day after Pope Paul VI had sanctioned the sainthood. Most of the medical panel who had been appointed to look into the case were there, as well as John himself, and his wife Mary, to give their side of the story. Cardinal Winning, Archbishop of Glasgow at that time, said they were not asking the public to believe that a miracle had taken place rather that, 'We only state the facts of the case and leave them to decide for themselves.'

John Fagan described how much he had changed since that night nine years ago. His religious convictions were much stronger and he hoped he was a more benign person than before. 'I can't offer an explanation as to why I was chosen to have this miracle, I can only suggest that the time was right,' he said. Going into more detail later, he added that his recollections of that night in 1967 were very blurry. 'I know I was close to the finish. I had a notion if I fell asleep that would be that. I was never fully conscious but I remember praying when I was. I was reconciled to death but then remember waking up and feeling better. I felt that once again I had the will to live. It gives me a feeling of humbleness that I should be part of this.'

The elevation of Blessed John Ogilvie to sainthood was not, however, widely received as good news. Certain among the Protestant community, including some notable scholars, were incensed by the announcement and so began a bitter and public wrangle over the affair, with the Protestant denomination demanding that the sainthood be denounced.

In what was described as 'an astonishing outburst', the editor of the Church of Scotland's official magazine, the urbane journalist and broadcaster on Christian affairs, Robert D. Kernohan, claimed that any future hopes of church unity were being threatened by the news that the Blessed John was being made a saint. 'If Roman Catholics are in earnest about church unity, they will proceed no further in the business of canonising John Ogilvie,' fumed his column in the magazine *Life and Work*. Among the many points put forward in the article was that

Protestants could not accept the mediatory role Roman Catholics allowed saints, the techniques by which they declared their status and the veneration which seemed to elevate saints above the rest of God's people, and that such canonisation would only widen the division between Christian denominations. The doctrine of sainthood was something the Protestant community could not accept.

Kernohan's views were backed by the distinguished William Barclay, professor at Glasgow University and one of the best-known and most revered biblical academics of his day, who commented that there were aspects of the Catholic Church 'which look to us Protestants like superstition. That's what we have here and you can't shut your eyes to it,' he pronounced.

The magazine's articles, however, not only upset the Catholic community but also caused considerable discomfort among many Protestants. The Right Revd. James Matheson, Moderator of the Church of Scotland, slapped down the writer of the piece, claiming that he spoke only for himself and not the Church. He said that the Catholic doctrine of sainthood was alien to that of Protestants, 'But,' he continued, 'if they believe so, why all the fuss? When we think of the really serious issues of faith and morals that face the churches today, one wonders why we should get heated about this one.'

Kernohan countered Matheson's comments by saying that he had spoken to 'large numbers of Protestants' and had consulted the seven-strong editorial committee appointed by the General Assembly before writing the article. Not only were they all in agreement but some members wanted the editor to take a harder line still. Predictably, the Catholic community hit back. The editor of *Scottish Universe*, the Catholic equivalent of *Life and Work*, stated that if there was no mutual respect between the two churches, then any form of friendship or sharing of Christian worship would be shallow and, at worst, hypocritical. Cardinal Gray, the head of the Catholic Church in Scotland at the time, pointed out that the campaign for Ogilvie's canonisation had been going on for more than 300 years and it hardly seemed appropriate that it be called off now. And Tom Winning, then Archbishop of Glasgow, soft-pedalled with a plea that patient, friendly, enlightened discussion had been the hallmark of joint conversations between the two churches up to that point, and he sincerely hoped this would continue. Meanwhile, the letters columns in various newspapers were packed with lively and varying public opinion on the controversy.

After a few weeks, however, the huffing and puffing died down and six months later John Fagan and his wife Mary left Glasgow to fly to Rome where, at precisely seven minutes past ten on the morning of Sunday, 17 October 1976, they played a central role in the colourful and moving ceremony at St Peter's where Blessed John Ogilvie was declared a saint by Pope Paul VI. Bagpipes were played inside the cavernous basilica and the 4,000 Scottish pilgrims who had gathered under the dome of Michelangelo clapped and cheered as John and Mary walked into the church and were ushered to the VIP enclosure for the ceremony. Also present were Cardinal Gray, Archbishop Winning, and other Scottish bishops, Princess Alexandra and her husband Angus Ogilvy, the new saint's direct descendant, and Glasgow Lord Provost, Peter McCann, with his family.

Amid the jubilance and celebration was one voice of protest, ringing out across St Peter's Square prior to the canonisation ceremony. It was that of another Glasgow man, the irrepressible voice of protest, Pastor Jack Glass. The pastor, representing the Twentieth-Century Reformation Movement, had driven all the way from Glasgow to join his followers on the steps of the world's biggest church and displayed a banner which announced that 'Four million Scots are against this canonisation. Ogilvie was a traitor, not a saint.' Predictably, as the newspapers reported the following morning, 'there were some minor scuffles' but, given Revd. Glass's reputation as an active protestor, it probably would have been more of a surprise had he and his converts not turned up.

After the events of that day in Rome, John Fagan quietly slipped into relative anonymity, moving house from Queenslie across the M8 to nearby Easterhouse, then later to a pensioner's flat in Ravenswood Rise in the new town of Livingston, near Edinburgh. His loyal friend and neighbour John Conway would accompany him to the Waverley pub. 'He was a great old fellow,' John remembers. 'He loved his regular bet and I would take his lines to the bookie. And do you know, he was really good at studying form and would have the occasional win for his efforts. John was the kind of man who never had a bad word to say about anyone, except Celtic that is, if they were playing badly! People from all over the world continued to write to him for years afterwards and each received a reply and a medal and prayer card from him. We often used to speak about what he had gone through and he would often say to me that he could never understand why it had been him that was picked out for the miracle he experienced. He would speak about the years that he lived after his miracle as his "bonus" years.'

John Fagan was 79 years of age when in 1993 he passed away peacefully from a stroke in a hospital near his home in Livingston. He had outlived his devoted wife Mary, a brother-in-law who was one of his closest friends, the Pope who had conducted the canonisation service, his faithful family doctor Archibald Macdonald, and Tom Reilly, the family priest at the time of his illness. His remains were taken to the East End of Glasgow to be buried alongside those of his wife, Mary, who had been dead for 14 years. At his funeral service in St John Ogilvie's, Easterhouse, his local priest from Livingston, Father Alan Chambers, spoke about the great humanity of a very ordinary man. Miracle or not, John Fagan was an archetypal Glasgow man who led a quiet, devoted life, devoted to his wife and family and whose down-to-earth humour kept people going when times were hard. As the priest went on to mention, he would frequently take communion to John on Monday mornings in his latter years and, had the Celtic result over the weekend been bad, John would refuse to talk about it. 'I would ask him why he didn't support a good team like Hibs,' said Father Reilly, 'and in that pawky way of his he would reply, "Father, if I had the strength, I would throw you out of this house."'

Chapter Three

Peter the Great

There's a good story told in Scottish boxing circles about the time that the great Sonny Liston – a formidable and fearsome bruiser, also a world heavyweight champion – was in Glasgow. As with legends like Sugar Ray Robinson and Muhammad Ali, he had come to the city at the invitation and sponsorship of the Glasgow boxer Peter Keenan, who had turned promoter on retiring from the ring. Liston was a man with a daunting reputation and had several associates in the criminal underworld. He was a world champion boxer, and had the kind of menacing face that could knock down a building.

As the story goes, Liston attended a function in an upstairs city lounge – the star attraction of a party thrown in his honour by Keenan. Not unusually, Liston was in one of his less congenial moods. He hated smoking and when someone near him was enjoying a cigar a bit too much he instantly flicked it out of the man's mouth. Then he noticed that Keenan was similarly smoking a cigar and loudly demanded that he, too, should put it out. What followed was the kind of showdown movie-makers dream about. Keenan instantly threw back his chair and marched over to Liston, shouting: 'Listen, you may be the heavyweight champion, but I have never lost a fight on the street in my life. If anything is going out, it's not the cigar. It's you.'

What makes the exchange all the more memorable was the entirely different physical make-up of both men. Liston stood at 6ft 1in, weighed around 16 stone, had a phenomenal reach of 84 inches and his 15-inch fist was larger than any previous heavyweight champion in boxing history. Keenan was 5ft 5in and weighed around 8½ stone. One wonders whether David and Goliath had such variance in proportions.

Stories of this ilk abound about Peter Keenan. For example, some years later I went to see him for some background information on a story I was writing. Peter told me to meet him in the dockside bar he owned at the time, in the Broomielaw – not the kind of place you would go for a dry Martini or a gin and tonic. While we were talking, a menacing-looking man, 6ft tall at least, entered the pub and walked up to the bar. Peter was having none of it and immediately jumped to his feet, ordering the stranger out of the bar. The man refused and went for Keenan. There followed what can only be described as a blur of a scuffle and, within seconds, Peter, completely unruffled, was back at my table, tidying his shirt cuffs, ready to resume our conversation. And the intruder? He was picking himself up from the pavement outside. The bar was hushed as the punters gazed at this fearless, little man, Keenan, with some considerable awe.

The best world champion Scotland never had was this handsome young man from Anderston whose biggest failing was that he was singularly independent minded. There are some, of course, who would use other terms to describe him – cussed, obdurate, pig-headed, difficult – and point out how often he had been publicly criticised for being brash and outspoken and on occasions just plain rude. Nevertheless, the boxer, Peter Keenan, could have been, would have been and should have been a world champion. The fact that he never was has little bearing on the exceptional skills, bravery and courage he displayed inside the ring. As it was, Keenan was one of the finest boxers Scotland ever produced. He made more money from the sport than any of the other post-war champions, certainly much more than world champions Benny Lynch and Jackie Paterson. For over a decade Peter Keenan was one of the greatest names in sport, capturing headline after headline, but not all of them for what happened between the ropes.

Peter Keenan was rebellious from a very early age. The second youngest in a family of seven – four boys, three girls – he grew up in one of the poorest parts of old Scotstoun. His background was Irish-Catholic – his great-grandfather had made the journey from County Tyrone in the latter part of the previous century – and so it was decided at the outbreak of the Second World War that some of the family might be safer in their ancestral land and were evacuated accordingly. That wasn't the first time the young fighter rebelled, but it was one of the first occasions that were to come to the attention of the authorities. The young Peter didn't like being away from Glasgow and promptly absconded from his new home in Ireland. It was some days before he was caught and he was eventually returned to Glasgow – all of which delighted Peter.

By now the family were living in Partick and Peter duly attended the local school, where he was described as 'wild and unruly'. One of the few things he did excel at was street fighting. For Peter, school was just one long wait until he was 14 years old and could legally leave. He was desperate to be his own boss and, with the help of his parents – dad sold fruit from a hawker's barrow – particularly his hard-wrought mother, that's just what he did. His mother was well aware of her second youngest son's temperament, his individualism and super self-reliance, and had scrimped and saved a little something to start him out in life. The money came from a dividend from the Co-op, that ubiquitous local saviour of the under-privileged in those days. The dividend – or 'divvy' – was similar in principle to supermarket loyalty cards these days.

Customers became members of their local Co-op Society and

were given their own membership number. Every purchase credited them with another few pence towards their quarterly share of the dividend. For many it was the only way to 'bank' money they knew of and Mrs Keenan had been saving her 'divvy' for Peter. It came to around £12.50, sufficient funds during the war years to purchase a small cart, and a horse to pull it. And with that Peter Keenan, aged just 14, was in business.

Scrap metal was needed for the war effort and dealers paid good money by the load. Wood could be gathered and tied into small bundles which sold as house-fire kindling. There were coal briquettes to sell – produced by the local cottage industry and manufactured from coal dust mixed with small amounts of cement – which were much in demand not only for the great heat they gave out but for their economy.

Peter would fondly recollect the end of his first working day with that little horse and cart when he counted out his takings, remembering to the penny the exact amount: £1, 14 shillings and 11 old pence. It was great money for someone so young. Much more than any of his pals would earn as apprentices, some of them hardly making that much in a week. With his independence firmly established, Peter turned his thoughts to the Army Cadet Force, a popular activity for youngsters then, and the local battalion in Anderston. According to his friends, the local unit was about more than marching and machine-guns, it had a great boxing club as well and, as Peter would often recall, the fact that they gave you a free uniform was as great an incentive as any to become a new recruit. 'It really is a fact,' he said, 'that the boxing business all began for me just because I wanted to get a couple of quids' worth of suit for nothing.'

His actual fighting career began many years before he joined an official boxing club, on and around the streets he knew as a boy. Maybe it had something to do with the pugnacious side of his character, whatever, but there was never any shortage of school playground punch-ups. Even as a young lad he was more streetwise than most, learning fast that to survive on the streets you had to be sharp, particularly if you were gathering wood and hawking steaming hot briquettes. It was that same survival instinct that gave him an edge in his early boxing matches – first of all with the Cadet Force and then as an amateur with the Anderston club. As well as skill and bravery, the boxer's natural asset is a streetwise mentality, an ability to predict and outsmart the moves of his opponent.

The Anderston club was renowned for its output of amateur and professional champions and its old-timers were some of the best coaches in the country. It was much frequented by managers and promoters scouting for new talent and its many champions were household names and headline news.

Peter progressed quickly in his training and fighting ability and was soon tipped for the big time. He wasn't particularly driven by boxing as a sport per se – his view was that when he was good enough to turn professional it would be just like going into business. He would be the boss, the managing director. He would collect the biggest wage packet and he would make all the decisions. As it turned out, boxing made him one of the wealthiest sportsmen Scotland has ever produced.

First, though, Peter had to learn the set-up – that in the world of professional boxing, the people that called the shots were the bosses, the managers and promoters.

There were few better to kick-start your career than the man who became Peter's first manager, the larger-than-life Brigtonian, Tommy Gilmour, who, like his dad Jim before him, was one of the best-known characters in the sport. His son, also Tommy, still carries the family flag in boxing as one of Britain's top promoters and managers. The Gilmour family, who ran the Premierland and National sporting clubs in Bridgeton, had been involved in boxing for years and were responsible in part for some of its great legends. They would point old Jim out and say how he had been the only man as an amateur ever to have beaten the great Alec Ireland. Stories abounded about Jim Gilmour, that when he worked at Fairfield's in Govan, he had sent a local gang fleeing up Govan Road after turning on them – with his riveter's hammer. It was said that in his boxing club on Barrack Street, just off the Gallowgate, Jim's old workmate and pal, Sammy Wilson, had first seen and discovered Benny Lynch. Tommy Gilmour became Keenan's manager after watching him in action as an amateur and studying him in training at his club, the Premierland at Bridgeton Cross. Gilmour liked what he saw, immediately recognising the potential of the young flyweight. And on a chilly Friday night in September 1948, the 20-year-old boxer from Anderston and Tommy Gilmour went into partnership when Keenan walked to the ringside for his first professional fight. It was one of the most successful – and certainly one of the stormiest – partnerships in the history of sport in Scotland.

Boxers always remember their first fight, perhaps more than any other, when their pastime becomes their pay packet. It wasn't until years later that Peter would describe how, despite assurances from an experienced manager like Tommy Gilmour, Keenan had never felt so alone in his life as Gilmour did that first fight. 'That was the strangest night of my life. I wasn't afraid. But for the very first time I felt very alone,' he later revealed. The man he faced that night was the seasoned Burmese flyweight, Al Hutt, a man who had fought in a score of different locations, against men of a multitude of nationalities. But the matchmakers were confident that Keenan could handle him. Not much was written about the Keenan–Hutt combat, but then what is there to say about a match that lasted only two minutes, except that Keenan had dominated from the moment they touched gloves, demonstrating the truly formidable fighting power he possessed. Manager Tommy Gilmour was more than impressed. By the confident way Keenan had handled the more experienced Burmese and the considerable ringcraft he displayed, Gilmour knew he really had a star on his hands.

Keenan's first fight with Al Hutt took place just two years after the death of Benny Lynch. At the time every flyweight boxer in Scotland was being eyed as the next potential champion. Tommy Gilmour, an experienced pragmatist, played his cards close to his chest with his young protégé, but he would always harbour great hopes for Keenan.

Following that first fight with the Burmese Al Hutt, manager Gilmour went on to arrange a series of contests for his new star, showing him to the crowds in Liverpool, Falkirk, Paisley and Glasgow. He had six rapid fights in less than four months, three of them ending much the same way as the Hutt contest with Keenan's remarkable punching power. One of his toughest matches around this time was against another colourful Scottish boxer who hailed from the Gorbals and who had a similar street-fighting background. Vic Herman, as the name might suggest, was Jewish – the Gorbals being the first home in the city of that community. As well as being a first-rate pugilist, Vic was also an active member of the local Jewish Lads' Brigade, a similar movement to the Boys' Brigade, and was a member of his battalion's pipe band. His famous hallmark was that he would enter the ring playing his bagpipes. The crowd loved it just as much as they loved him. In his first fight with Keenan, Herman knocked the young fighter clean out of the ring in the fifth round following a furious and prolonged assault. To Keenan's credit, he also gave an impressive display that night and took everything Herman threw at him right up to the final bell, his hand being raised by the referee for a points decision.

Tommy Gilmour progressed Keenan steadily, each fight matched against someone rated higher than the last, working confidently towards the supreme title of world flyweight champion. The title-holder at the time was Englishman Terry Allen, from Islington, London. Like Keenan, Allen was a former barrow-boy. His real name was Albert Edward Govier, but he adopted his ring name Terry Allen in tribute to a friend who had been killed in the war and whose name he had vowed to make famous – this he did in no short measure, having won 102 of his 107 fights. Four years older than Keenan and a professional boxer since he was 18, Allen had fought a draw in a world title fight in Belfast with the famous Irishman Rinty Monaghan who, in turn, had been one of the few men to have beaten Jackie Paterson. And now it was Keenan who was being lined up against Allen.

When word of the fight got out, there was much talk and debate but the general consensus was the verdict that a Keenan–Allen match would fall squarely on Keenan's side – and this from some of the best pundits in the sport. As fate would have it, it was Keenan's idolisation of another world champion that ensured the young pugilist never entered the ring for a world flyweight title. As a young amateur Keenan had watched his boxing idol, Jackie Paterson, train in the same gymnasium at Anderston. 'I was happy just to train in the same gym as Jackie. There was nobody like him,' he would say. If anyone had been a genuine successor to Lynch, it had been Paterson. He was the first Scot to win the world flyweight title after the famous Gorbals man, and even fought some of Lynch's old opponents. Even the scoffers and sceptics who had chanted the same things about him as they were now saying about Keenan – 'He'll never be another Benny' – had to confess that the new world champ had a killer punch. But Paterson's final failing as a boxer was something which bedevilled most of those small and lightly built men – keeping their weight. As they advanced into their mid- and late-twenties, so too would the natural tendency of their maturing bodies to gain weight. There was only one antidote known to work – starvation, a terrible catch-22, meaning that the less they ate, the less stamina they had for their arduous ring regimes. Paterson suffered greatly and in order to retain the world flyweight champion title he continually endured starvation and dehydration.

As a young fighter, Keenan had watched the agonies and anguishes of Paterson, as he sweated and suffered to lose just a few more ounces in order to get under the eight stone limit. Peter was obsessed with his own health and fitness and there was no way he would compromise it as Paterson had.

Gilmour and Keenan had now been together for two years, during which the boxer had established an impressive record, including several knockouts and, more importantly, no defeats. He had won victories over first-class fighters like Jackie Briers, Raoul Degryse and Emile Famechon, whose older brother Ray was the French and European featherweight champion.

Keenan's next fight has since been recorded as his most dreaded. This was less because of the strength of the opposition and everything to do with the fact that Peter's opponent was a friend of his. Joe Murphy, another Glasgow boxer, was not only Keenan's closest friend, but was also his best man at his wedding to Martha Gault, daughter of an Anderston metal dealer, better known throughout their long marriage as Cissy. The purse for the fight against Murphy was only a few hundred pounds – not much perhaps but still vital earnings in an unpredictable business – and Keenan knew he could easily beat Murphy. The only problem was Joe's dogged determination. Keenan knew he would keep going until he was either badly hurt or knocked out.

In later years, Keenan would talk about the quandary he had been in prior to the fight. While he always made it plain that he had never been involved in a rigged or fake fight, he had desperately wanted to throw that match with Joe Murphy. The fight seconds, knowing the score, urged Peter when he rose from his stool to 'do it quickly'. But Murphy fought on regardless. On several occasions Keenan looked pleadingly at the referee, begging him to stop the contest. He tried as hard as he could to end it himself but Murphy doggedly resisted. Eventually, in the sixth round, the referee stepped in to end the punishment – Keenan was overcome with relief.

There was little doubt by this stage that Keenan was a world-class fighter and that Gilmour had a contender. The next obvious step was a title challenge. When word at last emerged from the Allen camp that he accepted the challenge, everyone was quietly confident that Keenan would beat the Englishman and claim the title. Keenan's reaction to the news stunned everyone.

He did not want to fight Allen. His reason was all tied in with his weight. Up to this point he had managed to maintain the eight-stone limit for a flyweight, but his natural weight had been progressing and by now he was four pounds over. Keenan argued that he knew that he could lose the four pounds all right, but that this would be the start of the same dreadful cycle his idol Paterson had found himself in – he would have to lose the same, or more, for the next fight, and the next one after that. Keenan said at the time: 'It really hurt me to turn that chance down. But I remembered Jackie's suffering and I had sworn never to do anything like it. I know I could have made it but there was that thought that if I did it once . . . just once . . . and won the title, then I would be tempted to do it again and again . . . and break my health.' Gilmour accepted Keenan's decision, as all good managers do, but it marked a turning point in their relationship.

As it was, Allen's first defence of his world title was with Dado Marino from Hawaii who, three years earlier, with his manager, Sad Sam Ichinose, had come to Scotland to challenge Jackie Paterson for his world title. Due to Paterson's health and weight problems, the match was postponed and the party stayed in Glasgow longer than expected. Eventually, after a series of false starts, Paterson pulled out of the fight and was replaced by the Irishman Rinty Monaghan, who was disqualified in round nine for persistent holding.

Keenan had been training in the same gym as Paterson while he tried, without success, to make the weight for his fight with Dado Marino. He had watched him undergo the agonies of what the boxers called 'boiling down', that is, the process of sweating out every ounce of fat and liquid from the body. The price of achieving the optimum weight was severe dehydration and weakness caused by low blood sugar. It made them light-headed and lethargic, sometimes sickly. Many fainted. Training became a torturous ordeal, yet they were still expected to jump into a ring on a given night and fight for 15 three-minute rounds, expending as much or more energy than a runner would in a marathon. All of which Keenan had seen Paterson endure and he himself had sworn that he would never undergo similar agonies.

After reneging on the opportunity to challenge Terry Allen, Keenan renounced fighting as a flyweight, and became a bantam boxer instead, which allowed him the comfort of a weight limit of eight stone six pounds. One of his first major fights at that limit was with Dickie O'Sullivan from London, who he dispatched in three rounds at Paisley. It was a notable victory for Keenan – O'Sullivan being rated just three years earlier as the third best bantam in the world. Next he was tested against Jean Sneyers and Maurice Sandeyron, two hardy and highly experienced continentals, and he outpointed them both.

The fights were coming in thick and fast, some more notable than others. His fight against Jean Sneyers, a ruggedly handsome Belgian, and also a highly experienced and hardened battler, was the first time that Keenan had gone ten rounds, and the extra distance took its toll. Keenan was, nevertheless, declared winner but the following morning he was diagnosed with severe concussion. Speaking about it some years later, Peter noted that he 'felt sick and ill, and I could not remember a lot about the fight, although I did remember the most important things – that I had won and how much I was being paid'. A telling revelation of exactly where Peter's priorities lay.

Peter was always referred to as the man who hailed from Anderston, although by now he owned a large house on the more prestigious Grant Street in the Woodlands area and was in the process of converting its spacious basement into a boxers' gymnasium. The fans had taken to him too, referring to him by first name only, calling him Peter, or Wee Peter, never Peter Keenan, just like Lynch had always been Benny or Wee Benny, never Benny Lynch.

More matches, more victories. Yet another fight with the Gorbals Jewish bagpiper fighter, Vic Herman, which Keenan won on points, the referee commenting that Keenan's 'whole approach to the game had a flourish of the master craftsman'. He was now rated as the fourth best bantam in Britain and so his fights entered a process of elimination, similar to the latter stages of a football tournament. The first of these was against the country's third rated bantam, the Ulsterman Bunty Doran, a storming, non-stop, hurricane of a fighter who had beaten both Jackie Paterson – when Jackie was world champion at that – as well as the European champion Theo Medina. Then there was Tommy Proffit from Manchester, a former Amateur Boxing Association champ, whose long list of professional victories included the Scots Bobby Boland and Eddie Carson, and a pair of the very top-notch Canadian punchers, Fernando Gagnon and Charlie Savard. Proffit lasted only two rounds against Keenan. Next was the Frenchman Louis Skena, who was disposed of in an eight rounds points decision, then Jose Rubio from Spain, who went the same way. At Earl's Court, the Frenchman Armand Delanna went home via the canvas inside six rounds and, finally, in a championship warm-up, it was Amleto Falcinelli from Italy who paved the way for Keenan to bid for the British bantamweight title.

The British bantam champion at the time was Danny O'Sullivan, and manager Tommy Gilmour and the well-known Glasgow bookmaker and promoter Sammy Docherty arranged a title fight to be staged at Firhill stadium. O'Sullivan, from Finsbury Park, London, and elder brother of Dickie, who Keenan had beaten just a few months earlier, was another with the 'Paterson connection'. Ranked as 'a most intelligent and stylish battler', Danny O'Sullivan had fought Jackie twice, a knockout from one of the Scot's hammer punches ending the first, but Paterson bearing the brunt of it when they fought one year later. O'Sullivan had more than once demonstrated just how gutsy and clever a performer he was, having fought his way to the peak of the sport, putting up a spirited but unsuccessful challenge for the world title in Johannesburg against Vic Toweel, the first South African to win a world boxing title. O'Sullivan was famously contesting an important title eliminator and went into the ring with a pair of borrowed boxing boots which were too small for him. By the time the fight was midway through, his feet were so badly blistered he had to remove the boots and finish the contest in his bare feet.

The two men faced each other before a capacity crowd of 30,000. Keenan was in devastating form that night and the Londoner lasted only six rounds and was knocked to the canvas on several occasions before the fight ended. As Elky Clark, the *Daily Record*'s boxing writer noted, for a championship fight it was a very one-sided match. A Lonsdale Belt holder and one-time British, Empire and European flyweight champion himself, Elky knew the sport inside out and also had inside knowledge as to the circumstances of the match – O'Sullivan had been desperately trying to make the weight. Clark added that the boxer was severely weakened because of this and his form was jaded and sluggish.

As British champion, Keenan's prize-money soared, as too did his chances of challenging for the supreme title, still held by Toweel, the South African. En route, though, was the European championship title and Gilmour set about organising a match. Meanwhile, he was challenged to defend his bantamweight title by Bobby Boland of Dundee, who Keenan had already beaten. This was a harder fight, however, as a result of which the Dundonian retired in round 12, leaving Keenan dazed and staggering, with blood pouring from wounds to both eyes. The deep cuts required 20 stitches and he had to rest for several months – Keenan was paying the price of victory.

The European title was held by Luis Perez Romero, a tough little Spanish Moroccan who lived in Barcelona. Romero was one of the most experienced campaigners in the sport – he had fought in more than 100 contests and had been a professional boxer since before the Second World War. An awkward southpaw – meaning that, unlike most boxers, he led with his right hand – Romero was well known to Scottish fans for his fights with Bobby Boland and Eddie Carson, both of whom he had beaten.

Boland reckoned he possessed one of the hardest punches imaginable, but the same was also said about Keenan and, in front of another capacity crowd of wildly cheering home fans, he went on to become the new European title holder.

Meanwhile, Peter's continuing problems with manager Tommy Gilmour had worsened. Their dispute had become so serious Keenan had attempted to sever all agreements between them. No longer on speaking terms, they communicated by a third party. But agreements are agreements and in addition to being contractually united, the British Boxing Board of Control had their own jurisdiction over such altercations. The latest row stemmed from Keenan being under the impression that when his contract with Gilmour had expired three months previously, he was no longer under his control and he had asked the Boxing Board of Control to confirm this. In November 1951, just a little more than a month before he was due to fly out to Johannesburg for the most important fight of his career, Keenan engaged in a sensational 12-hour legal battle at a Board meeting in Central Halls, Bath Street, Glasgow. Both Keenan and manager Gilmour were there, together with their respective lawyers.

Keenan was the first to be called and was quizzed for more than three hours regarding his claims of poor management on the part of Tommy Gilmour. He said he was first introduced to Gilmour by two senior directors at the North British Locomotive in Springburn, where he worked at the time. The men had become his trustees and as a result of the introduction he had signed a three-year contract with Gilmour. At first everything had gone well, with Gilmour making all the arrangements for his early fights, including facilities for training, supervision and advice. But Gilmour never discussed Keenan's future or his plans for him. Peter argued that he only knew who his next opponent would be when he read about it in the newspapers.

Keenan trained at the Scottish National Club, owned by Tommy Gilmour, on Olympia Street, just off Bridgeton Cross. The club also housed a betting office – illegal at the time, though generally overlooked by the law. Keenan said that the training environment had been good at first and that quite a number of professional and amateur boxers used it but, as the duration of his fights increased, he was required to train more and more – his workouts being increased from three to seven days a week – and the Bridgeton club became more of a hindrance than a help. While sparring in the ring, the gamblers would crowd round to watch and his concentration was frequently interrupted by the announcement of race results over the loudspeaker. 'It puts me off my training,' said Peter. 'I like people coming to watch me, but most of them are drunk and they throw in some very rude remarks while you are training.' That wasn't the only complaint. 'The place was crowded with gamblers, drunks and was full of smoke. When I complained to my manager about the smoke – I don't drink and I don't smoke – and how it was affecting me and my training, I got no satisfaction. My manager said to me, "There will always be a Scottish National Club when there is no Peter Keenan going about."' Once, when he was preparing for a big fight in Liverpool he had been suffering from a cold and also had a boil on his face. But his manager had not taken any steps to check on his fitness. When they travelled to Liverpool by train they had gone by third-class sleeper and there were four people in the compartment including himself and Gilmour. The other travellers had sat up talking till the early hours of the morning and, when they had gone to bed, Gilmour had refused to put the light out, saying he wanted to read and so Keenan's sleep suffered.

Similarly, Keenan learned of his future fight with Joe Murphy at Paisley from the papers; this was the first time he had ever topped a bill. Recovering from injury, Peter escaped to Irvine with his brother for some respite. There was no contact between Gilmour and him during the time he spent at Irvine. No sparring partners were arranged until four days before the fight, after his return to Glasgow.

Asked about the money he was making, Keenan said he earned £250 for the fight with Dickie O'Sullivan, a fight that put

Keenan on the British boxing map. Gilmour subsequently suggested it would be good for him to be seen in London against a continental boxer. He arranged a purse of £125, admitting that the money wasn't much but that it would be a chance for them to 'show their wares' in London in an easy fight arranged more for publicity purposes. 'The next thing I found out was when I read the paper that I was top of the bill in Earl's Court, a place that holds 10,000 or more,' Keenan said. His opponent was the Belgian Jean Sneyers, one of the best flyweights in Europe. When he had tackled Gilmour about that, his manager said that they (the London promoters) had pulled 'a fast one on us'. But there was nothing he could do about it. Keenan couldn't understand how they could pay him just £125 to top the bill in London. When he threatened not to fight, he claimed Gilmour had warned that if he didn't, the London promoters would make sure he never fought again. The contest was arranged at a weight of 8 st. 3 lb but Keenan had been fighting heavier than that and was about 3 lbs over when he left Glasgow for London. On the train heading south Gilmour had handed him some pills, claiming they would help him lose the weight. But when he had taken them he ended up, as he recounted, spending most of his time in London sitting on the toilet. He had made the weight all right, but was physically weakened, despite going on to win the fight. He also argued with the promoters over his purse, only to have them respond that his manager had agreed to it. Keenan concluded that the 'fly boys' in London had taken Gilmour for a ride and he hadn't been clever enough to realise it.

Keenan admitted the relationship between the pair of them degenerated until they weren't speaking to each other. 'We were like a couple of children, passing each other and never speaking. If I had anything to say to Tommy Gilmour, I told my trainer and he told Gilmour, and the same in reverse. It was very childish between the two of us, I admit.' Eventually, one of his trustees got them together to thrash things out. Gilmour had said at this meeting that whenever anything was wrong, Keenan just shouted and bawled at him in front of other people instead of quietly talking it over. Keenan agreed that in future he would wait and discuss matters in private. Keenan said, however, that there had been a considerable change in Gilmour's attitude just before his fight with Danny O'Sullivan for the British bantamweight title. Gilmour would be down at the club every night watching his training, supervising things, personally bringing sparring partners and even taking them home again afterwards. And when Keenan had left for Troon to do some special training, Gilmour had come down with sparring partners. He was at the camp five nights out of seven during the three weeks Peter was there. He also laid on accommodation and facilities for boxing. 'Everything was great.' But, as Keenan pointed out, if he won the fight and the title, Gilmour had a clause in their contract which kept the two of them together for another three years.

Things changed again, however, for his next fight. It was the first defence of his new title against Bobby Boland, and Keenan had gone to Ayr to train, only to discover that Gilmour had left all the arrangements to a local priest. Despite being one of the biggest bookmakers in the very Protestant Bridgeton Cross area, the Gilmours, unknown to many, were Roman Catholic, hence the contact with the priest in Troon. His training was supposed to be done at a local army barracks but when he went along for his first night of training he was refused entry because they were using the premises for a whist drive. The accommodation was as cold as it was bare and it proved impossible to find another gym – they had wasted considerable time on his training programme because of the poor arrangements. When it came to the fight itself, Gilmour didn't show up because of the tension between the two. Keenan was also bitter about the proposed fight with Vic Toweel for the world title. He first found out about it by reading it in the papers. Keenan was furious and told his manager that he didn't want to fight as he needed a good rest. Gilmour replied, however, that as his manager he was the one who fixed the fight 'whether you want it or not'.

The chairman of the proceedings pointed out at this stage that their manager-boxer contract clearly stated that the boxer had to 'accept all and every match, exhibition or sparring, music hall, theatrical, cinema, film, wireless broadcast, literary or other contracts, made or entered into on his account by the said manager for the term of the contract'. Under cross-examination by Tommy Gilmour's solicitor, Keenan agreed that he had fought 32 matches since signing with the manager and that he had won them all. He also agreed that the fights came regularly, with no considerable gap between them and that he had won some £16,000 in purse money – equivalent these days to a considerable six-figure sum. He also consented that he was still completely undamaged, physically fit and capable – with any luck – of carrying on for some time yet, though he demurred on the last point, adding that things were not the way he would have liked them in the sport and that he would not be too much longer in boxing. The solicitor put it to him that the fights he had contested and the income he had made were down to good management and Keenan agreed that he was not complaining about the financial side of their arrangement, which he said had been 'very good', nor did he have any quarrel with his manager taking a 25 per cent cut of his purse money.

Keenan had spent four hours and 35 minutes giving his side of the story. It was now midnight and other witnesses were called throughout the early hours of the morning, including manager Tommy Gilmour. He said he was 36 years of age and lived at 682 Rutherglen Road and had been a professional boxing manager for 15 years. It was true, he said, that he didn't discuss future fights with Keenan. 'I discussed his opponents with the promoter, and I used my own judgement.' As for gambling at the club, it had been going on for about 40 years and hadn't just started up when Keenan had been there. There had, similarly, been no lack of consideration when they travelled to Liverpool.

'He got the same consideration as everybody gets.' Asked why he hadn't gone to see him when he had been training at Irvine,

Gilmour said there had been no need and anyway he had been busy in Glasgow with other boxers. 'For me to watch over a boy skipping, or out on the road, well, I mean, it is asking too much, in my opinion.' On another occasion, however, he had shown Keenan every support when he had been training, this time at Ayr. He had arranged the army gym and a house, but Keenan had been unhappy with the house and he had gone to see what could be done when Keenan had told him it was his job to find the boxer better accommodation, etc. At that time Gilmour had another boxer fighting in Leicester and he had to leave to look after the young lad there. The next he heard, Gilmour added, was the complaint about the whist drive at the gymnasium. It turned out, however, that the card tournament didn't start until 7.45 p.m., so Gilmour asked his boxer why he couldn't have started his training earlier. When questioned about the fight in London and the acceptance of a very small purse, Gilmour said that he didn't think it was appropriate but had consulted Keenan about it at the time and, because it meant showing in London, he advised him to take it, which he did. Gilmour said he couldn't understand his complaints about sparring in front of the crowd at his club as it was better for boxers to spar with an audience. The fact that there was gambling also going on shouldn't matter. Seven or eight other managers sent their boxers to the club for training and there were no complaints from them. Big champions too had worked out there, people like Ken Shaw when he was training for his British cruiserweight title against Freddie Mills. And other big names like Bert Gilroy, Jake Kilrain, Willie White and Harry Hughes. 'There is not a champion in the last ten years that hasn't trained at the National.'

Keenan then read an extract from the *Evening Times* about a police raid in which 78 men were charged for having been in an illicit gambling club and Gilmour, along with six others, was charged in relation to the management and running of premises used for the purpose of betting. He was asked if this sort of activity was meant to inspire confidence in his young boxers and whether such a newspaper report was a dignified one for a leading boxing manager. 'I don't see where it has any bearing on the character of me or my club. I am a tuppence-ha'penny bookmaker. There are bigger bookmakers than I am,' Gilmour responded.

Asked if he thought Keenan was looking for exceptional and preferential treatment, he said he thought the boxer had been. When he spoke about the lack of consultation over fight bookings and that Keenan more often than not would find out about his fights through the press, he said this was because some contracts were made around eight or nine o'clock at night and details of them would therefore appear in the papers before he could get notice to him.

Gilmour concluded by suggesting that Peter had exaggerated the differences between them and that he was temperamental and mercenary.

In summing up, Keenan's solicitor said that what they had heard that night had been a disgrace to boxing and if this degree of shoddy behaviour, invective and abuse was typical of the manager-boxer relationship these days, then the sport was in grave trouble. Gilmour's solicitor pointed out that a measure of the strength of the case which Keenan had brought could be found in the length of time it had taken to develop it. 'When you have a case that lasts from a quarter to seven one evening to a quarter to six the following morning, you may be well sure that it is lacking in solidity, and if ever a case was lacking in solidity and in strength this one is.' He suggested that there was no substance to the case and asked the council to dismiss the complaint by Keenan. By a majority, Peter's case was rejected. Undeterred, Keenan consulted his lawyer over accepting the Board's decision and was given the advice that he could appeal. The case was then referred to the Appeal Stewards in London, a group of 14 men, among them a sprinkling of former colonels, an MP, two High Court judges, a handful of Queen's Counsels, John Moores, the owner of Littlewoods pools, and one of the most eminent surgeons of the day, Anthony Dickson-Wright, father of Clarissa, one of television's *Two Fat Ladies*. A voluntary group, the Appeal Stewards met at the Boxing Board's offices on Hills Place, just behind the Palladium theatre. They dutifully listened to the plea by Peter Keenan but, because of a dearth of substantiations, they were left with no alternative but to adjudicate in favour of the manager.

The prevailing mood between the pair was, by this time, pretty grim and was fuelled just one week later by the surprise announcement that Alex Adams, Keenan's long-standing trainer, was quitting boxing. Adams had a long connection with Gilmour's National club in Bridgeton and had been there with Keenan in most of his big fights. But when the manager and boxer had fallen out, it had been Adams who was stuck in the middle and he had had enough of it.

The trip to South Africa was a sensational story at the time and not just for events inside the ring, behaviour outwith the ropes snatched most of the headlines. Whatever problems had surfaced when Keenan refused to contest the flyweight title against Terry Allen were nothing compared to the feud that now erupted between the two. Matters had deteriorated so much that Keenan declared shortly before leaving Scotland that he did not wish to see his manager in South Africa.

In a place like Johannesburg, thousands of miles from home, and with the prospect of the biggest fight of his life on the horizon, this kind of psychological pressure was the last thing Peter Keenan needed.

World champion Vic Toweel was from yet another legendary boxing family. He came from Benoni, the 'city of lakes', situated between Pretoria and Johannesburg, the second son of eight children whose parents were of Lebanese descent, his father Mike was also a boxer. Toweel had won his world title in his home city, taking the championship from Manuel Ortiz, a Mexican domiciled in Corona, California, listed as one of the greatest bantamweights of all time. Ortiz had held the title for eight years, losing it briefly to the Chicagoan Harold Dade from whom he recovered it in the return fight just two months later. After taking the title from Ortiz in 1950, Toweel had only defended it once, against Danny O'Sullivan, the man Keenan defeated for the British title. Of his three boxer brothers – Jimmy, Frazer and Willie – the latter was the most successful, following in older brother Vic's footsteps by becoming the South African bantamweight champion and a world contender before becoming the Commonwealth lightweight champion.

The fight had been scheduled for Saturday, 26 January, and Keenan arrived at the beginning of the month, accompanied by trainer Alex Adams who, by this time, had had a change of heart, in order to acclimatise while training. Johannesburg is around 6,000 feet above sea level – approximately one and a half times the height of Ben Nevis. Getting used to the altitude can take some time and, at its worst, it can bring on headaches and aching bones, loss of appetite and a feeling of breathlessness – none of which help ease an intensive training schedule.

As it turned out, however, there were bigger problems than rarefied air. Within days of Keenan's arrival in South Africa, and just hours after he had started training, a dispute flared between rival promoters over who would be staging the fight at the 30,000-seater Rand Stadium. The White City Sporting Club were claiming an alleged breach of contract by Keenan who, they said, had admitted he was obliged to fight Toweel under their auspices, but that his manager had concluded another contract with the Transvaal National Sporting Club, meaning that White City stood to lose some £5,000. They applied to the Supreme Court for an attachment order on Keenan, which meant that should the fight be promoted by another party, they could legally detain the Scottish champion in the country until there was a settlement – he could even be held in custody! The £5,000 claim may not seem like much money today, but in 1952 it totalled more than twice the purse for which Keenan was fighting.

All of this was taking its toll on Keenan and fortunately, a few days later, and to his great relief, White City officials withdrew their court action. On Tuesday, 15 January, eight days before the fight date, manager Gilmour left Glasgow for London to be in the corner with welterweight Danny Molloy, one of his other charges. Following the fight, he was intending to fly straight to Johannesburg, despite the fact that he was still at loggerheads with Keenan. 'Although Peter Keenan and I are not on speaking terms and there is no sign of any reconciliation, it is my duty to be at the ringside on 26 January,' he said. 'I will definitely go and see him as soon as I arrive, but I don't expect he will want to talk to me.'

Meanwhile, 6,000 miles away in the Transvaal, yet more unsettling problems were being aired and would emerge in the following day's newspapers. The fight was now in serious doubt, with a strong possibility of it being called off because the Toweels were demanding a new clause in the contract guaranteeing a return fight within two months. Such stipulations are common in fight arrangements, but are mutually agreed when the original terms are drawn up. As there had been no such agreement in the fight documents, the Scots party rightly refused, Keenan telling reporters there had been no question of a return match in their negotiations. 'I will sign no contract binding me to fight in Johannesburg,' he maintained. 'I shall get little enough out of this month's fight as it is, the £2,000 purse will barely cover my expenses, unless, of course, I get the title. If I beat Toweel he will have to go to Glasgow to try to regain the title, otherwise there is going to be no fight.' From London, Gilmour insisted that unless the match went ahead according to the original conditions, there would be no fight. On hearing this, the Toweel clan, headed by their tough-talking father Mike, and Vic's manager – brother Maurice – besieged the Orange Grove Hotel where Keenan, his trainer and sparring partners were based, demanding to be heard.

Before Gilmour could get to Johannesburg, further developments suggested that Keenan had changed his mind and was now reported as saying that he didn't blame Toweel for wanting such terms. The arrival of Tommy Gilmour less than one week before the fight was billed brought yet more headlines – the Bridgeton man making it abundantly clear that, despite his boxer's views, the fight would only proceed on the original and agreed terms. 'I never agreed at any time to a return fight clause,' said Gilmour.

As time marched on, the Toweels became increasingly frustrated and returned once more to the Orange Grove Hotel to issue an ultimatum to the Scots party: the fight would definitely be off if they didn't get their way. Just as they were leaving the hotel, Keenan stopped them. Looking remarkably relaxed, tanned and impressively fit and dressed in a floral shirt, Keenan nonchalantly announced, 'Okay, you win.' The Toweels got their precious return clause, and the fight was on.

Although none of it had been good for the boxer's morale, the pre-fight publicity, including the disputes, was to make this one of the most anticipated post-war world title bouts. Keenan, with his steamrolling career, was now one of the most popular boxers in Britain, though bizarrely enough the enthusiasm of his fans was completely overlooked by the BBC who made a cavalier decision not to transmit radio coverage of the fight. Instead, fans would have to wait for the Sunday morning papers, only to be confronted with a fuzzy, picture-by-wire photo of Keenan, his knees folding under him, as he fell to the canvas – in round one! That wasn't the end of the fight, merely an indication of the final outcome – a handsome points victory for world champion Toweel, who fully lived up to his nickname, 'Little Dynamite'. All the fuss about the return fight had been for nothing.

Sadly for Peter it had not been the best of nights or fights for him. The South African had dictated the pace and the man from Glasgow had been out-thought and out-fought, to such an extent that he had resorted to spoiling tactics and fighting-on-the-run methods which met with little approval from the fans, who booed him as he left the ring. Obviously the pre-fight tensions and traumas, the arguments and the anxiety had taken their toll.

Peter didn't allude to them when asked to comment at the end of a bruising 15-round battle, saying only: 'I just could not get going somehow, and I felt tired.'

It was the first time in three and a half years and thirty-three fights that he had been beaten. Many years later, however, when Keenan and Gilmour resumed their relationship, Peter confessed that things might have been different in South Africa, 'but I was young and I thought I knew best'. Gilmour, too, said latterly that Peter was a greater fighter than he was ever given credit for and that he really should have gone on to become world champion. He is also reported to have told his closest friends that he considered Keenan an even better fighter than Benny Lynch.

Losing to Vic Toweel that night in Johannesburg was the end of a chapter in the fight career of Peter Keenan, but certainly not the end of the story. He was just 24 years of age and at his peak physically – robust and tough, able to take what he could hand out. Provided there were no serious injuries ahead, he still had a good future ahead of him. Peter Keenan was every bit the fighter in spirit as he was the battler in the ring. And being the business-minded person he was, he looked on the defeat by Toweel as similar to losing out on some company deal. You just shrugged your shoulders and got on with it. There would be plenty of good paydays ahead, plenty of other titles.

Back home in Glasgow and four months later, Peter Keenan was back in action again, once more in the familiar surroundings of Firhill Park. His opponent once again was the rugged Belgian, Jean Sneyers, the man who had given him concussion in London. Sneyers was after Peter's European bantam title and Keenan, ever confident, knew that having beaten the Belgian once, he could do it again. The fight went well for Keenan until round five, when the crowd was silenced, as the local man suddenly slumped to the canvas, unable to rise. It hadn't been a punch, so what was going on? He looked pale and frightened as he watched the referee make the count, all the while struggling to get back on his feet. But he couldn't make it up before the 'ten', and Sneyers was the new European champion – Peter had lost his second fight. Keenan suffered a ruptured knee cartilage and two weeks later had an operation to remove it completely. Afterwards he revealed that what had really terrified him as he lay immobile on the canvas was the fear that he had been paralysed. 'I thought one of Sneyers' punches had somehow paralysed me and even though my title had gone, I've never been so happy and relieved when told by the doctor what it really was.'

It was the autumn before he fully recovered from the knee problem and was back in action, this time against another old foe, the Italian Amleto Falcinelli. The run of bad luck continued and Peter lost once more, making it three defeats in a row. The reason once again was injury, with the referee stopping the fight because of a bad cut to one of Keenan's eyes which required outside ring attention. By now it was October 1952, and because of the eye injury, there would be no further fights that year. Undaunted, however, Peter instead started planning for an eventful 1953.

The 'earhole blowers', or whisperers, had a field day, of course, claiming that Keenan was finished, that he'd never be the same again, but Peter was confident that the good times would roll again. And they did. He was still one of the most charismatic figures in sport and one of the most popular and most sought-after fighters in the game. Fans knew that when Keenan was on a bill they would see some real boxing, some real fighting. Similarly, promoters knew that when they had him on their programmes, the money would come rolling in. There were fights in London and in Paris and in the South of France, out to the Far East and on further to Australia, collecting more titles en route, and regaining the European championship he lost to Sneyers because of that bad knee. He won the Commonwealth title in Sydney and retained his British bantam crown on sufficient occasions to win outright two of the coveted Lonsdale Belts.

His career continued in the same controversial fashion with Peter making the headlines for events occurring outside the ring as much as inside it. He refused on two further occasions to contest world title fights. The first was with Robert Cohen, the French domiciled Algerian. Cohen was the French and European bantamweight champion, and had outpointed a Thai boxer in Bangkok to win the world title. Idolised in France, Cohen had made a small fortune from boxing and was a successful businessman. Promoter Sammy Docherty tried to organise the terms for a title match. Cohen was keen, but Peter, surprisingly, refused to accept the offer, despite the lure of the world title. Still the fights came. The most personally memorable for Keenan was his combat with Jake Tuli, another South African, but a totally different breed from Toweel. Tuli was a Zulu who more than lived up to his warrior-nation background. The fight had been scheduled for Cathkin Park, home of the late Third Lanark Football Club and one of the more popular venues for boxing matches. Peter had only just arrived back from his victory over Bobby Sinn in Sydney to win the Commonwealth bantam title when he was informed that the fight might be cancelled due to a shortage of promotional money. To ensure that the contest went ahead, Peter invested some of his own money in the match, his first defence of his new Commonwealth title. It was a wise move as an investment, so much so, in fact, that Keenan admitted that when he went into the ring and even after the fight had started he could hardly concentrate on his opponent for looking at the number of people in the stadium and working out what his financial return might be. Given that a sell-out crowd of more than 30,000 paid to watch the contest, one can assume it would be no small pittance!

Tuli quickly prompted Keenan's concentration, however, by swiftly knocking him down in the opening minutes, then doing it again, and yet again, in the first round. Round two and Keenan was floored once more, this time blood oozing from a cut in his right eye. Tuli came on the attack again in round three and Peter went down, this time for a short count. You needed flair and skill to survive this battling Zulu, and Peter, despite bad cuts to both eyes, went on to demonstrate he had plenty of both. As the rounds progressed, he slowly gained control and by the twelfth it was the flagging Tuli who went down, taking a count of eight. Elky Clark himself best described the ending of that contest in the opening paragraph of his report in the *Daily Record*: 'I saw the punch of the year at Cathkin Park last night. It came from the right hand of Peter Keenan. It landed on Jake Tuli's jaw and it sent South Africa's little coloured bundle of energy flat on his back for the count of ten.' The punch had come in the fourteenth, testament yet again to Keenan's guts and determination. Both of these were on display in front of a packed Firhill Park some months later when he defended his British and Empire bantam titles against Johnny Smillie of Fauldhouse, one of the most promising bantams of his day. The headline in one of the papers the following morning perhaps best told the story of Peter that night. It read: 'HIS LEFT EYE CUT, HIS HOPES FADING, THEN THE CHAMPION MAKES AN AMAZING COMEBACK'.

They called Keenan 'the merciless and magnificent' for his showing that night. Smillie, the challenger, had been leading on points in four out of the first five rounds, they were sharing the fifth. He had opened up Keenan's left eye – his vulnerable one – in the first three-minute session and the Anderston man had looked worried for the remainder of the early rounds. Then, in the sixth, he fought back, launching a magnificent attack on his younger opponent who could find no answer to his superior punch power and his remarkable ringcraft. The well-known reporter and broadcaster, Jimmy Sanderson, said of Keenan's comeback:

> Smillie, young, strong and flushed with the knowledge that he was comfortably ahead on points, came out confidently for the sixth round. Then, in a matter of seconds he was a husk of a fighter, a shell of flesh with his brain numbed and his body unable to answer to his will . . .
>
> In the time it takes to lift a phone, turn on a tap or

perform any of the mundane actions of everyday life, the world crashed down about the Fauldhouse miner's ears. He got up at the count of nine, climbed gallantly to his quivering, protesting legs, but the waves of sound, like the surf crashing on the shore, rolled over him. He heard nothing. He saw only the menacing figure of Keenan – his Nemesis in gloves.

It was his defence of the British title which won Peter a second Lonsdale Belt, the first Scot ever to have done so. Graham Van der Walt, yet another prolific and highly talented South African boxer, was to figure in more than one of Keenan's classic fights. Van der Walt was subsequently rated by commentators as one of the gutsiest fighters ever seen in a Scottish ring, but when they met that cool night in April 1958, at Paisley ice rink, the South African was facing a Keenan at his invincible best, a Keenan that had the scribblers lavishing their home man with unprecedented praise. 'Peter Keenan, the handsome, skilled matador, floating an invisible red cape to lure on the bull,' was the way one of them described the British champ. Others had him 'gliding gracefully' and being 'superb and supremely confident'. Van der Walt had an impressive reputation, not in the least that he had never been knocked down. The fight did nothing to tarnish his name. 'We thought he was cocky,' said sportswriter Tom Nicholson about the game South African. 'We suspected that in the finer points of the fight game he was a tyro. The one thing we did not know in advance about Graham Van der Walt was his guts.' Nicholson added, 'In his brave challenge of Keenan he gave a display of cold courage that Scots boxing fans will seldom see equalled.'

If the South African displayed his courage, Keenan showed his control, countering his opponent's pluck with proficiency and his courage with cunning. Another of the scribes wrote of Keenan: 'He was choosing his moments. He slid out of the way of punches. And whenever he wanted it seemed he could plant his own power-laden rights and lefts on the South African.' In a rare tribute after the fight to the two boxers, the master of ceremonies saluted Van der Walt 'for a display of courage and fighting spirit which has never been equalled let alone surpassed in Scotland' and Keenan for 'a display of precision boxing and punching which must entitle him to rank among the world's best'.

Just over six months later, aged 30, Peter faced the 20-year-old Irish-Canadian Pat Supple at Paisley ice rink and suffered yet again another eye injury – the left eye once more. Despite his supreme fitness, it was during this fight that commentators started to suggest that Keenan was perhaps past his best and that only his vast experience and physical prowess had helped him survive the 15 gruelling rounds and points win. Worse still, two further fights demonstrated that the fans too were beginning to lose heart.

In yet another duel with his old Glasgow rival, Jewish bagpiper Vic Herman, the fans booed, slow handclapped and sang derisory songs about the lack of action. Nothing upsets boxing fans more than a fight which isn't, and this was one. Even the referee had to warn the pair to 'make a fight of it'. But they didn't and it dragged on for ten rounds, with Peter winning an unremarkable victory. He was similarly booed by a large French crowd when he put on a rare display of action-dodging in a ten-round fight with the Algerian Alphonse Halimi who, at the time, was the world bantamweight champion. His runaway tactics were caused by that same old injury, his left eye, which was opened up by a savage punch he took in the early rounds. His subsequent attempts to keep out of trouble, however, did nothing to please the crowd, who hated it, booing and whistling as Halimi, the man they nicknamed the Tiger from Constantine, chased Keenan round the ring for the rest of the fight. It was the only time Keenan had gone the distance against an opponent without winning a single round.

Less than two months later Peter was back in the ring for what turned out to be a hallmark fight – his last contest as a professional boxer. For the past 13 years he had averaged something like five fights a year, and had scored 23 knockouts from 54 victories. While he had not intended this next fight to be his last, he was aware that time was against him and had vowed that, should he lose, he would call it a day.

Peter lost the fight and took his bow from the sport that night in a manner befitting the champion that he was. The match was at the King's Hall in Belfast and his opponent was local boy Freddie Gilroy, one of those remarkably tough ring warriors Ulster keeps producing. At stake were Keenan's British and Commonwealth titles. The match was bloody and grim as Peter Wilson, boxing writer for the *Daily Mirror*, noted:

> His left eye was like a red crayon smudge in a child's exercise book. His face was as bumpy as the shell of a tortoise. His right ear was a purple bell, its colour so different from the pallor of his cheeks that it almost seemed to have a separate existence of its own . . . He was Peter Keenan and he had just finished taking a savage 11-round battering from the numbing fists of Belfast's 22-year-old Freddie Gilroy, who has ripped the British and Empire bantamweight titles away from the perky Scot.

At the end of the fight, his legs like lead, his head and upper body badly marked by the mauling he had just taken, Keenan, amazingly and to the astonishment of the fans, went to the centre of the ring and joined the young Gilroy in singing 'When Irish Eyes Are Smiling'. Then, with a touch of inspiration, Teddy Waltham, secretary of the British Boxing Board of Control, led the crowd in a rendition of 'Auld Lang Syne' in tribute to the retiring Keenan, following which the ecstatic crowd in a spontaneous and equally inspirational gesture of their own, lustily sang 'I Belong to Glasgow'. It was a fitting and deserving tribute to one of the bravest men to have graced the sport.

Boxing had taken its toll and the various injuries he had collected along the way left their mark. His eyebrows alone had collected a massive 67 stitches over the years. Not being one to glory in such war wounds, Peter underwent plastic surgery; tidying it up as it were. He had made an estimated £100,000 from his fighting days, which was considerably more than any other Scottish boxer had achieved and would have amounted to around £1 million today. Boxing was only over for Peter inside the ring. There was still good business to be had out there in the sport and for as many years as he had been a fighter, Peter Keenan became a promoter, a leading fixer of both boxing and wrestling matches. He branched out further, managing an up-and-coming pop group, becoming involved in the pioneering days of televised football, and making considerable investments in property. For a while things were on the up. He owned a large red sandstone house in Pollokshields, went horse riding at the weekends on his country property at Aberfoyle, and owned a lot of land in Giffnock. His only vice seemed to be the big cigars he enjoyed.

But luck just wasn't on Peter's side. The second-hand car business in which he had bought a share failed. So too did his considerable property speculation at Giffnock. Other investments fizzled out. Then, tragically, his only son, Peter Jnr, received crippling injuries in a horrific car crash. His finances spiralled into bankruptcy. Meanwhile his divorce from Cissy was described as 'acrimonious' in the newspapers.

Latterly, there was a second and happy marriage to Jean, but he never experienced again the great prosperity he had once enjoyed, living out his days in comparative obscurity in a small flat in Anniesland. It says much for the man whose ultimate years were dogged by such a catalogue of misfortune that so much remained of the optimistic and cheerful character they once called 'Perky Peter'. His popularity at the height of his career had been such that one recent boxing promoter enviously commented that this truly great Glasgow champion could attract more people to watch him get his hair cut than he could for one of his fight shows. After a long and debilitating illness, the best world champion Scotland never had died, aged 71, in July 2000.

Chapter Four

The Man with the Golden Charm

He was the kind of man not normally associated with Glasgow – fabulously wealthy, handsome and dashing, enterprising and entertaining. A genuine, ten-carat playboy of the highest order, there was nothing 'wannabe' about Sir Hugh Fraser.

Throughout his comparatively short life, he occupied more news space than any other Glasgow citizen of his era. His life story was as sensational as a string of instalments out of an American soap opera – he was, after all, extremely rich and a shrewd wheeler-dealer. Women flitted in and out of his life with enviable regularity. Had a TV series been made based on the various episodes of his life, it would probably have outrated Dallas. When it came to matters relating to business, bets and boudoir, there was no one quite like Sir Hugh Fraser – he had it all and blew it all in his lifetime.

If he had been a rogue of sorts, perhaps his extraordinary lack of success may have been more understandable, but he happened to be one of the most charismatic of figures. The man with the golden charm was as liked by the general public as he was loved by so many women. Sir Hugh Fraser's story is classic Hollywood – a Beverly Hills scriptwriter couldn't have done a better job, but the unlucky events of his life, which were played out in and around Glasgow, were entirely of his own making.

Hugh Fraser was born into a distinguished Glasgow business family and though he was never referred to by the title, he was officially Hugh Fraser the Fourth. His ancestors were the Frasers of Dalcattoch, Boleskin, Inverness-shire, who were displaced from their homes in the early nineteenth century because of famine and the Clearances and migrated south to settle in Glasgow.

Glasgow was a booming city at the time, with the industrial revolution in full swing. Numerous shipyards and engineering works sprang up along the banks of the Clyde, with settlers arriving in droves for work and a share in the burgeoning wealth. The city was teeming with entrepreneurs, inventors and creators, pioneering the new industrial age.

The first of the Hugh Fraser dynasty was Glasgow-born, his parents having made the long trek south from the Highlands. As a young lad he left school and found work as an apprentice draper in Stewart and McDonald's store on Buchanan Street. He showed early promise in the trade which which was to make his family's fortune. From apprentice he became the company's lace buyer and was eventually promoted to warehouse manager, by which time he had gained enough experience in the trade to go into business himself. Buchanan Street was always one of Glasgow's better and more refined shopping thoroughfares and in 1849 Hugh Fraser acquired small premises on a site which is still home to House of Fraser.

A lifelong dedication to his profession – something which filtered down through the generations – enabled Hugh Fraser to make his draper's store one of the most successful on Buchanan Street, and when his son, Hugh Fraser II, was old enough, he too joined him in the business. The family prospered enough to purchase a splendid house at No. 3 Kensington Gate in Hyndland, and the pair of them would ride in a horse-drawn carriage every morning to be at the store long before it opened.

After an early-morning inspection of the premises and staff, they would take their place by the stairway just inside the main entrance, checking a gold pocket watch before giving the manager an authoritative nod to open the doors for business. Senior and junior, both dressed identically in dark, formal business suits, with their trousers crisply pressed and their shirt collars starched enamel white, would welcome the first shoppers with a pleasant 'good morning', cultivating an air of inclusion and respectability that their customers grew to associate with the store.

At the turn of the twentieth century, Hugh Fraser III was born – Sir Hugh Fraser's father. The Fraser store had prospered and grown to the extent that it was now one of the most prestigious of its kind in the city. After three years at Glasgow Academy and a spell at Warriston's, near Moffat – a popular boarding school with wealthy Glasgow families and an experience he particularly enjoyed – Hugh Fraser III was raring to get into the business. By the time he was 16 years of age he was pleading with his father, chairman of the company, to allow him to leave school and start work, and pretty soon Hugh Fraser III was learning the ins and outs of the business by working his way through the departments of the store he would one day inherit.

Hugh III was just 23 when his father died in 1926. He immediately took over as chairman of the company and, despite the fact that a major depression was looming, which would see more than three million unemployed nationally, Hugh Fraser put his faith in the future, financing the building of four extra floors in their Glasgow store and launching one of the biggest advertising campaigns of its day. Post-depression and the House of Fraser prospered further and its chairman started looking into expansion. His ambition, as he put it, was to be the greatest draper in the country – Hugh always preferred the old term for a department store and its reference to artistically draping the fabrics and clothing for sale on display in the shops.

The Fraser family work ethic was strong in Hugh Fraser III

and he worked incredibly hard to realise his ambitions. In those days the main road to the south of England was merely a B-class two-lane route, yet Hugh would regularly motor down to London overnight in his big powerful Chrysler to be the first customer the following morning at the outlets of major clothing and fabric wholesalers in the city. Few knew their prices better than he did. He was always up front, fair and honest and would name his price on a 'take it or leave it' basis. His early trading principles served him in good stead as he went on to build his empire and finance bigger and better projects. His success was attributed to his three great strengths – a courage and readiness to take risks, his complete and utter integrity, and his originality in the world of finance. It was the latter skill that would anchor Hugh Fraser's expansion programme. The key to his financial success was his inventive harnessing of the property boom to retail store development. By selling the freehold of his store properties for cash while, at the same time, obtaining long leases for them, he could be provided with large sums of money, not only for development but to make for further acquisitions. When he completed one programme of selling, leasing and developing, he would embark on another in exactly the same way. His reputation remained rock solid – there was never any duplicity, double-dealing or deceit with this sober-suited, clear-minded, no-nonsense talking Glaswegian.

Hugh Fraser III and his wife Kate, daughter of one of the wealthiest families in Aberdeen, settled in a large house in Bearsden before moving to a palatial estate at Mugdock called Dineiddwg (a Welsh name describing a hill fortress), where they raised a son and daughter. Like his forebears, their son, born on 18 December 1936, was also called Hugh and was looked on by the family as the fourth successor in what was now one of the most prosperous companies in Scotland. His father was eager for him to join the fray and, as he said in later life, from the age of ten all his father spoke to him about was business 'and all I wanted to be was a farmer'.

According to locals in and around the prosperous locale of Mugdock and Drymen, Glasgow's stockbroker belt, the young Fraser paid a heavy price for being the son of a mercurial business tycoon. The little lad was never allowed out to play with other kids, never seemed to have a real childhood and was forever accompanied by a chaperon, an employee of the company. Notwithstanding, his father was delighted when his son enthusiastically entered the competitive world of business.

The young Hugh, like his father, was sent to boarding school at an early age, attending St Mary's Preparatory School at Abbey Park in Melrose, and completing his education at Kelvinside Academy. He didn't go to university and at age 17 he began work in the Buchanan Street store as a counter salesman in the dress fabric department. Thereafter he was swiftly moved around as many departments in the store as possible in order to gain a thorough understanding of the business. In 1959, when he was 23 years of age, he was the assistant managing director of the House of Fraser, his father confident that he had not only learned enough about the workings of a store, but that he was also showing more than a lively interest in the company as a whole and where it might also be heading.

That same year the House of Fraser made its most significant acquisition, the takeover of the Harrods store in Knightsbridge. Put in perspective, a similar deal today would be worth around £225 million. The acquisition was made in typical Hugh Fraser style. He had set his sights on owning Harrods but was snubbed by the store's chairman, Sir Richard Burbridge, who told Hugh that Harrods and the House of Fraser were 'different in origin, conception and practice' and that there was no basis on which they could do business. The tart rebuff from the Englishman merely made him all the more determined to succeed. The story goes that Hugh Fraser reminded Sir Richard of the victory of David over Goliath and, before taking his leave, announced that he would be going to Hyde Park to 'collect a couple of chuckie stones and you'll be hearing from me'. And at that he donned his black homburg at a jaunty slant and left the building. But he would be back. As one of his former senior staff put it, when he was around life was full of interesting things, 'but when he goes on holiday, I almost die of boredom'.

The company sharpened their tactics for the takeover and in September of that year Hugh Fraser won over his shareholders. The acquisition secure, he rose early one morning, dressed in his customary business suit – striped trousers and a dark jacket, his favourite tie, the red, white and black Warriston school tie – and went out to the greenhouses by the side of his mansion to collect a fresh, dark red carnation for his buttonhole. Then, accompanied by the young Hugh, they took the first flight to London and briskly walked through a side entrance of the Knightsbridge store to avoid the formal welcoming party at the main entrance. They strode briskly to the escalators and arrived on the fourth floor, where they turned sharp right at the sign announcing 'Senior Staff', and walked straight into the boardroom, the elder of the two doffing his homburg and puffing his cigarette. It was Hugh Fraser's way of saying he was in charge now.

Hugh Fraser became one of Scotland's wealthiest and most successful businessmen and entrepreneurs. He was made a knight in 1961 and a baron three years later, taking the title Lord Fraser of Allander, named after the charming little river which flowed past their home. At the suggestion of his wife, the motto on the baron's crest was 'By courage and endeavour', two qualities he displayed throughout his many transactions.

The House of Fraser continued to expand, acquiring more and more retail outlets: Daly's and McLaren's in Glasgow; Binns, Smalls and Patrick Thomson's in Edinburgh; Bairds in East Kilbride; stores in Aberdeen and Stirling and others in country towns, until there were only two towns left in Scotland without a major Fraser interest. They spread throughout England into stores that were household names in Plymouth and Newquay, Manchester and Kendal, with others in Wales, Northern Ireland

and Eire, even in Denmark, all coming under the House of Fraser banner. By the early 1960s, his empire of 67 stores dominated the high streets of every major town in the country with an annual turnover exceeding £100 million. There seemed to be no limit to the success of the company and Lord Fraser branched out, recognising the great potential of tourism in Scotland, urging for more facilities and investment, and boosting the popularity of the Cairngorms with the creation of the ski resort and centre at Aviemore. He also became chairman of a wide variety of prosperous Scottish and British concerns, including what was then known as George Outram & Co. (publishers of the *Glasgow Herald* and *Evening Times*) and Associated Fisheries, forming and bringing to the public his own investment company, Scottish and Universal Investment Ltd. (SUITS), as well as chairing a varied collection of prominent boards, including the Highland Tourist Development Company, and Cairngorm Development Ltd. He was national treasurer of the Scottish Conservative Party, and the Automobile Association and was on the board for Films of Scotland, Scottish Tourism and the National Export Council.

Hugh Fraser was 26 years of age when, in what was called the wedding of the year, he married Patricia Bowie, whose father owned the well-known dry-cleaning firm of that name. It was a huge wedding in Glasgow, with newspaper coverage rivalled only by the royal family or Hollywood. After the service at St Mary's Cathedral on Great Western Road, large crowds cheered the couple as they stepped into the gleaming black Daimler, lead transporter of the House of Fraser's prestigious car-hire firm. Squads of extra police directed 200 car loads of guests to Mugdock, where a special car park was arranged in one of the fields surrounding the family's rambling mansion, Dineiddwg, and where they enjoyed a lavish reception. The fairytale couple had a beautiful home bought for them near the family estate at Mugdock and got down to the business of married life.

In 1966, just three years after the wedding, Hugh's father,

Lord Fraser, died of a heart attack – news of his death wiped almost £2 million off the company shares. He was just 63 years of age, but looked ten years older, his pressurised lifestyle and smoking habit – at least 60 a day – had taken their toll. The young Hugh refused the hereditary peerage in the belief that the title should die with the man. He chose instead to be known as Sir Hugh and he inherited all of his father's business interests, becoming chairman of the House of Fraser and SUITS (Scottish and Universal Investments), his holding company, with some 85 per cent of its resources invested in trading companies, the rest placed in investments. As well as being its chairman, Sir Hugh was SUITS' biggest shareholder, possessing in excess of three million personal shares plus more than seven million as a trustee. Under Sir Hugh's guidance, SUITS continued to expand and diversify with the younger Fraser emulating the entrepreneurial ways of his father, winning the award for Young Businessman of the Year. In addition to George Outram newspapers, bought by Lord Fraser in 1964, SUITS bought into a huge chain of local newspapers in Renfrewshire, Lanarkshire, Ayrshire and the Borders. They branched into insurance (Leslie & Godwin, a fast-expanding general insurance broker); into cleaning (A. & J. Macnab Ltd., with 15 laundering and dry-cleaning branches in the east of Scotland); into soft drinks (Strathmore Spring Ltd.); into liquor (the Tomintoul–Glenlivet distillery, Whyte & Mackay blended whisky and Dalmore malt); into textiles (Shetland cloth manufacturers Adam Paterson & Sons of Haddington); into engineering (Nicol & Andrew, ship repair specialists, with yards in Glasgow, Hull and Singapore). They had their fingers everywhere, it seemed, including a half share in Glasgow's Craigton crematorium. The SUITS group employed around 4,500 people with an annual wage bill of nearly £13 million.

Just as he had emulated his father in business, so too did he inherit Lord Fraser's love of the good life – the holidays at St Moritz and Monte Carlo, the occasional flutter at the tables of the Casino and National Sporting Club in Monaco, then going along the Corniche to dine in the very best restaurants, like La Reserve in Beaulieu, in the shadow of Cap Ferrat. Like everything else his father had done, young Hugh had to do it better, more exuberantly, more flamboyantly and, alas, more carelessly. Hugh worked hard and played harder. He had a passion for skiing in the priciest of Swiss resorts, for attending the best of the horse trials, owning five showjumpers and ten racehorses, and generally living what the tabloids would describe as a jet-set life. In itself, this wouldn't necessarily lead to a millionaire losing his fortune – but Hugh just seemed to be desperately unlucky.

Initially there were no outward signs of anything untoward in the burgeoning House of Fraser. In 1976, however, stories began appearing in the press about share and loan irregularities within the Fraser empire. The problems turned out to be much worse than first anticipated. SUITS had provided a loan of more than £4 million to a property company jointly owned by another property group in which Sir Hugh had a major stake. Shareholders were not informed about the loan, only discovering in August 1976 that the advance had been written off. It had also not been revealed in the company's annual accounts from the previous year and, as a result, the company auditors resigned. Details of the loan and other irregularities on the part of Sir Hugh, including some under-the-table share dealings, were revealed in an eight-hour emergency boardroom meeting he had with the directors of SUITS. Seldom had such a prolific businessman been so embarrassingly exposed. As one newspaper put it that morning, 'Who wants to be a millionaire!' before going on to cast an investigative and cynical eye on dealings in high finance. It was rare for a millionaire to be under the spotlight and Sir Hugh gallantly admitted that he was 'in the firing line – and not trying to duck'. At the same time, the tabloid papers were also digging the dirt on his private life.

After nine years of marriage, during which he had fathered three children, Sir Hugh had divorced his first wife for adultery.

He then courted showjumper Aileen Ross, who became the second Lady Fraser following a secret Caribbean wedding in November 1973. Now, however, there were stories about her involvement with a village blacksmith. Between the missing millions, his divorce and subsequent second marriage and the tabloid pursuit of the village blacksmith, his life had all the makings of a soap opera.

When the Stock Exchange were informed about the revelations which emerged from the SUITS emergency board meeting, they immediately set up a three-man investigation committee. They found that the loan had been wrongly described in the company's accounts as 'cash at bankers and on hand' and that Sir Hugh had been privately selling SUITS shares, worth around 90 pence per share at that time. Unfortunately, he wasn't just disposing of the odd few. In one month, it was revealed, he had sold off half a million company shares. A few weeks later he had then bought many of them back, buying more a month later, and again the month after that. When they examined his dealing record, they could hardly believe what had been going on and the investigation committee described it as 'haphazard and extraordinary'. In a five-hour private session with the inquiry team as to his odd business behaviour, Sir Hugh eventually confessed, with 'natural reluctance', that the sell-offs had been to meet gambling debts. And so the rumours, it seemed, were true.

The Stock Exchange investigators kept digging. They ordered him to hand over his personal bank books, two of the major London gambling clubs were contacted and instructed to supply details of the 'financial results' of Sir Hugh's visits. Two months later, the inquiry team released a report on their findings.

It was the biggest financial scandal in years, the report described in a press release as 'strange reading'. The sensational news was that the 40-year-old Glasgow tycoon had sold off some 1,620,000 shares of SUITS and 636,899 of House of Fraser. According to the report: 'The committee could determine no particular pattern in Sir Hugh Fraser's transactions. There were occasions when both buying and selling transactions would be effected on the same day through different brokers.' They also discovered that when he had sold the House of Fraser shares from his own personal holding, he was then buying them in his role as chairman and managing director of SUITS. The only logic in his behaviour was that he bought and sold the shares according to his luck on the tables of London casinos. It was as though he had been playing real-life Monopoly with hard-earned cash instead of tokens.

The committee reported they had, nevertheless, found no evidence of 'insider' share dealings – a most serious financial offence – but did consider his dealings 'undesirable' and his conduct 'haphazard and extraordinary'. They reported a breach of two sections of the Companies Act and a further breach of the Stock Exchange Listing Agreement. Immediately following their inquiry, a 40-page report was sent to the Department of Trade.

As always in financial scandals of this nature, it wasn't long before the opportunists and predators waded in. The vulture in this instance was another financial giant, a certain Roland Rowland, much better known by his nickname 'Tiny'. Rowland, a self-made man, was 60 years of age and knew all he needed to know about making and breaking in business. Having made his fortune in farming and mining in Rhodesia, he went on to head finance, industrial and mining giants Lonrho – the company name taken from London–Rhodesia – which had experienced its own cash crisis some five years previously. Hard times resulted in a share slump and eight of the company directors tried to have the boss, Tiny, sacked. However, he took out a High Court order to block the move and in the bitter battle which ensued it emerged that some of the top Lonrho directors had part of their salaries paid directly into banks on the Cayman Islands in order to avoid paying tax. The scandal inspired the Prime Minister of that time, Edward Heath, to make his legendary comment about the Lonrho group being the 'unacceptable and unpleasant face of capitalism'. Tiny Rowland was a shrewd and calculating mover

– he knew that with falling share prices and a loss of profit, the House of Fraser had no option but to do a deal.

Following a meeting between the two directors, Rowland put up sufficient cash to acquire Sir Hugh's 24 per cent SUITS holding, an acquisition of more than seven million shares in the company, making him the largest single shareholder The deal caused quite a few ripples, with bankers who acted as financial advisers to SUITS threatening to quit following Fraser's sell-out. Things were never the same again for Sir Hugh, who stepped down to allow Rowland to become chief executive of SUITS, but continued in his role as chairman of the House of Fraser. Just over a year later, their business arrangement turned sour when three of Sir Hugh's own directors proposed a deal whereby Sir Hugh, now the company's vice-chairman, would hand over complete control of SUITS to Lonrho. Lonrho then owned 29 per cent of SUITS and were offering a straight shares deal in their takeover bid. The proposed acquisition of SUITS was referred to the Monopolies and Mergers Commission who approved the deal. Sir Hugh's family trusts, who still controlled almost 9 per cent of the SUITS shares, also gave the venture their support.

One month later, the Department of Trade came to their conclusion regarding the Stock Exchange report, and Sir Hugh Fraser and five others were charged with offences under the Companies Act involving more than £4 million.

The charges against Sir Hugh and the other directors alleged that they had failed to give a true and fair view of the company's state of affairs. Pleading guilty to the charges, their trial was heard at Glasgow Sheriff Court. The trial lasted eight days but it was a further two months before Sheriff J. Irvine Smith issued his reserved judgment on the case. Two of the directors were cleared of the charges, but Sir Hugh and three of his associates were found guilty and fined a total of £885. The sheriff commented that it had been 'difficult to resist' the conclusion that many questions had not been answered and that many others had not been asked during the trial which he described as 'almost unprecedented'. Despite his scandalous and highly unusual conduct over share dealings, it is worth bearing in mind that Sir Hugh Fraser had taken the House of Fraser much further than his father. Under his chairmanship it had prospered and expanded, becoming the largest department store group in the United Kingdom with 122 shops, including Harrods, employing a vast army of some 28,000 workers, with annual sales of more than £700 million and pre-tax profits of nearly £40 million.

Sir Hugh Fraser's story was as colourful and dramatic in his private life as his public persona ever had been. While many might have said that his first love was gambling, he was also a man about town with an eye for the ladies and an appreciation of having attractive women by his side. More often than not he would make the headlines as much for the beautiful women he associated with as he would in his business affairs, leading one punter to say: 'He had big problems with both lumbers and numbers.'

Aged just 26, he had been labelled Scotland's most eligible bachelor when he married Patricia Bowie, whose father owned the famous dry-cleaning firm. They had three daughters, but were divorced in 1971, on account of her adultery, after nine years of marriage. Two years later, Sir Hugh married a second time, to Aileen Ross, a top Scottish showjumper, who shared his stately home, Dineiddwg in Mugdock. Aileen Ross had been in his life, in one way or another, for many years, as both a neighbour and as a prominent showjumper, one of the social circles of which Sir Hugh was very much a part. She was among his closest friends before their marriage and their story was a sensation in itself.

Aileen was the daughter of one of the tenant farmers on the estate the family owned around Mugdock and Drymen, just north of Glasgow. She was well known with the horsey crowd as an accomplished showjumper and was part of the inner élite socially. Aileen accepted her first social invitation from Sir Hugh when she was just 18 and was whisked off to St Moritz in

Switzerland along with his wife, Lady Patricia, her sister and some other guests. Following the breakdown of his marriage to Lady Patricia, their subsequent divorce and her emigration to Canada, Sir Hugh set about in no uncertain terms pursuing the girl from Drymen, with no expense spared.

There were gifts galore and nights out to the most exclusive restaurants and clubs. He bought her a magnificent maroon horsebox-cum-mobile home, one of the most sumptuous vehicles of its kind and which was the talk of the stables among the showjumping set, its presence drawing as much attention from the crowd as some of the jump-offs. Then there was a horse. Not any old filly, but a very special horse. A thoroughbred that had a family history that read like royalty and cost him more than £50,000 – that would be around a quarter of a million today. The engagement ring was something else again. It had sculpted into it a unique heart shape – almost unique that is, for in all of Europe there was just one other like it. Somewhat sedately, he proposed to her inside the horsebox as she was preparing her mount for an event. The engagement party which followed, however, was anything but restrained. It was held inside a stone barn on his estate, which had been transformed by function specialists into an exotic Arabian Nights fantasy, including hired models in the most spectacularly revealing dresses. The supper was gourmet, the champagne sparkling. And endless. It would have cost Sir Hugh about the same amount as the thoroughbred horse.

The fairy tale continued with the wedding itself. It was one of the few secret events of Sir Hugh's life. He was still on friendly terms with his ex-wife Patricia and his daughters, and he and Aileen had gone to visit them in their new home in Vancouver. From there they travelled to Mustique in the Caribbean, the remote holiday home of the Queen's younger sister, Princess Margaret. Mustique is pretty much of a closed island to holidaymakers unless you happen to own a house on the island or be invited as the guest of someone who does. Sir Hugh was friendly with Colin Tennant, the wealthy Scottish landowner, hence their access to this exclusive resort. Tennant welcomed the pair on arrival and Hugh announced his intentions to perform the wedding ceremony there. Given that neither parents had been told, let alone consulted, it would have to be conducted in secret. And it was, not a whisper escaping from the registry office on neighbouring island, St Vincent. Princess Margaret was there on Mustique with a kiss for the bride at the reception organised by their mutual friend, Colin Tennant, which took place at the island's only hotel. Again, the guests were reminded of the utmost secrecy and they all cordially obliged.

Like so many fairy tales, however, the reality of their marriage was very different. After all the trips, the magic of Mustique, their romantic hideaway haunts, diamonds in the horsebox, the bouquets and the society friends, life back in the outlying districts of Glasgow wasn't quite so easy. As Sir Hugh had moved out of Dineiddwg, the family seat at Mugdock, following the breakdown of his marriage to Patricia Bowie, the pair had returned from their wedding to live temporarily at the farm owned by Aileen's parents. They had apparently agreed before marrying that his new wife would never have to take up residence at Dineiddwg, the Fraser family home. Aileen hated the place and they planned instead to stay for a short while at her family home until they bought a new house.

Within a month, however, Hugh was already showing that he was not happy with their living arrangements and insisted that they leave the farm and settle in the Fraser family home. Aileen still refused to go to Dineiddwg, which resulted in the first of a series of showdowns between them, this one culminating with Hugh packing his bags and leaving the farmhouse, announcing somewhat dramatically that she knew where to find him should she change her mind. Reluctantly, she did just that, resenting all the while that she had to live in the dour greystone mansion. When she first arrived on the doorstep of its vast entry hall she was greeted by seven members of staff, a scenario which she later told friends reminded her of something out of *Upstairs, Downstairs*, a popular TV series at that time. Dineiddwg had all the makings of a castle, including the gloom, and for Aileen there was the additional emotional burden of it being the home of her husband's previous wife. She attempted to modernise the place and add a bit of much-needed cheer – everything seemed so grey, brown and drab. But Hugh wanted it kept just the way it was. She thought it dull and dour, he thought it friendly and familial. And so the gulf between them widened.

While he genuinely loved his home and all that it meant to him, he also found it hard to settle for any length of time and was continuously on the move, attending numerous business meetings in various cities around Europe, many of them home to well-known casinos. It was around this time, shortly after their marriage in 1973, that Sir Hugh entered his most profligate gambling phase. By then he had become a betting junkie and, when the chips were down, the urge increased. He couldn't walk away from the table, believing that the next spin, or the one after it, or the one after that, might be the big one, might provide the all-time high. He described to friends the guilt he experienced when he was on one of his gambling sprees. He thought of it in terms of Harrods, the store his father had fought so hard for. 'And when I lost one big pile of chips,' he said, 'I thought . . . here goes the lingerie department. The next heap went and I thought . . . that's the furniture department – ladies' coats next!'

He played the tables for days on end, his gold Cartier flaming a steady supply of cigarettes. He would play four tables at the one time, losing simultaneously on each one. By now he was gambling to an uncontrollable degree and in one night alone he lost £500,000, equivalent to four times that amount today. He would hit all-time lows the morning after a bout, with extreme depression setting in, alleviated only by another spin of the wheel or shake of the dice. So started his illicit share dealings as a means of funding those benders – the start of the end of his reputation as a successful businessman.

It was around this time that Aileen Ross and Sir Hugh Fraser parted, officially separating in 1976. Before that was the tabloid suggestion of her illicit affair with the local blacksmith, which Aileen hotly denied and insisted there had been nothing between the two. They had been married for only three years when they separated and the marriage was dissolved in 1982. Just two years after that, in 1984, came the tragic news that Aileen Ross was missing, feared dead, following an accident during a flight in a microlight craft. The pilot was Alastair Milne, from Dundee, generally thought to be one of the most experienced pilots of the tiny planes. It was believed that, together with Aileen who was training for her pilot's licence, he had been trying to break an altitude record at the time. Their microlight was last seen plunging into the sea off Inverbervie – it was a further seven weeks before Aileen's body was found at Stonehaven.

Post-separation and before Aileen's terrible death, however, Sir Hugh revealed another woman in his life. Someone who had been helping him beat his gambling addiction. Despite the bitter experience of two unhappy and unsuccessful marriages, Sir Hugh remained undeterred and seemed on course again for another heady romance. Sometime around Christmas 1978, 32-year-old Lynda Taylor, a farmer's daughter from Hertfordshire, was rumoured to become the third Lady Fraser. By this time he had sold his family mansion, Dineiddwg, and speculation continued as to whether his new ash-blonde companion would share the beautiful new home he had bought, a sumptuous ranch-style house called Cattermuir Lodge, near Drymen, overlooking Loch Lomond. Lynda Taylor, a former air hostess with one previous marriage to an airline pilot, had been accompanying him regularly for some three months. Journalists who had been in their company said they were very much in love and, when interviewed, Sir Hugh had introduced Lynda as 'the girl who has stopped me gambling'. When one of them asked if she would become the third Lady Fraser, Sir Hugh coyly replied, 'Who knows? Anything can happen.'

But tragedy and headline news struck again for Sir Hugh. On the morning of Monday, 19 March 1979, the sensational story was that Lynda Taylor had been found dead in her car behind the closed doors of the garage of his new house, Cattermuir Lodge. A hose connected to the exhaust pipe led into the car interior. The news left the media baffled: what had happened to her during the last hours of her life? And what drove her to such a lonely death in that fume-filled car and garage? When he was eventually contacted at the family home in Frogmore, Hertfordshire, Lynda's father, Geoffrey Taylor, surprisingly revealed that his daughter was intending to end her relationship with Sir Hugh. He was quoted as saying that the previous week the family had learned from their daughter that there had been some sort of rift between the couple. On the Friday she had left their home at Frogmore bound for Scotland to collect her things, and on the Sunday she had phoned to say she had everything and would be coming home. Her mother said that she had spoken to her daughter by phone twice on the Sunday and that she had seemed quite cheerful, although she had expressed concern about driving back through the snow which had fallen that weekend in the Scottish borders. The next phone call was to announce the shocking and tragic news of her death. Friends of Lynda and Sir Hugh were as baffled as the police, the consensus being that she was genuinely in love with Sir Hugh and, to all intents and purposes, the pair were intending to marry once divorce proceedings with his current wife Aileen had been finalised. On Thursday, 29 March that year, ten days after they had found her dead, Lynda Taylor was buried near the family home at Frogmore. Sir Hugh, accompanied by his mother, Lady Fraser of Allander, attended the funeral and placed a wreath of red roses, carnations, daffodils and other spring flowers by the graveside bearing the message, 'With deepest sympathy from the Fraser family'. A rather sad chapter in the life of Sir Hugh Fraser came to a close.

The same day that the news of Lynda Taylor's suicide was

made public, Tiny Rowland's company, Lonrho, launched the £56 million takeover bid for SUITS, a financial tussle which dragged on for the following two years. Meanwhile, Sir Hugh, who had taken some time to get over the devastation of Lynda Taylor's suicide, put Cattermuir Lodge up for sale, the house where his lover had been found dead. The newspapers called Cattermuir, appropriately enough, his 'heartbreak house'. The sniping and arguing between the two great business rivals reached new heights when, in May 1980, Sir Hugh announced his resignation from SUITS's board only to find himself replaced in the most brazen of moves by Rowland – the man named as Sir Hugh's successor was, remarkably enough, yet another Hugh Fraser. Bearing no relation to the Mugdock Frasers, this Hugh Fraser, who was also knighted, was a well-known Member of Parliament and former husband of Lady Antonia Fraser, the writer and daughter of Lord Longford. His family lineage was the prestigious and illustrious Clan Fraser of Lovat, the House of Fraser successor being the son of their chieftain, the 16th Baron Lovat.

The tussle between the two culminated in January 1981, in a showdown battle over a decision made by Sir Hugh to sell their London Oxford Street property, the department store known as D.H. Evans, for £29 million – then lease it back. This strategy was a favourite device of his father and had been the bedrock of his empire building. However, Rowland, whose Lonrho company now had a 30 per cent holding in Fraser, opposed Sir Hugh's decision and forced a shareholders' meeting in Glasgow the following week. After nearly two years of financial wrangling it appeared that a decision was finally being made. Prior to the shareholders' meeting, Sir Hugh confidently predicted he would win the battle for power over Tiny Rowland – a poll of shareholders had shown him to be comfortably in front of his rival. It was him, he used to say, who was the draper, using the old and favourite term so favoured by his father, and he knew the business better than Rowland. Which was probably indeed the case, but Sir Hugh didn't reckon on the ruthless, merciless nature of big business. Commenting on their relationship, he agreed that a decision had to be made as the conflict between the pair had been bad for business and had been making life 'very difficult'. Sir Hugh went on to confess that with hindsight it had been a mistake to become involved with Mr Rowland. 'He was very plausible,' he added. 'We had dinner very frequently and were great friends.' He admitted that perhaps he should have considered things 'very carefully before doing what I did. He [Rowland] was very friendly as long as I could provide a useful service.'

Six days after he had confidently predicted victory, the shareholders' votes were counted and Sir Hugh had, as forecast, won with a comfortable majority. That battle had been won but, as Tiny Rowland added, the war would continue. 'This is only the second round,' he said. 'It is only the beginning and Sir Hugh knows it.' Just over a week later, at the House of Fraser head office in Kensington, the directors met and in a swift, cut-throat decision, Sir Hugh was ousted from his post as chairman. Control of the huge shopping empire, carved out by his father and his grandfather before him, was now no longer in the hands of the family. Just minutes after Hugh's dismissal, Tiny Rowland announced a dramatic £155 million takeover bid for the company as a whole. Sir Hugh Fraser's days as a big business entrepreneur were over – his biggest single wrong decision was entering into the partnership in the first place.

Despite his very public fall from grace in the business world, his private life continued to attract huge media attention. That same January in 1981, Sir Hugh revealed that there was yet another woman in his life. At that stage he wouldn't say much, only that she was the daughter of one of his father's friends and was much younger than him, she was also separated from her husband, with no children. He said he wished he could have met her 20 years previously. Yes, they intended to marry, he said when asked, 'that is, when we are both free'. In his inimitable style, Sir Hugh handled the affair like the gentleman he was and called a press conference in the most unusual of venues – in the middle of Rouken Glen Park, on the south side of the city. The new woman in his life, it was revealed, was blonde schoolteacher Annabell Finlay, and for the immediate future, he said, they would be considerably preoccupied with plans for their wedding which would be sometime that summer of 1981.

His friends sincerely hoped that things would work out for him this time and there seemed every possibility that they would. Annabell was 25 and Hugh was 44 and could remember the day she was born – his father had given her father, who had been a friend and one of his senior business partners, a silver cup to mark the occasion. They had met again recently, the previous November, just weeks after Annabell had split up with her husband Douglas. The occasion was the Scottish Variety Club ball in aid of handicapped children, a glittering social event held in the former Albany Hotel. Sir Hugh had left the top table of guests, including civic dignitaries and showbusiness personalities, when he spotted Annabell and her party. He stayed with them for the rest of the evening and the couple literally danced the night away. Four days later they were at the Drapers' Ball, run in aid of the Cottage Homes Fund, to which the Fraser family had donated countless thousands, and Sir Hugh appeared to take considerable pride in introducing her to family and business friends. Answering questions at the somewhat novel press-in-the-park conference, Sir Hugh said they couldn't put a date on their wedding until both of them had completed legal formalities of their respective divorces.

Over a year and a half later the couple announced a date of Friday, 20 August 1982, at the Turnberry Hotel. However, on the very week of their big day, another announcement from Sir Hugh caused the first flutter of speculation on the romantic future of the pair. It was on the Wednesday, just two days before their wedding and the extravagant reception at Turnberry, that Sir Hugh announced that their arrangements had to be postponed.

The official reason was that his divorce from the showjumper Aileen Ross would take longer than anticipated and because of that they would have to delay the wedding till the autumn. 'Annabell is very disappointed too,' he added. 'But she understands that it is a technicality.'

Meanwhile, Sir Hugh was in the process of getting back into business again, having acquired several stores, including the old Paisley's at the corner of Jamaica Street and Broomielaw, an old-fashioned but prestigiously traditional store where, among other things, almost every pupil at Glasgow fee-paying schools was marched by aspiring parents for their uniform and sports kit. Sir Hugh had plans afoot for the store and for his business. He had already opened a menswear shop in Ayr, and together with Paisley's his hopes were high that he would one day be the owner of another huge chain of shops.

When he was ousted from the House of Fraser, Sir Hugh still retained a number of other assets and businesses. There were farms in Stirlingshire, the Winnock Hotel in Drymen, a specialist shop for the horsey crowd (jodhpurs, riding boots, the inevitable waxed coats, waxed hats, waxed jackets), a garage in Perthshire, a herd of cattle, at least 20 horses worth a small fortune, a small building company and a cluster of small shops and flats, an Aberdeen knitwear company, large holdings in two clothing manufacturing firms and an ample house and surrounding 6,000 acres in Killin, Perthshire. He planned to make Paisley's, which would be his stores' headquarters, a mini-Harrods, upmarket and prestigious. He changed the name to 'Sir Hugh', intending later, when they had converted the upper floors for female fashions, that that section would be called 'Annabell'. Despite reports regarding low sales from his new shop in Ayr, the conversion work on 'Sir Hugh' in Glasgow still went ahead, and opened later that year – stylish and exclusive as planned, but pitched, it was generally thought, at the wrong end of town, the brand of shopper the store aimed to attract were difficult to lure from around Buchanan or Gordon Streets. The wedding to

Annabell was postponed for a second time. Having set a date for November, Sir Hugh claimed that 'business pressure' meant the ceremony would be delayed again. Sir Hugh was still actively engaged in the establishment of his new 'Sir Hugh' stores. Shortly after the New Year of 1982 the rumours were substantiated and the wedding was called off. There was no Rouken Glen Park press conference this time, just the tearful revelations of Annabell Finlay herself telling a reporter that Sir Hugh had told her that he didn't want marriage or a family and that the difference in their age had been of vital importance in his decision to end the relationship. 'But he is still the only man in my life, although I will never be his mistress,' said an upset Annabell, tears streaming down her face and who was now back home living with her mother. She went on to tell newspaper reporters that it had not been until she had tried to force Sir Hugh into a definite date for their marriage that he had announced to her it was all off.

When journalists contacted Sir Hugh about the reasons for the surprise news, he was more guarded than usual about making a comment, saying only that he did not want to be involved in a third mistake, a reference to the breakdown of his two previous marriages. And of Annabell all he would say was, 'She's a lovely kid.' The following day, however, he was slightly more disposed to clarifying the position, telling one journalist that he was not 'the big bad wolf in all this'. And because Annabell had given up her work as a schoolteacher, he revealed he would be 'looking after her until she gets herself fixed up again'.

For the remainder of that year, Sir Hugh concentrated on what he had earlier said had been the reason for his wedding postponements – business. He was determined to try and restore some semblance of the family's previous success and he had every faith in the new 'Sir Hugh' being the salvation of his diminished business reputation. But there were problems getting the project off the ground, with deals for shops in Bearsden and Largs falling through and another in Edinburgh not eventuating.

The yuppies had arrived in force on the London scene that year, but there weren't many to be found in the West of Scotland, which was experiencing a poor trading year. His upmarket venture racked men's suits with price tags that didn't fall below £130, which was 'big bucks' money for the time. Neither the Ayr nor the Glasgow shop – the former Paisley's – were reported to be doing good business; notwithstanding, there was no dwindling of Sir Hugh's confidence and he was planning to buy two more shops in Alexandria and Helensburgh. Despite his optimism, however, it appeared that perhaps all was not well with the news later that year, in the summer, that an Arab sheikh had bought his prestigious Mugdock estate, including Dineiddwg House, and that another of his investments, the sporting estate at Killin, was up for sale. He insisted that the slack summer trade had not been the cause of the property sale at Mugdock. His surprise explanation was that he had been interested in buying Turnberry Hotel and the neighbouring lands of Turnberry Farm. This had been just one of a series of property deals and proposals in which he became involved in the process of trying to rebuild his own personal business empire. He had sold Fraser Stock Ranches, a prosperous estate of six farms in the Drymen area. He had also sold a country mansion at Croftamie in Stirlingshire. He then went on to buy the Winnock Hotel at Drymen and the 400-acre Boquhan Farm near Kippen. Dineiddwg, the family mansion, had previously been sold then bought back in April 1982, only to be sold again 16 months later, this time to the wealthy Arabian sheikh, Basrahil of Makkah.

Sir Hugh's dreams of realising his former business empire and position did not, however, come to fruition. The main Glasgow 'Sir Hugh' store on Jamaica Street failed. While the building itself, built more than 130 years previously, was architecturally handsome and ornately decorated, looking every bit the part of the mini-Harrods he had spoken of, the venture lasted only six months. The old Paisley's had been a crowd-puller in its day, but that area of the city centre just wasn't popular anymore. The irrepressible Hugh decided to concentrate instead on regrouping his outlets into smaller stores – mainly in the West of Scotland – and as part of this move he acquired the 'Sir' male boutique chain from Austin Reed.

By the spring of 1984 the media were showing interest in yet another woman in Sir Hugh's life. She was Janis Sue-Smith, a smiling and glamorous blonde whose professional past had included being a beauty queen, a dancer and a prominent and highly paid model, one of her most publicised assignments was her selection as one of the Tennent's lager can girls. The 26-year-old was not, however, linked to Sir Hugh on a romantic level. Janis was a company director and fashion controller for Sir Hugh's new chain of fashion stores, making it plain to inquiring pressmen that she certainly wasn't there to beautify the boardroom. 'You can forget the dumb blonde bit,' she told one. 'I'm here to make a success of this job, for the company and for myself.'

Later that year came the tragic news of his former wife Aileen Ross's death on the microlight plane flight near Stonehaven. It had been two years since their divorce and the news visibly shook him. By now he looked much older than his 48 years – his head of wavy hair which had progressively greyed was now turning silvery white and, like his father before him, he was never photographed without a cigarette in his hand.

While his first major Glasgow shop may have flopped, his empire building, second time around, continued apace and by the end of 1984 he had an impressive and growing retail chain of 31 stores, having added the 13 Caird shops to the group. Word emerged that the House of Fraser was considering closing some of its stores and he even inquired whether he could take them over. Later came the news that Lonrho, who had taken over his House of Fraser and its gem, Harrods, were now under threat of losing the store with other business parties coveting the outlets. The new financial giants on the scene were three brothers from Egypt who had established a business and property empire spanning Egypt and the United Arab Emirates to Switzerland, Paris and London. They were called Fayed – Ali, Salah and Mohammed Fayed, and much would be heard about them in the coming years. Sir Hugh also expanded his diversified interests, mainly in the clothing manufacturing trade, owning or having interests in a variety of companies in places like Aberdeen, Tillicoultry, Stirling, Belfast and Northern England. His father, Hugh Fraser III, who had been one of the country's notable philanthropists, would have been proud of his son's attempts to rebuild his assets and would have been even more delighted that Sir Hugh continued his father's charitable ways, maintaining the Fraser Foundation and continuing, under his direction, to give away at least £500,000 a year to various worthwhile causes.

Unfortunately, Sir Hugh never did emulate the success of his former years and by the time he was 50 he looked at least 60. His chain of stores was shrinking and the 31 outlets operating in 1984, just two years previously, had now been reduced to just 12. His fashion director, Janis Sue-Smith had gone elsewhere and his private life seemed barren and empty. There was a short-term relationship with another blonde – another divorcee and a model. Nothing ever came of the affair. Despite commenting that he would like to slow down his business activities when he reached the age of 50, the old enthusiasm remained and, while there had been a variety of setbacks, money was still flowing into the Fraser fortune from a wide variety of successful interests. He even bought his way into the world of football by investing £60,000 of his own cash into Dumbarton FC and becoming its chairman. He admitted that he had been to just ten football games in his life and that prior to making the investment he didn't know where Boghead, their ground, was located. The reason, he said, was simply that a business contact – a former Aberdeen player – had convinced him it would be a good idea to be connected with Dumbarton and he quite sincerely hoped his relationship with the club would sharpen up its finances and its sporting future, perhaps even rejoining the Premier League.

In the autumn of 1986, Sir Hugh was once more page-one news – the receiver had been called in after the Clydesdale Bank refused to cash a cheque from his dwindling fashion stores chain and so ended his business dream. Thereafter, newspaper interest was strictly of a non-business variety: the surprise pre-birthday party thrown for him at a country restaurant which took the form of a theatrical 'sting'; another short-lived romance; taking part in a dieting stunt by jogging round his Dumbarton FC's track; and speaking about his future after 50.

The real character of Hugh Fraser was revealed to me by Sandra Ratcliffe, who was a close friend. She was a journalist who perhaps knew him best of all in the latter years of his life. He confided many 'off the record' revelations regarding his true feelings, particularly those relating to the succession of misfortunes in his love life. He even talked about his alcohol consumption, that he would have a few drinks and then fall asleep in the bath. 'I drink sometimes to forget everything,' he told her. 'I hate going home and being alone when something has gone wrong. When I am not sleeping, a couple of drinks help me. But I get worried when I wake up and the bath is freezing cold. If my mother knew, she'd be so worried.'

His mother, Lady Fraser, was a dignified, gracious woman. She died in 1999, in her 90th year, and according to Sandra Ratcliffe her only son was a constant source of worry to her – his health, his business acumen and his various disastrous relationships with women. The daughter of Sir Andrew Lewis, the wealthy Aberdeen shipbuilder and Lord Provost of the city, Lady Fraser was the ultimate reason that the book of Sir Hugh's stormy and controversial life was never published. He had been enthusiastic about the idea when it had been suggested to him by two journalist friends, Phil Davies and Norman Lucas, and he immediately co-operated with them in the lengthy process of recording all his various business and romantic adventures. It was virtually completed when Lady Fraser found out about it. She was furious with him and, because of his great respect for his mother, he assured her it would not be published in her lifetime. He commented at the time to Sandra Ratcliffe: 'It will be some book! Am I the hero or the anti-hero? Well, I won't be James Bond, that's for sure. He always gets the girl.'

It was precisely for this reason – not getting the girl – that Sir Hugh and Sandra met in the first place. She had put it to him that she felt he wasn't getting the chance to give his side of the story following a recent break-up. 'I know this is a line many journalists feed but I genuinely meant it. I knew he was basically a decent man who would not deliberately do the dirty on anyone. To my surprise he agreed to the proposal and we met for lunch at what was then the Albany Hotel. He arrived a little late, apologising profusely. He was, as always, immaculately dressed. He was not an unattractive man. But he never struck me as being the "smoothie" womaniser type. He didn't have any chat-up lines, not like many other rich personalities I have interviewed. I felt he was really quite shy. He didn't exude confidence. On the contrary, he often looked so very sad.' In this rare meeting Hugh went on to reveal more about his human frailties, particularly in relation to women, than in any other interview he gave. 'I've hardly slept,' he confided to her. 'This situation [with his latest girlfriend] is a nightmare. I am hurt and angry. I know you are going to write about it. I wasn't going to say anything, but I need to talk to somebody. I have been a very, very stupid man. It just seems that every relationship I have turns to disaster. I just can't trust myself to get involved with anyone else ever again. I try to be nice to people, but once again I've been kicked in the teeth. I don't know where I am going wrong.'

Throughout their lunch together, he chain-smoked, his hands shook, his voice was shaky and Sandra believed he was very close to tears. 'I felt desperately sorry for him,' she says. 'I realised then that he was a very vulnerable man. He was the rich kid who was blowing everything. And he knew it. "I've had it all," he told me off the record. "All the chances, all the money in the world, a lovely family . . . and I still can't find the answer to anything or how to make it all work. I look at others and wonder how they manage to achieve anything. I want to ask them their secret. But Sir Hugh can't do that. Sir Hugh Fraser can't go up to someone he admires and ask them for a few hints on how they manage to go through life without all the personal and business flops I've had."'

Sandra Ratcliffe felt he was at rock bottom that day. He was so depressed she advised him to see his doctor as soon as possible. 'But he was a stubborn man. He hated showing weakness in public. No matter how many times his weaknesses hit the headlines, he always picked himself up and charged on to the next project . . . or girlfriend. It was almost as though he could wipe it away like wiping a tape, and he could almost convince himself that the press and the public would do the same. But, of course, the press never forgot.'

Sandra later experienced Sir Hugh Fraser's unbridled generosity, something of a trait in the family, his father being a munificent benefactor. It had been over yet another lunch, this time in his favourite Italian restaurant, the Parmigiana on Great Western Road, where with his favourite fried plaice lunch he ordered a large Bacardi. The reason for the lunch was that he knew of the journalist's personal work in aid of a charity connected to Nuffield Hospital and he had indicated he would like to make a donation from the Fraser Foundation. In view of the circumstances, she anticipated a donation of reasonable dimensions, but nothing like the figure written on the cheque he handed over to her. It was for £10,000. 'I was absolutely stunned by the donation,' Sandra recalls. 'But that was the measure of the man. If there was something he thought he could do to help, his generosity was almost boundless.'

It was through Sandra Ratcliffe that he was introduced to the American knitwear importer Dan Laytham. Sir Hugh was enthusiastic at that time about the prospects of a knitwear factory he had taken over in Tillicoultry. He had great hopes of increasing exports and optimistically believed that this time he had a business venture which would be a real winner. The American visited the factory in Clackmannanshire and the two struck up a business partnership with goods from Tillicoultry being exported to the States. He was delighted at the new association and invited both Sandra and Laytham to be his guests for lunch at Duck Bay Marina on Loch Lomond followed by a visit to a Saturday match at Dumbarton Football Club, which he now enthusiastically owned.

Sandra remembers how unwell he appeared that day. It was bitterly cold, yet despite that he had insisted on taking off his coat and giving it to her while they were seated in the draughty directors' box. 'He had looked so drawn during lunch but still he persisted I take his coat. Again, a measure of the caring and gentlemanly side of the man.'

He also talked with Sandra about ageing and getting older. 'Turning 50 is terrible,' he said. 'I have always hated growing older. I have loved life. I wish I was 25 again. But if anything happens to me, no one need have any regrets. I have had a very full life, even if I have been very silly at times.' His father, he said, would most certainly have disapproved of his gambling, but there was comfort in knowing that he would have been thrilled that the charity work of his Fraser Foundation continued under his son's guidance. Shortly afterwards, Sandra Ratcliffe received a call from Dan Laytham following a business meeting he had just had with Sir Hugh in Dublin. At dinner Sir Hugh had confided how worried he was about his health and that he was afraid to go to the doctor. He had said his legs were affected and showed him his grossly swollen ankles. Fearing he had heart problems or severe kidney disease, Laytham insisted he must go to his doctor without delay.

Not many months after that last interview with Sandra Ratcliffe, Sir Hugh died suddenly. His lifelong chain-smoking habit, up to 100 a day, finally caught up with him at just 50 years of age. On a visit to a specialist on Friday, 1 May 1987, he was told that he had developed lung cancer and that in all likelihood he had only a few weeks left. That same day he had met a fellow Dumbarton FC director and, with his inimitable style and confidence, told him that, despite the terrible news, 'There's a lot of life left in me yet'. Just five days later he was dead.

There was a genuine feeling of sadness about his death. Perhaps Glaswegians had warmed to the shopping magnate who, despite his background and his wealth, didn't come across as a city slicker, preferring to remain, at heart, a Glasgow punter. He was honest and candid. He had been foolish, but was never the fool. He gambled and he lost – monumentally lost – yet he was the first to admit it. He enjoyed £50 bottles of wine but would order fish and chips in his favourite Italian restaurant. He adored his father and would often say that the elder Hugh had handed him a crown to wear . . . 'but it never fitted'. They liked Hugh Fraser for all these things, and more.

Chapter Five

You Ain't Heard Nothing Yet

In many ways he was the father of modern sports journalism, the man who knocked the stuffiness and formality out of reporting and became one of Scotland's most colourful characters. Even today, more than three decades after he reported on his last big soccer match and championship title fight, the words of Robert E. Kingsley, better known by his legendary pseudonym of Rex, are as fresh, stirring, thought-provoking and invigorating as ever. Compared to the formalised prose of the sportswriter of his day, Kingsley emerged on the scene with a far lighter pen and a mischievous typewriter, preferring to look at sport with a smile rather than a snarl. He saw the sporting world as showbusiness, as entertainment, as something exciting to be reflected in the style of reporting.

It was Kingsley who pioneered and revolutionised a new approach to popular sports reporting which was decades ahead of its time. For more than 30 years he was the man connected with every major sporting story. In the flamboyant world of the sports star, he was as big a name as any of the major players he mixed with and wrote about. Bob Kingsley was a man you couldn't miss. He was straight out of the pages of a Damon

Runyon book, the kind of dynamic character people often lament 'they don't make them like that any more'. He was as Runyonesque as Harry the Horse, the Lemon Drop Kid, Okay Okum or Dapper Don. Nothing could have been more appropriate for him than his pseudonym Rex. It was a byline which summed him up. For if ever there was a king of sportswriters, he was the man. When I started this story I was in New York and from the window of my room just off Broadway I could look out on 8th Avenue at the point where it fringes on the district once known as Hell's Kitchen. It was the area in and around here that many of Damon Runyon's fabled individuals used to haunt. Glasgow's Robert E. Kingsley was a perfect match for one of the American writer's eclectic characters. On many occasions he would come to New York on assignment from Glasgow and walk the very same streets as his fictional counterparts. Despite his familiarity with the streets of the Big Apple, it was in his home town of Glasgow that Robert E. Kingsley – Rex – made his name. That's not to say someone else may not come along to rival him but that there just hasn't been anyone quite like the legendary Rex.

The Sunday columnist became a household name throughout the country from the 1930s to the late '60s. He viewed sport as a branch of showbusiness and with his own showbiz background – he was Scotland's first radio announcer – he treated those columns like a performer would their show, with him playing the 'star' role. He even referred to himself as being the 'Walter Winchell of Scotland'. Winchell, it so happened, was not only the doyen of American columnists, he was also the most powerful and influential of American writers, personified on screen by Burt Lancaster in the hit Hollywood film *Sweet Smell of Success*. His egotistical, arrogant character was all part of his 'act' and was never meant to be taken seriously. Given the kind of man he was, Rex would probably have presented himself as the Al Jolson of sportswriters. Jolson was the original jazz singer and the man who insisted on being billed as the world's greatest entertainer.

As the story goes, he was playing at one of the largest fund-raising concerts staged in the States and his act followed that of legendary Italian tenor, Enrico Caruso. The crowd gave the illustrious Italian an ecstatic reception and a cheering standing ovation at the end of his magnificent performances. Then Jolson, absolutely unimpressed and unfazed, coolly walked on stage with a sly grin and announced to the audience: 'Folks, let me tell ya something. You just ain't heard nothing yet!' Rex would have liked that. That was the kind of man he was.

Until he appeared on the scene, there never had been a sportswriter so well known to the public. There hasn't been one like him since. Television, of course, has thrown up a froth of personalities, a few of whom have made a genuine contribution to the art of conveying the action of a sporting event in an interesting and entertaining fashion, but none have come close to the kind of wit and vitality of a character like Rex. His writing never seems to date – even today his commentaries, the way he expressed his forthright opinions, his fearless approach to sporting bosses, his effervescent humour, all survive the test of time. In his own day – the mid-'30s – they were nothing less than sensational. Not only did he become the country's No. 1 sportswriter, in the close season he turned to showbusiness writing and mixed with the major film and Broadway stars of his day in New York and Hollywood. He was even introduced to the President! Such was his meteoric rise to fame as a writer after just four years as sports journalist, the Sunday newspaper which hired him devoted the largest column space in the paper's history to the life story of a certain R.E. Kingsley.

Here's how that serialisation began:

From the moment I started writing, I've been publicised all over the country. I've been described as 'the writer who is different', 'the Walter Winchell of Scotland', 'the inimitable Rex', etc., etc. Every time I made a trip abroad the world was told about it. And I wrote reams about it. I have a fan mail – newspaper and radio. I've been photographed in every charming atmosphere with film stars, football stars, golf stars, baseball stars, and Sid Montford's stars! I have broadcast in the United States and Canada.

People think of me as a human dynamo. Unapproachable because I'm being approached too much. They come to see me, hesitantly. I won't keep you a minute . . . know you're a very busy man. I've signed thousands of autograph books. Sent out dozens of autographed photographs. I've given hundreds of lectures both as a BBC producer and newspaperman . . . I am the only Scotsman who has ever been invited to broadcast the greatest sporting event in Britain – the Scotland v England football match at Hampden.

His cleverly constructed persona was merely Rex's way of celebrating the point that in truth he was, as he put it, 'plumb lazy'. Similar to Jolson asking for the theatre house lights to be put on so everyone could get a better view of how much the rest of the audience was enjoying him, Rex put the razzmatazz into being a newspaper columnist, and his readers were hooked.

R.E. Kingsley – Bob to his friends, Rex to everyone else – was from that old breed of Glasgow showmen. They were the genuine Barnum and Bailey characters who banged the drum and craved the spotlight because they genuinely had something to offer – rare talent or a magnetic personality. Bob Kingsley was first and foremost an entertainer, latterly with a pen. When he started out in showbusiness it was by more conventional means, in front of a live audience. It was on stage and, later, as the first BBC radio announcer in Scotland that Bob Kingsley got his taste for the thrill and satisfaction of being a showman.

The young Kingsley began life in 1901 in a tenement house on Calder Street, Govanhill, his dad a hard-working postman. His family went without to afford the fees for an education at

Hutcheson's Grammar, but Bob later confessed he had no academic flair. His first job was as a ten shillings (50 pence) a week apprentice in his uncle's chemist shop. He hated that job as much as he did the next, a junior salesman in the millinery department of a Co-op warehouse. He did, however, enjoy the nights he spent at the classes he enrolled in at Percival Steeds' Drama School which were conducted at the Athenaeum, a small theatre on Buchanan Street and later the workshop for students at the Royal Academy for Music and Drama. The drama classes at Steeds' helped him to secure roles in the evening variety concerts, and while his weekly full-time job paid just ten bob (50 pence), he could earn as much as £3 on his evenings off playing in a concert party. He was left in little doubt as to his chosen career in showbusiness.

Around this time a new form of communication was revolutionising everyday life. The radio – or 'wireless' as it was called – was becoming a household appliance by the mid-'20s in Britain and the British Broadcasting Company, as it was known then (it didn't become the Corporation until granted its charter in 1926) was establishing relay stations throughout the country to satisfy demand. The BBC's first Glasgow studio opened in a humble office on Bath Street and they began recruiting for an altogether new kind of person – a media personality – to convey the message. They were called radio announcers. By coincidence, Percival Steeds' troupe, including the young Kingsley, had just broadcast a radio performance of Romeo and Juliet. Elocution was a much more essential part of the young dramatist's training than it is today, and Kingsley's stagy, plummy voice, the *de rigueur* articulation of the time, caught the attention of D. Miller Craig, the BBC's Scottish Controller, who invited him, along with 49 others, to audition for the role of Scotland's first announcer. At this early stage he was informed that if he got the job, he would have to do something about 'that name'. His family had the somewhat obscure name of Quaey and he was, consequently, Robert Elliot Quaey. So when those first historic words were announced – after a polite 'good evening' that is – 'This is 5SC, the Glasgow station of the British Broadcasting Company', the owner of the young thespian voice was none other than a certain Mr R.E. Kingsley. It became his adopted name from then on. After a six-week probationary period, Kingsley was contracted for £5 per week – ten times the wage he had been getting as a junior salesman. Despite his drama school elocution lessons and the work he put into smoothing out traces of his Glasgow background from his voice, it was his accent that proved to be the Achilles' heel of his BBC career. The general manager of the company at the time was a giant and dour Scot, John Reith, who became the Corporation's first Director General, and is best remembered as Lord Reith, the revered father of the BBC. It was Reith who laid down the early guidelines of broadcast material and the performance and behaviour of the Corporation's staff. It was on his insistence that announcers be accentless, a speech variant which rarely existed outwith the studios of the Broadcasting Corporation.

Kingsley settled into his job and all was going well until one of his broadcasts from Scotland was overheard by Reith himself. His pronunciation of the name of the composer Bach had upset the general manager, who phoned immediately from London demanding to speak to the unorthodox announcer. Kingsley had merely said 'Bach', with a short 'a', in the manner any well-intoned Scot might. Reith demanded it should be enunciated with a long 'a' as in 'Ba-a-a-a-ch' and that in future he should pay more attention to such detail.

Sometime later Reith came to Scotland and the pair met, the 6ft 4in figure of Reith towered over Kingsley and he was obviously displeased with the latter's enunciation. Shortly afterwards, Kingsley was sacked but was soon surprisingly reinstated following a spate of letters to the editors of some newspapers about his dismissal. He went on to spend the next six years with the BBC, becoming a senior sports broadcaster before eventually being dismissed a second time when the company 'rationalised' in order to concentrate their efforts in London.

Out of work for the first time in years, Kingsley was determined to continue in some form of showbusiness and managed to get bookings for a string of revue performances, some of them in London's top theatres, including one in a show starring the legendary Jack Buchanan. He loved the theatre, but up to that point hadn't realised just how much he enjoyed commentating on football during his radio years. While visiting Glasgow he met up with a former journalist with a Glasgow newspaper who suggested that if Kingsley could only write with the same flair with which he had done his radio commentaries, there could well be a big future for him as a writer. He encouraged him to try submitting a report for the *Evening News*, one of the three newspapers owned at the time by Kemsley Newspapers and printed in Hope Street. The editor loved it, telling Kingsley – as he later recalled in his autobiography, *I Saw Stars* – that his column had broken new ground in sports reporting, combining 'facts with comedy, punch and reasoned comment'.

Sports reporters of the day mainly wrote under assumed pen-names – bizarre and baffling pseudonyms which often left you wondering what the connection was. One newspaper's collection included such byline gems as Nimrod, Spike, Cromwell, Bedouin, The Ace, Jack Trot, Westward, Dreadnought, Old International, Famous Referee and Clarion. Some of their names sounded more like brands of whisky than those of press reporters.

Rex too, of course, came with his own nom de plume, but in his case he was quick to show that the name did mean something and that if there really was going to be a king of sports writers then it was R.E. Kingsley.

He was introduced to Sunday newspaper readers in April 1936, in a news story headlined 'The Writer You'll Wait For At The Weekends'. The paper then went on to record its pleasure in announcing that 'Mr R.E. Kingsley, the famous BBC sports commentator and critic', would be joining the staff of the *Sunday*

Mail. The column added that their new signing was '. . . the friend of players and officials throughout Scotland and England' and was 'the sports reporter with a laugh in his lines'. From his very first report under the byline 'Rex' – printed at least twice the size of any other writer in the paper – it was clear that he was everything they had imagined. The match was Celtic v Arbroath, the latter being a top division team at the time, and began: 'That million-dollar head again! It belongs to McGrory, and lucky Celtic to hold a still unexpired lease of it! That famous head scored a goal yesterday fit to be photographed and hung in the Parkhead pavilion.' Snippets from the rest of his report summed up the man's style and flair: 'At times they showed as much inspiration as a glassy-eyed cod on a fishmonger's slab'; 'Had it not been for McGrory's superhuman effort at the end, the post-mortem at Parkhead tomorrow would have cracked the pavilion windows'; 'Celts first goal was the type that makes you mutter "Ach" in disgust and feel for your cigarettes'; 'Arbroath only had one forward with ideas – Brand . . . They should handcuff him to the boardroom table till he re-signs!'; 'Once again Becci [Arbroath] kept the crowd roaring. I wouldn't like to foot his bill for pants. Those ferocious sliding tackles must play havoc with 'em. Mebbe he'll find a corduroy pair hanging on his peg one day!'; 'If Celtic treated this game as their only remaining "dangerous" fixture, they can now go ahead with a spot of whitewash for the flagpole!'

Having covered a Celtic game for his first assignment, it was perhaps more than obvious that his next match report would involve Rangers, which it did, the Ibrox side playing at home to Third Lanark. Again, it was one of those snappy, on-the-button reports that made easy and entertaining reading for the fans. This time it was the Rangers goalkeeper, the legendary Jerry Dawson, who had Rex enthusing as only he could.

'Immaculate Jerry Dawson,' his report began. 'A goalkeeper in a thousand – and a thousand goalkeepers in one! I see him yet in those testing moments when the wind, sun and Cathkin courage threatened to crash through the Rangers defences. I see him picking the wind-swept, jerky ball out of the air or off the ground with a grace of movement which hid the grim tenacity of those masterful hands. And, most memorable of all, I see his six-foot muscular body hurtle through space to bring off the save of the match. Old-timers can wheeze about "so-and-so's" save in 1887 and tell me I was born too late. My answer is that I saw Jerry Dawson's save in 1936 – and thank heaven I wasn't born late enough to miss it!'

Aberdeen was the venue for his third report, firmly establishing Rex as a favourite among readers. The Dons were playing at home to St Mirren and Rex began his report with the startling introduction: 'I grabbed Paddy Travers, the Aberdeen manager, at half-time. "Come clean, Paddy," I demanded. "Where have you been hiding this fellow Strauss all this time?" Paddy smiled in that way that speaks volumes yet leaves your notebook empty.' Strauss, it emerged, was a youngster from South Africa and was playing his first game for the Dons, as well as any of their regular stars it would seem. 'I don't often get burned up about a newcomer, because it's bad for him – and it makes me thirsty! But this sun-tanned young fellow with the flying legs and hearty physique may become a personality in our game very soon.'

Within a year of branching into sports journalism, Kingsley was not only writing lively match reports but, at his request, had been given a full page of his own to indulge his readers with comment and chit-chat, prattle and tattle, blabberings and backbites, rumours and romances. The fans loved every word of it. It was billed as 'My Page', perhaps somewhat egotistical but then that was the point. 'My Page' became one of the mainstays of the newspaper with fans eagerly devouring it for football gossip before turning to the columns informing them how their team had fared. His popularity rose yet further with the launch of 'Your Space Boys', a section of the paper where the fans could sound off about all the usual things with Rex replying to each and every one of them in his own inimitable style. Even in those days, back in the 1930s, fans were complaining about the dominance of Rangers and Celtic on the Scottish game. One griper wrote from Buddon Street, right next to the Parkhead stadium, complaining that: 'On behalf of the small fry who visit Ibrox or Celtic Park. Is it not about time the "Old Firm" racket was handicapped? My suggestion is to allow the visiting team to Ibrox two extra players – namely one forward and one defender. In the case of the visitors to Celtic Park, I would allow them one extra forward and two goalkeepers. What is your opinion about this?'

Rex replied: 'Pal, the only difference between you and me is that I get paid for being daft!'

Another fan, around the same era, complained about the bigotry of the songs sung by both sides at a Rangers–Celtic game and suggested there should be loudspeaker music of another sort to drown them out. 'Old pal, you're an optimist,' Rex retorted. 'The only thing that would drown these ratchet-throated choristers is a good going hose-pipe and plenty of water!'

They would tease him about his vanity, as much professed as it was confessed. 'Dear Rex. Is it true that every time you look in the mirror you shout hip-hip-hooray?'

'Certainly,' responded a typical Rex. 'And maybe if you saw what I see you'd do the same!'

As well as his football columns, his 'My Page' and varied other writings, Rex did an irregular series of open letters to sportsmen who he considered needed his guidance. One of his first correspondees was that famous Gorbals lad, the irrepressible and legendary Benny Lynch. At the time the youngster had made it and was not only the world champion but was rated as one of the best flyweight boxers ever, adored by the whole country. But to insiders like Rex, he knew that warning bells regarding Benny's future were ringing. And ringing loudly. It was in March 1938 that Rex penned his open letter to Benny. It had been just five months after the boxer defended his world title in what was reckoned to be one of the greatest fights of all time: his knockout of Peter Kane at Shawfield Park, watched by a capacity crowd of 40,000 with almost as many turned away. On this occasion Lynch was fighting Kane yet again, this time in a non-title bout at Liverpool. Sadly out of condition because of his drinking, Benny turned up overweight and put up the most mediocre performance against the Golborne man, the fight being declared a draw. Afterwards Rex took him to task in a public letter.

Dear Benny

Are you proud of your display at Liverpool? If you are, then I've nothing more to say. It is in the hope that your disappointment is as acute as that of your admirers I pen this note. When you smote Peter Kane into submission last October we hailed you as the greatest flyweight in the world. You are the greatest flyweight in the world. But only when it comes up your back!

You made a bad start at Liverpool when you stepped on to the scales a pound and a half overweight. You may think you lost only £100 [the sum he was fined by the boxing authorities]. You lost a lot more than that – as you may learn to your cost if you repeat this blunder . . . I think I know the public. They don't know what to make of you. They don't know when they are going to see the world's champion flyweight, or just a fellow called Benjamin Lynch . . .

In my personal association with you, Benny, I have always found you a fine little sport. A top-notch display in your next fight and all will be washed out. Another careless one – and we'll all be washed up! Come with a straight right, Benny!

Yours sincerely

Sadly, it was too late to stop the downwardly spiralling career of Lynch and just three months later he forfeited his world title by turning up overweight again for the challenge by Jackie Jurich, after that he fought just two more official contests.

Many years later, another legend to receive one of Rex's public reprimands was the late Jim Baxter, playing for Rangers at that time. Baxter was a favourite among Ibrox regulars, but Rex considered that he needed to be taken down a peg or two for his less than sportsmanlike play, particularly so after his club's game against Monaco in September of 1961. It prompted this letter.

Dear Jim

You've been snowed under with 'credits' since the season started. Some of them very extravagant and even fulsome. I may have been guilty of this myself. Forgivably so, for when you are moving that ball you can be the smoothest thing since velvet.

Why spoil it? Why is it that you seem to resent opponents occasionally doing to you what you so often do to them – outwit you by skill.

The first Monaco player who did this to you in the early minutes at Ibrox was fouled by you. It was the first foul in a game of many fouls, and may have some bearing on the subsequent deterioration.

A fellow with your natural soccer gifts should be ready to accept an occasional outwitting, confident he has the skilful qualities to weigh the balance heavily the other way. Indeed, no one more so than yourself. For throughout a game your tantalisingly brilliant dribbling must reduce opponents to the verge of frustration.

But you can't have it all the one way, Jim. The footballer who can never be beaten is still unborn . . . There are few players who give me so much pleasure. You mean a lot to Rangers and to Scotland. Hence the reason that every little thing you do on a field is widely noticed – and noted.

The Baxter I prefer to see is the player who does the things beyond the scope of so many – the Baxter I don't like to see is the player who does the things within the scope of the least skilled.

Yours sincerely

Having established himself in a remarkably short period as the best-known and certainly the most entertaining sports commentator in the country, Rex spread his writing wings even further. He just couldn't bear to be out of action during the close season, so he became one of the first international columnists. He was tossed the keys to the world and went on to report on numerous famous personalities from Hollywood stars to Broadway performers, Madison Square Garden boxers and Wall Street tycoons, senators, mayors and Bowery characters. He met them all. In a world of movers and shakers, Rex could move – and shake – with the best of them. As he wrote in one of his first columns from New York, he had just stepped off the gangway of the Aquitania – you sailed to New York in those days – and before the day was out he had lunched with Burris Jenkins, America's top newspaper cartoonist, had dinner with Babe Ruth, not only the legendary baseball hero but billed as 'the most popular man in America', enjoyed the company of the actress Myrna Loy, at the time one of the biggest names in Hollywood, and had made arrangements to meet the President of the United States. Being Rex, the meeting with the man in the White House actually happened. Then again, when the likes of Joe Louis, one of the greatest world heavyweight champions, invites you to join him in his private box at a Detroit–Yankees baseball game, as he did Rex, then perhaps meeting the President isn't all that much of a big deal! He also met the man he had so famously compared himself with, the *Sweet Smell of Success* columnist Walter

Winchell. This happened at the famous Twenty One Club in New York, where he was also introduced to a variety of other stars, but by this time Rex was on top and had to dash off to yet another renowned location, this time the Cotton Club, accompanied by the glamorous star Ella Logan, from the famous Glasgow showbusiness family – she was Jimmy's auntie – where he met jazz legend Cab Calloway. The presence of Ella, a genuine Hollywood and Broadway star, attracted the attention of a press photographer on the lookout for celebrity personalities and he snapped her as she enjoyed a drink with Rex before they dined. A typical Rex would say that the only reason he was in the picture was to make Ella look better.

While he did a number of 'celebrity' tours, meeting and being photographed with the rich and famous, it was his blunt, candid and, for his day, outspoken views on football, the sport he loved so much, that won him so many readers. He was forthright, frank and fearless when it came to expressing his opinions on the game and the way it was run. His columns endeared him to his readers as much as they enraged administrators. Not long after he became a regular columnist, two of the biggest and most influential men in football refused to speak to him, one of them even banning Rex from their ground, the incidents almost bringing an end to his career as a sports journalist.

In the 1930s, as it is today, football giants came from either Rangers or Celtic. Two of the most influential men in soccer at that time were Willie Maley of Celtic and Bill Struth of Rangers. Both were the longest-serving officials with their clubs, the former for more than 50 years, the latter for some 40 years. Both had the title of manager. In those days they ruled their clubs like autocrats. A journalist wouldn't dream of approaching any member of either club, unless Mister Maley or Mister Struth gave their blessing. Even Rex obeyed the code, except on one occasion. Celtic player Charlie Napier had gone into a nursing home for a cartilage operation and Rex, quite naturally, wanted to let the fans know how he was progressing. He had tried his best to contact Maley, making six attempts in one day, but without success. His deadline was approaching and so he decided he would just go and see Napier in hospital instead, and was delighted to find the operation had been a success. Mindful of protocol, Rex contacted one of Maley's friends and asked him if he would mind going with him to the Bank Restaurant in the city, owned by Maley, and introducing him to the Celtic boss. At the same time he could show the manager what he planned to write about Napier. Maley nearly had a fit when Rex told him that he had seen and spoken to his player. The story is best recounted in his own words as he described Maley's reaction when they met in the restaurant and Rex handed him the typed story he had prepared for his paper. 'His eyes popped. He stepped back. Then he thundered: "How dare you go to see one of my players without permission!"' Rex informed the manager that considerable efforts had been made to contact him beforehand but without success. That only served to make Maley even more furious, who erupted once more: 'The press think they can do anything they like, but not to Celtic players so long as I'm in charge,' he roared as he marched up and down in the middle of the restaurant, glass in hand, furiously denouncing Rex, the press, his paper and everyone concerned with it in front of the other diners, watching in hushed silence.

Unperturbed by Maley's fury, Rex snatched back the piece of paper with his story and tore it up before the furious manager. 'When I came here I thought two gentlemen were going to have a talk,' he shouted back. 'Now I know there's only one – and he's going out. Good night!'

The pair didn't speak for the next ten years. The ice was finally broken when Maley called at Rex's newspaper building on Hope Street and inquired whether it would be possible 'to have a word with Mr Kingsley'. When phoned at his desk, Rex asked for Maley to be sent to his office, though he never called it that, always referring to it as 'the den'. Not a word of the incident the previous decade was mentioned, neither were any of the criticisms Rex had made over the years about the club. The purpose of Maley's visit was to ask whether Rex – one of the most prodigious charity fund-raisers in the country – could arrange one of his regular shows for a particular children's hospital which Maley supported. Rex said he would be delighted and took his show to the hospital. Thereafter the two men became, and remained, lifelong friends.

As any Rangers fan will tell you, anything Celtic can do, Rangers can do better. Which was certainly the case when Rex had his fallout with Ibrox manager Bill Struth, shortly after his conflict at Parkhead. The bust-up between the two was so serious that the Ibrox manager ordered that Kingsley should not be allowed into their press box, and made a bitter complaint about him to his editor at the paper. Once again the ruction was caused by Rex being 'ahead of the game', as it were, as a journalist. He had heard that Rangers were interested in an American soccer player called Jimmy Coubrough and that the club had invited him to Glasgow for a trial. As it turned out, the American had already arrived when Rex was tipped off about the story. He immediately headed to Ibrox to see Struth. When he arrived at the impressive entrance to the stadium there were no staff on duty at the front office. Rex wandered instead into the stadium. He strolled down the players' entrance to the field where the team training was in progress. The Rangers' chairman at the time was Bailie John Buchanan, who was watching the practice match from the running track. As soon as he noticed Rex come into the stadium, he went over to him, greeted him with a friendly slap on the back. Rex asked what the purpose of the match was and the chairman informed him that they were giving a possible new player a trial, the young Coubrough from the States. Manager Struth was there, too, but made a concerted effort to ignore the pair. Rex returned to his den and wrote a piece on the American and how he had viewed his trial, the only paper to carry the story. Struth was furious when the article was published as he had informed other journalists that the game was private – when photographers had turned up at the park he had personally chased them out of the stadium – yet had said nothing to Rex when he turned up. Struth had never been so furious with a pressman. He complained angrily in a letter to Rex's editor about 'his conduct', demanding to know why he had defied instructions, overlooking the fact, of course, that Kingsley had never been in receipt of any instructions. However, he made sure that Rex received his latest instruction, which barred him from any future mid-week visits to Ibrox. It was a long time before there was any rapprochement between the two, Struth taking the initiative many years later by having a waitress deliver him tea and some cake when Rex had been making a BBC broadcast at Ibrox. At the time, for a sports writer to be shunned by the two most influential managers in the sport was most certainly an impediment to his career and only the respect and backing of an understanding editor persuaded him to withdraw his offer of resignation. Despite being declared *persona non grata* by the dominant duo, Rex continued to write about the two clubs, and was more determined than ever to be seen as the most scrupulously fair commentator in the business.

Incidentally, it wasn't just Rangers and Celtic who were over-sensitive to criticism in those days. A variety of other clubs would regularly take umbrage with anyone who dared challenge them – editors regularly receiving communiqués from irate boards of directors. One of the most furious of these came from Hearts, following up their complaint by posting an official at the entrance to the press box at Tynecastle to bar Rex, all because one of his colleagues had censured them for their play the previous week. Rex was secretly delighted with the ban, knowing it would guarantee a sensational column in the paper. With his route to the press box blocked, he immediately headed for the public turnstiles to compose his report on the terraces. However, Willie McCartney, the Hearts manager and one of the great characters of the day, spotted him. Realising the kind of headlines that would have resulted from that situation, he grabbed hold of Rex and practically frogmarched him to the press box, flouting the exclusion ruling of his directors. McCartney then stood guard over the controversial journalist to ensure he didn't escape back to the terraces and the punters.

The domination of the game by Celtic and Rangers was as prominent then as it is now. Rex was there for that memorable match in 1938 when, after a decade of poor performance in the derby games, Celtic trounced Rangers 3–0. His coverage of the game was one of his classic reports. It began:

> Rangers got a proper dusting yesterday. Brilliant goalkeeping, desperate clearances, and barrowloads of luck prevented the game from being all over before the interval.
>
> Celtic went daft. Rangers played daft. It has taken Celtic ten years to manage a win over Rangers in a Ne'erday game. It will take Rangers ten years to live it down!
>
> I have never seen a Rangers team so easily hoodwinked, outmanoeuvred, and even 'kidded' as in this first half. Rangers can have no excuse. They were whacked in the arts of the game. When they did start to get on the lines again, the number was engaged. I lost count of the breathless escapes and thumping fine saves by Jenkins . . . most of the Rangers' players looked as if they were 'hitting the hay'. A sleepy, drowsy, heavy-footed bunch . . . It was Celtic's day all right. They played on their toes and in doing so put Rangers on their backs. Heaven only knows what might have been the score if regulars Delaney and Geatons had been playing!
>
> Despite Celtic's superiority over most of the game, it was always worth watching. Loads of clever interpassing, slick lobbing and thrilling runs . . . The best thing Rangers can do is to try to forget about this game as quickly as possible, that is, if their friends will allow them.

When the boot was on the other foot, as it were, and Rangers were playing well, they too would be accorded the praise they deserved. Although he tried his best to be the most neutral of game observers, fans would quickly take offence at his comments if their team happened to come under fire. Their letters would feature regularly in his 'Your Space Boys' page.

'Jolly little fellows, some of these Rangers and Celtic fans,' Rex announced on his page one week. 'They take their football so happily! A few quotations from this week's mail:

'"Your report proved you have no time for Celtic . . ."; "Even you with your green specs and green pullover should have seen that this tripe about Celts' wonder inside trio is a lot of boloney . . ."; "You said if the referee made any mistakes he must have made them at half-time. You're right – he made a mistake in coming back to the field again!"; "I sincerely hope Celtic don't score more than six goals in any game you attend as I would hate to see you left with writer's cramp."'

Writers would often ask why he published so many letters from the fans of the two Glasgow teams. The simple answer to that, he wrote in reply, was because he got so much correspondence from them in the first place. 'If Rangers and Celtic fans show that interest more than the supporters of other clubs then I must pay respect to them. They are to be commended in their enthusiasm for their club which encourages them to go to the bother of writing.' There were no commendations, however, for those fans associated with the darker side of the game. Although the atmosphere these days at Old Firm games remains much the same as it always did – the descriptive word is vitriolic – better policing and improved ground facilities have considerably reduced the kind of scenes which were all too frequent in former times. Disturbances in and around the stadiums and later in the evening in various parts of the city were regular occurrences and pitch invasions, either by groups of fans or kamikaze soloists hell-bent on some form of deranged 'kill', were all too common. Such behaviour was the scourge of the game during the four decades Rex was star reporter on the matches. He regularly lambasted them in print. 'Yes, I knew it,' he wrote in 'Your Space Boys', 'knew I'd get a load of letters about the tykes parading as Celtic fans at Parkhead last week and the Rangers ditto at Falkirk . . . Hooligans can never change their technique. They don't have the brains. If they had, they wouldn't be hooligans. And if they weren't hooligans they wouldn't be noticed. And there you hit the guy right betwixt his fish-supper and beer. For when you see a terracing mug blurting profanities to the heavens you are watching a nonentity trying the only way he knows to become a lance-corporal.'

In addition to the hooligans on the terracing, there was apparently no shortage of them on the field, judging from Rex's reports written more than 60 years ago. On the park the action could occasionally be as violent and ferocious as some of the post-match skirmishes, Rex regularly making the point that there would be fewer hooligans off the park if those on the field behaved themselves. 'When we lash at the guys who create trouble on the terracing, we are whipping a cow who goes through a window when prodded in the hindquarters by a hayfork. I've said this till I'm sick, and I'm still sick. Club officials who refuse to see how that trouble starts are blind enough to be admitted to the German Air Force.' (Note: The comment was made just prior to the Second World War.) Rex would often accuse the club officials themselves as being the real culprits in the continuing disorder between the two clubs. It wasn't so much what they had done for the game but what they had done to the game. Onus was put on everyone, except the real culprits, the respective club managements, he would say. 'They have done nothing to reduce the religious heat which brings huge crowds to these games – one would almost think that they encouraged it to ensure such crowds, the game itself seems now to be merely a thin cover for the "Billy" or a "Dan" challenge.' A sentiment which still rings true today.

Following a minor riot at Ibrox stadium, Rex launched one of his most trenchant denunciations of fan violence: 'Rangers–Celtic games have done more to foul the name of Scottish football than any others. The Hampden instance on Wednesday last (a fan attacked the referee) contrived to introduce an even more vicious element. I never imagined I'd live to see the day when a person could dive on to this famous ground and at close quarters attempt to assault a referee with a bottle. Rangers–Celtic games should be "under new management". I'd start with the refereeing angle. We have too many officials who can referee a Rangers–Celtic game – and too few who can control it.' At the time, he reckoned, there were only three referees in the country able to control Old Firm matches (for the aficionados he named them as Craigmyle, Calder and Webb) and the reason, Rex suggested, that there had been so much trouble at the last derby was, not surprisingly, because none of the three had been in charge. Incidentally, one of that refereeing trio, namely Peter Craigmyle, was rated by Rex as not only one of the greatest umpires in the game, but also one of its great characters. Rex described his refereeing as peerless, much of it due to the astute warnings he would discreetly hand out to the players as he ran alongside them. He would often tell the story about the time Craigmyle caught the great Celtic winger Jimmy Delaney, one of Rex's friends in the sport, play-acting an injury. The incident occurred during a game at Fir Park against Motherwell. With just minutes to go, Celtic were a goal down and hell-bent on getting the vital equaliser. Delaney had the ball out on the right wing and was racing in towards the goal when Ben Ellis, the Motherwell left-back, went in for the tackle. It was a precision, by-the-book intervention, Ellis retrieving the ball in the process. Delaney, however, did a spectacular tumble about two yards inside the box and lay perfectly still with his face buried in the grass – years before today's continental players mastered the art.

The fans screamed for a penalty as Celtic left-half Chic Geatons raced over to help his injured teammate. Running just as hard from the other direction was Craigmyle, reaching Delaney just as he lifted his head an inch off the ground and whispered audibly to Geatons, 'Is he gi'en us a penalty?' To the amazement of the fans, instead of signalling to the dugout for help, Craigmyle gave Delaney a firm tap on the shoulder and uttered something sharp in his ear, whereupon the player jumped to his feet and play was immediately resumed. It was never revealed just what was said, but it's pretty easy to speculate.

The bloody rivalry of the Old Firm continued and by the early '60s, Rex was advocating that, having tried every other approach imaginable, the only way to halt the thuggery was to have the perpetrators face judges of the calibre of Lord Carmont, a notorious High Court judge whose stiff sentences in the post-war years did much to diminish the activities of the infamous Glasgow razor gangs.

'Nail 'em and jail 'em,' Rex urged. 'Cut out the wet-nursing, pandering and poppycock. Stamp them for what they are – outcasts of society and mass morons.' Yet still, half a century later, the violent tribalism continues, amply demonstrated in one of the first games of the new millennium. The same old sectarian chants dominated, the same old tiresome taunts prevailed and afterwards there were 62 arrests, one man was stabbed to death in his home, another kicked senseless by a gang of supporters, and another was attacked with sticks and golf clubs. Even one of the star players from the game was involved in a post-match inter-fan fracas.

Fortunately, there were other happier events for Rex to write about. During the six years of the war, sport was considerably curtailed and with less reporting in his usual sphere, Rex devoted his spare time to supporting and encouraging the forces. Having been proclaimed medically unfit for the army, he contributed to the war effort in other ways. He organised concert parties around the barracks, ships and airfields for the men and women in uniform – he could play the piano, he could sing, he could be the master of ceremonies. When he wasn't performing he would be involved in some kind of fund raising.

Prior to the war he had raised huge sums of money for the blind and had founded the organisation known as the Rex Blind Parties, organised football outings for the sightless accompanied by a host to provide a running match commentary. For more than 50 years, until the advent of miniature headphones and other aids, those outings were a source of great enjoyment for countless thousands without vision. He expanded his charity work to cover the armed services, perhaps his best-known project being the outstanding 'My Shilling Fund'. It was unveiled through one of his famous open letters to readers, taking up an entire page of the paper. 'Times have changed,' he told readers. 'I'm a beggar from now on. I'm not ashamed. Proud rather. No longer will I claim that I can get money without appealing. I'll appeal, work, organise, do anything, in fact, for your money.' Which he did. And for the next six years he developed the venture into a large-scale fund on behalf of those forces. He charged fans for his autograph, he made them pay for his jokes, his songs, for his piano playing, for being a master of ceremonies, with every penny raised going towards his 'Shilling Fund'. For his tireless work and enthusiasm in fund raising, Bob Kingsley received an MBE. The award was presented by the Queen at her very first investiture as new monarch in 1952.

With the cessation of war in 1945, a sports-starved nation was desperate to reinstate Saturday afternoon normality. By 1946, two of the most popular sporting events of the era, the soccer and rugby internationals against England, were resumed. The anticipation was great and was heightened all the more with the announcement that both events would take place on the same day.

Saturday, 13 April, came and promised to be one of Scotland's more memorable sporting occasions. At Murrayfield, the Scottish rugby side played better than they had in a good while, vanquishing the visitors 27 points to nil. As for the football match, only Rex could describe just how brilliant and momentous an occasion it was. A real nailbiter, Scotland had easily been the best team, but suffered that same old problem – the inability to score goals. Fortunately, England weren't doing much better. With barely half a minute till the final whistle, it was Celtic legend Jimmy Delaney that won the home team the justice they deserved. The game and its fantastic conclusion even had the usually verbose Rex stuck for words: 'For the luv o' Mike, will somebody tell me how to describe this game! Only an artist could give you that scene half a minute from the end when 140,000 went stark, staring mad and waved, yelled, spluttered and prayed for strength to wave, yell and splutter some more. When Delaney scored that goal nothing else mattered. This was the greatest game in the world. Hampden the greatest place. And those 11 Scots the greatest players.' It was Rex at his major league best. He made the reader feel like they were actually there, waving, yelling and spluttering. The team that early spring day in 1946 was: R. Brown (Queen's Park); D. Shaw (Hibernian) and J. Shaw (Rangers, captain); W. Campbell (Morton), F. Brennan (Airdrie) and J. Husband (Partick Thistle); W. Waddell (Rangers), N. Douglas (Birmingham), J. Delaney (Manchester United), G. Hamilton (Aberdeen) and W. Liddell (Liverpool). The players' clubs perhaps, summing up the changes in Scottish football since 1946. Such is the nature of the Scottish side, however, that victory is never a certain thing. In the 1950s Rex wrote about another Scotland v England performance. It was in the days of Brown, Mackay, Docherty, Evans, Collins and Ormond. Despite the stars in the line-up, they put on a dismal showing in a 1–0 defeat against England at Wembley. As Rex wrote: 'Our selectors are still looking for miracles – instead of footballers. But for the grace of the football gods, and the brilliance of Bill Brown and Bobby Evans, this could have been worse than Flodden.' That single-goal victory by England was as laughable, he said, as was some of the Scottish side's play. He went on to castigate our team, saying that man for man, the English line-up had been in a different sphere of football from ours. We did have friends on the park, though – the Portuguese linesmen and referee who had surprisingly nailed England for 'fouls'. But then, in one of his quips, Rex reckoned that the ref's mother had come from Scotland. He thought too that one of our forwards must have been wearing weighted boots with square toes, judging by his kicking accuracy.

While football was his first love as a sportswriter, Bob Kingsley also covered other major sports, boxing being one of his favourites. He didn't cover many big fights, however, boxing writing protocol at that time being very much left to experienced men on the newspaper's staff who specialised in the sport, and who were often ex-champions themselves, for example, the *Daily Record*'s Elky Clark, a great boxer and former British, Empire and European flyweight champion. He was a holder of the Lonsdale Belt and only lost on points in a world title fight against Fidel La Barba, a tough and gritty South American at Madison Square Garden. Unfortunately, Clark not only lost the fight, but his career abruptly ended that night when he received an eye injury so severe that he lost the sight of one eye. Despite the calibre of talent available to write about boxing, Rex knew, appreciated and could describe a fight as well as any of them – he was there when that other great flyweight, Jackie Paterson, won his first major title. Paterson was just starting out in his boxing career at the time and was still undecided whether or not his future should be that of a professional boxer or in the back shop of a Glasgow butcher in which he worked on Canal Street, just off Dobbie's Loan, Port Dundas. His fight that last day of September 1939, against the British flyweight champion Paddy Ryan of Manchester, finally made up his mind.

The 15-round match against the English champ was billed for Carntyne dog racing stadium. Rex summed up the future champ's display in classic style, describing the blow that ended the fight in the 13th round as 'a punch that shouted for a camera'. His report went on: 'As that shattering left cracked on to Ryan's chin, there was a gasp from the crowd. Ryan's knees straightened up, and he toppled flat on his back like a wooden soldier. There he lay, arms outstretched, his face sprayed with blood, his eyes wide open to the heavens, but seeing nothing. It was the blow of a champion wonder, the crowd jumping to its feet waving programmes and hailing hysterically this new Scottish hope in boxing.'

As Rex predicted, Paterson went on to win the Commonwealth and world titles and was eventually hailed as the second Benny Lynch. (The full story of Paterson's boxing life is told in *Great Glasgow Stories II*.)

Rex's snappy, vivid style was his hallmark as a writer. To Rex it was showbiz. Sport was about entertainment, and writing about it should be entertaining. He had a typewriter that hammered out jazz, not symphony. His words were flashy, never fusty; gaudy but never grandiose. He had an exuberance that grabbed you, hooked you and made you want to read to the end. For example, after Rangers had been trounced by the Dutch team Eintracht in a European Cup contest, there had been much critical talk about the Ibrox side. Rex honed in on the controversy: 'You need a sense of humour in this world. Poor old Rangers are being tossed and bandied about since that Eintracht licking almost as if they'd sold our birthright by distributing bad whisky among the Jerries . . . yet nearly all the people whose pre-match forecast was that Rangers would at least draw, if not win, had never seen Eintracht play. But they had seen Rangers play . . . and while Rangers are taking it as a bad football beating, which is all it is, others are crying their eyes out about being "ashamed", etc., etc. See's a len' o' yer hankie, hen.' Similarly predicting great things for UK soccer in the coming year, his first column of 1961 would have enthused even the most cynical fan: 'Good morning, chaps! Ease the ice-pack off your cranium and listen to me. As we grab this babe of 1961 by the legs and smack it gently to hear its first call, let's ponder what is promised in our soccer world by the time these same legs can carry the weight of its own body. ME! I declare this may well be the year when British football will burst its way through the continental code of soccer for a new and revolutionary blueprint stamped "Made in Britain".'

His commentary on the problems of soccer managers displayed a similarly eccentric style: 'Knock on any door – any manager's door – and you'll soon be on talking terms with an ulcer. The football escalator grinds on relentlessly, hooking up the successful in its ascent, sending the failures spinning away. Till the next time round. Then – who knows? You could run a toy railway on the "marshalling yards" above a manager's eyebrows.' In the early '60s there had been a reluctance by many Scots players to re-sign with clubs until they were offered better wage deals. Rex took the less talented of these players to task: 'Scottish football has gone completely haywire. Never before have so many players refused to re-sign. You'd imagine this little country was jammed full of crackerjack performers just waiting for the swoop on their services. Lumme, if some of these reluctant guys are stars then they must have come out at night – I ain't seen them through the day. What's got into them? Do they really think they're in the Joe Baker–Jimmy Greaves class? I look at the list and wonder. Wonder at the bigheadedness, or pigheadedness, of very ordinary players who appear to have extraordinary ideas of their own importance.' A report from the States while he was covering the game between Bangu (Brazil) v Dynamo (Romania) in an international soccer tournament at the Polo Grounds in New York read: 'So far the tempers in this tournament have been hotter than the play. Bangu led the ill-tempered parade in this their first match with Dynamo. Playing like tired tomcats who'd had an uneventful night prowl, they flared up easily.'

And his comment on the hiring by Celtic of manager Jock Stein was a classic: 'The Celtic signing of Jock Stein may be the best thing that happened this year – to Rangers! It has certainly stuck a hayfork in the Ibrox pants. Now there's real action there. The decision to appoint a public relations officer, like Celtic have done, is a step in the right direction, leaving manager Scot Symon to do the job for which he was surely engaged, complete concentration on fielding a team worthy of this great club.' Rex's match report on the Third Lanark–Rangers game (score 1–2) which appeared on 3 September 1939, the first day of the Second World War, offered a somewhat different take on the treatment of war: 'Doesn't it get you down? Just when the youngsters in football are busy earning their spurs – and how they're earning them – this German clown [Hitler] upsets everything. Here was a game where youth looked old in football skill. The field was sprinkled with youngsters – Waddell, Sinclair, Thornton, McNee, Stephenson, etc., youngsters with talent bursting for release. The halt in their football career which seems imminent may spoil everything.' His dispatch from Madrid on the SFA decision to drop legendary Scottish captain George Young from the national team is palpable in its disgust: 'This is really a sodden, tarnished world. The SFA selectors have something to answer for. In their complex and mysterious wisdom, they have decided that George Young will never play another game for Scotland. Of all the cruel, heartless, almost criminal indiscretions, this dropping of the big chap for tonight's return game against Spain is the sorry limit. The only people happy about it (additional to the men who made it) are the Spanish selectors and their players who almost can't believe it.'

Realising that Rex had potential far beyond that as a mere sportswriter, his employers at Kemsley House, the former newspaper HQ in Hope Street, Glasgow, sent him on regular trips abroad where he would report back on a wide variety of matters, including the world of showbusiness. These dispatches before and after the Second World War would fill innumerable pages during the summer months when football had shut up shop. It was America he loved most of all. To appreciate the impact of his reports is to appreciate that in those days Rex was a rare breed altogether – not many had visited Broadway, the White House and Hollywood, or had rubbed shoulders with the rich and famous, even the President himself. Rex enjoyed his time in the States. He even had a perma-groomed American look about him: forever the natty new suit, the tailored shirt, the silk tie, the ever-coiffured hair. America was his kind of country. He liked the pace, the way it moved, the way things worked. He loved the service, the style. He captured the spirit of the place to perfection in a report from one of New York's most renowned sports arenas, the famous Polo Grounds. The attentions from the staff there obviously overwhelmed him: 'There was I hammering away at the old typewriter like an enemy's teeth were the keyboard when a steward in the lofty press box laid a can of beer in front of me, all opened and ready to be swallowed. Next came another steward with a plate of ham and beef sandwiches that melted in the mouth. I forget when that first happened to me back home – indeed, I forget when it ever happened at all! In this brash city of New York, where you never know when the boss will barge in and holler "You're fired, turn in your ulcer", courtesy is in violent contrast.' He went on to rave about the manners of telephone operators and hotel staff, eulogising the expression 'have a nice day' more than half a century before it became common.

And, of course, the showbusiness stars he met rattled from that old typewriter of his almost on a personality-per-paragraph basis. He didn't just meet the likes of superstars David Niven and Loretta Young. No – they invited Rex to lunch, and at one of Hollywood's legendary meeting places, the Brown Derby. Well, come on, you wouldn't catch Rex in company like that anywhere else. And when they were there, they were joined – naturally! – by a collection of other superstars of the day. First came Alice Faye, a pre-war star who might equate nowadays with the likes of Meryl Streep; and if the awesome company of Niven, Young and Faye wasn't enough, who else should come along to their table but Groucho Marx. But that wasn't to overwhelm a guy like Rex. Hell, no. As he reported, they had already met! The last time had been on a Hollywood film set in a film starring the legendary Marx Brothers. That had been when Groucho had told Rex one of his famous golfing stories because, being from Scotland, he knew he would appreciate it more than most. This time, at the Brown Derby, he had another 'tale' to tell. Appearing as though he had just run in from somewhere, his hair over his eyes, gulping, panting and swallowing hard, he said, 'I've just seen a terrible accident. As I came along the road there was a man in front of me smoking a cigarette. He threw the stub down a manhole – and then he tramped on it.'

Despite his love of the States and its stars, Rex was never happier than when he was at home and in the company of the great characters in football. He was one of the first to welcome to Scotland the most famous footballer of his generation, Stanley Matthews. Matthews was in Glasgow for what was to be a unique occasion: his appearance at Ibrox as a member of the Rangers team.

Stanley Matthews playing for Rangers! Apart from those pundits who know every dot and comma about the club, people are rarely aware that the great Englishman did once pull on the light blue jersey to play for the team. It was in 1940 while he was on the staff of Stoke City and awaiting his call-up to the forces that Matthews had come to Scotland for a few days. Hearing of the visit, the Ibrox manager, Bill Struth, invited him to turn out in that Saturday's league game against Morton – which sounds a bit like asking David Beckham if he would fancy a game at Ibrox, perhaps against Kilmarnock, on his next weekend trip with Posh to Gleneagles. But it was different ways, different days back in the '40s and Matthews told Struth he would be delighted to play for the team he had always admired.

Predictably, Matthews' presence packed Ibrox that Saturday, 30 March 1940, with everyone keen to see the soccer legend join in with the other ten in the home side of the day: Dawson; Gray and Shaw; McKillop, Woodburn and Symon; Duncanson, Thornton, Ventners and McNee. But life is full of anti-climaxes and that late winter's day at Ibrox was to be one of them. Despite its boost from the mighty Matthews, the home side's 1–0 win was to be the most mediocre of games, one match report describing it thus: 'Not a game that entranced as a spectacle . . . play went along on ragged lines . . . passes went wrong . . . a pity the Ibrox game didn't run on the lines favourable to him [Matthews] showing all he can do with a football.' Matthews was to admit afterwards that it hadn't been one of his best days. But then, that's football.

Rex loved the great characters of the game, many of whom became genuine friends. The Scottish captain George Young had been one, which was why Rex had been so particularly upset when the SFA announced they no longer required him for the Scotland team. He had sincerely felt for the way Young had been treated and had berated the officials accordingly: 'Young has done nothing to deserve this shoddy treatment . . . he is thrown on the heap in the most callous fashion. Ach, it would make you sick. Nobody can tell me that George Young is not the fittest man to skipper Scotland.'

Tommy McInally and Charlie Tully of Celtic and Torry Gillick of Rangers, names to make older fans swoon, were among others on the friendliest of terms with Kingsley and men he considered as great and genuine characters. In the '60s, when all these names were long since gone from the scene, he would write that Scottish soccer was a considerably poorer place without them and the individualism they had brought to the game. They were among the most memorable of people, he would say, and they pulled in so many fans to see them in action with their teams. Tully, the great Celtic character renowned for his cheeky capers, like bouncing the ball off an opponent's back after being handed it for a throw-in or cheating from corner kicks, was a regular visitor to Rex's den and would feature in his columns, usually favourably of course. 'But if I dared to criticise him I was bang in trouble,' he wrote. 'Even rusty razor blades were sent to me by incensed Celtic fans advising me to use one "when your hand is shaky".' When he told Tully about the abuse he got over him, and about the razor blades, the jovial Irishman roared with laughter and told Rex he should be getting himself an electric razor.

Torry Gillick of Rangers was one of the great stars of the Struth era and would always go to training carrying a brown paper bag. Mandatory dress for the Ibrox men in those days was the wearing of a bowler hat but Torry would have none of it, at least till he was within sight of Ibrox, whereupon he would doff his cloth bunnet and swap it for the bowler he had in the bag. Rex would write that the very name of Gillick conjured up all the things older fans were missing from the game in Scotland. For example, the straight-talking Gillick would criticise others in his team who, when passed the ball, would in turn pass it back to him. He would say that, in his consideration, if he passed the ball to one of the forwards, then it was up to him to do the rest. 'If you yank a piano up a stair surely you're not expected to play the damn thing as well,' he would say. It was the same Gillick who caused a sensation at the legendary Rangers–Moscow Dynamo game in 1945 by ignoring a ball that had been passed to him because he was too busy finger-counting the opposing Russian team. Unnoticed by the referee, they were playing with 12 men, a substituted player having 'forgotten' to leave the field.

The irrepressible Tommy McInally of Celtic was another of the Tully–Gillick calibre. He was a man who could be as impudent with his moves as he was with his mouth, once stopping a game in a five-a-side tournament by sitting on the ball because he considered he had run enough. His observations were as legendary as Shankly's, one of them being that referees were people who found out early in their lives they couldn't play football, then studied the rules so they could stop others playing the game too. And when he once appeared before an SFA disciplinary hearing, accused of calling a referee a disreputable name – a charge he in all honesty denied – he was asked after the evidence had been heard if he wished to make a final statement before the committee passed their judgement. Once again he denied the allegation but as he walked out of the room he turned to the panel with the comment: 'Mind you, I thought he was one just the same!'

Towards his retirement in the early '60s, a period when football was suffering a dearth of fans at the same time as it was experiencing the beginning of the metamorphosis which was to lead to the game as we know it today, Rex was to do much crystal-gazing about the future of the sport. The golden days of club soccer were fading, he would say, and when the platinum days arrived they would mean glory only for the few who toiled and sweated on the training ground and expanded outwith the Scottish circuit to entice the continental showpiece teams. The trunk of the Scottish soccer tree, he said, was top-heavy, all the fruit being at the top and carried by too few branches. 'It's a small country, Scotland. In the easy-easy days of the past it could carry all these mediocre clubs just and no more.' And he warned Scottish players that their days would be up unless attitudes changed. 'Some of them seem to spend more wind arguing for extra money than proving they are worth it.' There were too many artful dodgers during training. Once they had re-signed for a new season, they would amble through training because they considered that was them set for another year.

There was talk about involving the Scottish teams in a British league but Rex would have none of it: 'They're throwing out the old lifebelt again. The moment Scottish clubs start floundering desperately in deep water, out comes the lifebelt inscribed "SS British League" . . . It's supposed to have some magic formula to bring Scottish football home to calm waters. I don't get it. Chairman Bob Kelly of Celtic has often been quoted as saying it is bound to come. And now Tommy Docherty, the Chelsea boss, claims it as a solution to the fading attendances . . . For years English clubs have been scoffing at including Scottish clubs in a newly conceived British league. Why the change? Is it that some of the top clubs down south are finding it tough to pay their players all the incentive bonuses etc., and are casting a greedy eye on the two big fish up here, Rangers and Celtic? For, frankly and bluntly, this is all we have to offer them – Rangers and Celtic. And believe me, the Old Firm would have to find some real magic to fight their way above the middle of a British league.'

It was Rex who was first to reveal the initial plans by the Scottish Football Association to take over and move to Hampden Park, albeit that it was just talk at the time. He backed the suggestion enthusiastically: 'If the SFA bought Hampden, I'd say they should immediately sell their £35,000 white elephant at Park Gardens and move their administration offices to Hampden where tickets etc. could be more easily handled.' He wrote these words in February 1959. Forty years later that move finally transpired. And had only Rex been here to see it. 'He really was a man way ahead of his time,' says one of his contemporaries, the sportswriter, broadcaster and commentator Alex Cameron. 'He really was the most entertaining of writers. And essentially that's what he was – an entertainer. He was a proper showbusiness character. Loved coming in that wee bit late at big sports occasions, like championship boxing tournaments, and to be seen being recognised by all his many friends and acquaintances as the well-known character which he was. And when you read some of his material now, it's as refreshing and contemporary as anything that's being written. He really was a one-off.'

Rex – Robert Elliot Kingsley – died on Christmas Eve 1974 at the age of 73.

Chapter Six

The Best Cop We Ever Had

He was the best-known cop Glasgow ever had. He was so famous, in fact, they knew and liked him not only in every part of Britain but in 44 countries throughout the world. They watched him in Dublin, Dubrovnik and Dakar, in Turin, Toledo and Toulouse, and as far away as Shanghai and Sydney and the South Island of New Zealand. They dubbed him in Catalan Spanish and Mandarin Chinese as he bossed the team of detectives who were regularly in pursuit of a variety of violent criminals. His worldwide audience amounted to tens of millions. Just think about it: more than 12 million in Britain alone were his regular audience. In one series it was nearer 20 million. Glasgow has never had a policeman as celebrated as Taggart. And more than likely never will again.

Actor Mark McManus, who died in 1994, the man who made Detective Chief Inspector James Taggart a household name to millions, was Scotland's first-ever international television star. And he would have been the first to have laughed in your face if, as a young man working as a labourer unloading the timber ships in Govan docks, anyone had suggested to him what the future might bring. For acting was one of those things which just happened to Mark McManus. There was no drama school, no thespian lessons, no planned studies, no acting courses. In an industry where fortune is as much a factor in success as talent, Mark had his share of the former as much as the latter. Take his face, for example. Looks are of vital significance on TV, as every female newsreader's face can testify. Faces tell stories. And TV cops' faces tell special stories. McManus's could show feelings that flitted from scorn and loathing to disdain, contempt, abhorrence and now and again humour with all the facility of some superb mime artist. Along with the sophisticated Morse, who could do it with barely moving his handsome facial muscles, the rough diamond Dalziel and that gorgeous bag of spanners face of his that spat out the expressions with gunfire velocity, and Frost's mobile moustache, Taggart's face told it all. The stony visage with its classic in-built Glasgow stare and its menacing and summarising silence. A face that knew what it was like to come from the Maryhill tenements. A face that could say 'don't mess with me, pal' one minute, and the next show care and affection. A face too which didn't require any of the other ruses they devised for the TV sleuth to make them distinctive and worthy of your attention – like the corpulence of Cannon, the old coat of Colombo, the crotch of Dalziel, the Mozart of Morse, and the like. Taggart didn't need gimmicks, not with that face, that look. They were the key ingredients the producers had been searching for in someone who could portray the role of the tough, hard-nosed Glasgow cop with an image that would say as much about the city as it would the man himself.

Back in the early 1980s Scottish Television producer Robert Love, with the lofty title of Controller of Drama but more appropriately nicknamed 'Mr Drama', was planning future programmes for his department. He wanted to create something the station could sell to the main network. Something they would find irresistible. And he thought something along the lines of a series about a hard-nosed Glasgow detective might be the right idea. Love had already tried out a young Edinburgh writer called

Glenn Chandler for some previous programmes put out under the title of *Preview*, a series of half-hour plays, and had liked his work. He thought he would be the man to write the new programme he had in mind and Chandler accepted the challenge. The requirement had been for a mini-series murder drama set in Glasgow, a task Chandler tackled with some dedication.

Chandler was from the kind of Edinburgh family which was as far removed as you could imagine from the sort of Glasgow criminal and underworld types who were to be the fodder for his TV writings. The Chandlers were musical people, a grandfather leading an orchestra which used to play in the city's Caledonian Hotel, his dad being a member of the band, mum being the bandleader's daughter and a well-known amateur opera singer. Being from Edinburgh and that sort of background, Glasgow wasn't really his scene but he applied considerable dedication in changing that, soaking up what he could of the atmosphere of the city, particularly Maryhill, where the fictional cop he had in mind would have grown up, and wandering around the local cemetery taking names from gravestones for the names of his cast. The one he chose for the name of his detective chief inspector had been a man called Taggart. James Taggart. There was no searching required, however, for the man he wanted to play his new fictional character. Chandler already had that man in mind, an actor who had impressed him so much in recent TV drama performances – Mark McManus. The name of the resulting STV drama viewers were to see was entitled simply . . . *Killer*.

The response was such that the Glasgow TV station immediately ordered more works from writer Chandler and seriously considered investing in a long-term future for the policeman who had been received as such a believable character. A TV legend was in the making. Chandler, who confesses to a macabre bent in his writings, went on to write many more episodes of the ongoing series. Each would take about two months in the planning stage, during which he researched and consulted police on their attitudes and reactions in certain situations. Many of the stories would be based on real-life murders, the writer having an impressive collection of true crime books, many of which he would earmark for future *Taggarts*.

A lot had happened in the life of actor Mark McManus from those days when he had come to Glasgow from his native Hamilton and laboured in the Govan docks. His dad was a miner, a staunch socialist so dedicated to the cause that when he collected money from fellow miners to help republicans fighting in the civil war in Spain he travelled there himself to hand over the funds. Before moving to Hamilton the family had lived in Cumberland Street, one of the main thoroughfares in the Gorbals, and it was there that Mark remembered his earliest days at work, picking 'totties and tumshies', as he would say, on a Newton Mearns farm during his summer holidays from school. He had enjoyed that but had the opposite attitude when making a living at the Govan docks, work he described as 'a hell of a job'. Perhaps it was just as well he did see it that way, for the need to escape was what started him along the long road that was to culminate in his being one of the most recognised figures on television. The first stage along that road was taken in 1960 when, aged 26, he headed by ship to Australia, the ironic end result of that being that he found himself back working in the docks, this time the ones in Sydney. Instead of unloading timber planks in the wind and rain, he was now loading wool bales in the heat and dust.

Life on the old Sydney docks was an On the Waterfront existence. The wharfies operated in gangs, each with a gang number, and McManus, together with his team, would be there every morning at six o'clock in the hope there would be work. They would mill around with hundreds of others waiting for their gang number to be called. Often it wasn't, however, and that would be another day without pay, another trudge back again the following morning at six, another lottery for a job.

Australia, being the kind of place it is, gave McManus the

chance to change his job as often as his location. A fit and active man, unafraid of hard labour and with no qualms about travelling, could always find a job and he made working trips to the outback, remote places like Broom, which is somewhere at the back of beyond, and after that even further away when he landed a labouring contract on an oil company project in Papua, New Guinea, which was under Australian administration at the time. Being the convivial sort of bloke he was, McManus also found those experiences in such outlandish parts to be great source material for the stories he would regale his pub pals with in later years back home in Scotland. 'See in the jungle,' he would tell them, recounting his time in New Guinea, 'everything moves and everything bites you. It was murder! At night we'd sit in a clearing and try to relax. But no chance. For at six o'clock the fruit bats woke up – hundreds and hundreds of them, all flapping about above our heads and dropping more guano than a million Glasgow pigeons.'

Another story went down even better. It had its origins in Tahiti. Mark had gone down there on leave from New Guinea and while in a bar in Papeete, the island capital, he had met what he described as a stunningly beautiful girl called Seline. They stayed together and Mark was to describe that experience as being like all his Christmases had arrived at the one time. 'For a week I was unbelievably happy and was madly in love. Seline was absolutely gorgeous,' so he said. Twelve years later, however, together with his first wife, Paulette, Mark had gone on from Australia on a Pacific island tour and stopped off at Tahiti. 'We wandered into Duffy's Bar, a well-known sailors' haunt, for a drink and were sitting quietly at a table when the place went absolutely dark. I looked up and saw this monstrous, massive 20-stone woman looming over me. She was so fat that she was blocking out all the light. Then she says to me, "Oh, Mark, cherie. Don't you recognise me? I'm Seline."' When he recovered his composure, Mark asked the lady how on earth and after all those years she had remembered him. Despite the company of his wife, she wasn't slow in explaining just why. 'Because,' she answered, 'you are the worst lover I ever had in my life.' It was a hard story for any pub mate to top.

It was in Australia too that Mark McManus was introduced to acting. Being the gregarious group they were, the dockers had a variety of side interests when work was over and they had slung their hooks. Among such activities was their own theatrical company and one of its producers asked Mark if he could help out with one of their shows, behind the scenes that is. It's a story as old as showbusiness itself, of course, the man at the side of the stage being asked to fill in and next thing you know he's the star actor. In Mark's case it happened when the company were staging Brendan Behan's *The Quare Fellow*. They needed someone with a good Irish accent and all eyes were on Mark. 'Near enough' was their view of Mark's broad West of Scotland tones and he got a main part. 'It was like putting a peg in a hole just made for it,' said Mark about that first time on stage. 'I just slipped into acting and loved it right from the start.'

The rest of Mark's tale goes along similar lines to that old showbusiness story, except for the stardom bit, which wasn't to happen for many years. Getting to the top, for him, was to come gradually. Very, very gradually. He became involved with a theatrical company which had been a regular supplier of talent for TV soaps and children's programmes. As he had next to no acting experience, Mark was to take the lower end of the trade. One role was as a dog, one that barked and didn't bite. In another he played the part of a witch. Yet another saw him together with a crocodile puppet. It seemed at first he had difficulty getting away from animals. Even in his first proper acting job he was involved with them in the kids' programme *Skippy*, one of the first big successes of early Australian television.

From barking dogs to squawking crocs and playing second fiddle to a kangaroo called Skippy – not the kind of roles you think would lead to playing in Shakespeare, or *Taggart,* but that's showbusiness. Mark certainly had no regrets about his strange introduction to the business, not with the wealth of those great yarns he so much enjoyed telling. Like the one about that crocodile puppet. 'I did it for the money because I was hard up, but I hated it,' he would say. He hated it so much that one night when the credits started rolling on the screen at the end of the show, Mark faced the puppet croc and told it what he really thought about it. Only thing was, the show hadn't really ended and his outburst was broadcast to the nation. And it wasn't the kind of stuff suitable for young ears. So he was instantly sacked.

Then there were his stories about *Skippy*, although being a genuine animal lover, these were stories he didn't enjoy retelling. Skippy, it turned out, was actually 14 different kangaroos, that number being necessary because their accident rate was upsettingly high. 'I lost count of the number of animals that died through rough handling,' Mark would say. 'One was supposed to jump on the back of a moving lorry and when it kept refusing, one of the crew picked him up and tried to throw him on to the truck, but missed and the poor beast got run over. Another died when it fell from a tree.'

By now he was at least getting a living, though. It was much better than being a docker or wharfie. To Mark, totin' barges and liftin' bales had about as bleak a future as it had for Ole Man River himself. And you know what happened to him after he got a little drunk! Showbusiness offered amazing diversity and opportunity. Life was never dull and full of the unexpected. By 1970 he had become well enough established with the theatrical agencies which supplied bit actors that his name kept coming forward for various small parts. One which would go down well in his burgeoning showbiz CV was playing alongside none other than Mick Jagger. Mick was obviously looking for satisfaction of another kind and was playing the starring role in the movie *Ned Kelly*, the story of the legendary Irish–Australian bushranger. And there was Mark riding alongside Mick in his role as one of the leaders of the gang which for years had terrorised the backwoods of New South Wales and Victoria. And when the cameras stopped rolling for the day, there were all the accompanying perks of handsomely budgeted movie-making, like sumptuous parties in the Outback, iced oysters and the finest wines. Playing crocodile puppets and barking dogs had never been like this.

The roles got bigger and more varied, and when he auditioned for the Australian tour of a big West End stage musical it wasn't a bit part he got – he was to be the star. With his fair hair and boundless energy, the producers saw him as another Tommy Steele, which was just what they wanted, for the musical happened to be the hit that Steele had written for himself, the flash-bang-wallop Cockney show *Half a Sixpence*. Mark had to be truthful with them, though, when he was asked if he could dance and sing: 'I told them I couldn't, but that I would learn.' And learn he did, taking dance lessons and working hard at the likely routines for the show. The singing bit was easier, though: 'Well, I was a good party singer,' he said. In any event Mark and the show were to get rave reviews, and *Half a Sixpence* was to have one of the best runs of any touring musical, playing to full houses for the next two years.

With that experience, plus his film and TV parts, Mark began thinking about trying his luck as an actor back home. With his Australian wife Paulette and their two children, Christopher and Kate, they set up home in Radlett, Hertfordshire. There was more work than ever for aspiring actors, with the boom in television, and within months of his return a selection of roles were to come his way. There were parts in a series of stage plays, including long stretches at the Royal Court and the National Theatre, appearances as Macbeth with the Scottish Theatre Company and in the Greek tragedy *The Bacchae* at the Edinburgh Festival, in which he played Dionysus, the god of wine, fruitfulness and vegetation. And you can imagine the stories playing that kind of role was to provide! Then there was Shakespeare's *Macbeth*, a part he had also played in an

Australian outback touring company, and *Benny*, that being a portrayal of the legendary Glasgow boxer Benny Lynch. He had particularly cherished that role for there was a lot of Lynch in Mark McManus himself. He was a drinker, a legendary drinker at that, but the boxing part of his story was told in some detail when he spoke to a Sunday newspaper about the time he made it to the semi-finals of the British championships and took part in a contest in Madison Square Garden, New York, backing up the story with an actual photograph of himself in an amateur ring contest, and with his opponent on the floor at that. He was to tell this same writer that one of the two reasons why he had quit the sport had been a man called Walter McGowan, who any fan will tell you became world flyweight champion in 1966 as well as being a British Commonwealth flyweight and bantamweight champion. The second reason was another man, this time with the eerily portentous name of McTaggart. He was Dick McTaggart, an outstanding Olympic medallist and generally regarded as the finest amateur boxer Scotland has ever known. Mark's story was that his misfortune as a fighter had been meeting these two champions in contests and, as he put it, 'How the hell was I to get past the likes of them?'

It was at this point in the story that I wanted to know more about Mark's boxing prowess, especially his fights against McGowan and McTaggart, two of the most illustrious ever of Scottish pugilists. I wanted to know their memories of being in the ring with someone who had become such a TV legend. To make sure his own memory was right on the score, Walter McGowan had to do some research for me. 'I know who you mean,' said Walter, 'but I don't remember having fought the man.' The former world champ then checked his records but there was no trace of any fights with an opponent called McManus. 'He must have been thinking of somebody else,' said Walter. Dick McTaggart, on the other hand, was to meet the inquiry with a gentle laugh. 'Aye, I've heard it before. He was supposed to have fought Walter then myself shortly afterwards.

But Walter was a flyweight and I'm a lightweight, so how could that have happened?' (There's more than a stone and a half weight difference in these two boxing divisions.) Dick did want to add, however, that he had met the actor on a couple of occasions and found him 'a really nice fellow. No airs or graces about the man.'

I spoke too with a number of Scottish amateur boxing officials but none remembered McManus taking part in contests here, giving him the benefit of the doubt that most of his fighting must have been done while he was in Australia. Perhaps an explanation comes from the story told by a showbusiness friend of how Mark, being the amiable and helpful sort of man he was, hated to disappoint journalists always on the look-out for new angles for their articles. 'I often make up wee stories to keep them happy,' he had confided to the friend. Well, those fights with the superchamps McGowan and McTaggart appear to be two of them. Or maybe those stories about the ones that got away are not just confined to fishermen!

In later years, however, McManus did have a genuine interest in boxing and amateur officials here do remember him on many occasions being one of their staunchest supporters and speaking knowledgeably about the game. And he did go into great detail about the fights in which he took part in Australia, where he used them as a means of supplementing the meagre wages he earned there as a docker. These were mainly rough-house matches around the Sydney boxing booths, a form of boxing popular at the time in which the challengers came from daring punters among the booth audiences, and his face was to clearly bear some testimony to those brawling days, the customary pugilist's trophies, such as a rearranged nose and a variety of wounds which had required multiple suturing. He told one journalist that, in all, he had more than 70 stitches as a result of his ring conflicts. But then again, maybe that painfully large total was another of those 'wee stories'. . .

By the 1970s, Mark's reputation as a reliable journeyman

actor was sufficient for him to qualify for auditions in the active
TV market and when he landed the title role in a drama called
Sam, producers and directors began taking note. There was a
presence he exuded whenever he was in a scene, the youthful
elfin face giving a rare display of all the emotions that came with
the script. After that he was chosen for a key role alongside the
well-known TV series star Don Henderson in a show called
Strangers, Mark playing the part of Superintendent Lambie, a
tough Glasgow detective. After having been co-star to a
kangaroo and an animated reptile doll, getting a role like that felt
like he'd achieved Hollywood status.

It was around this time that STV started considering making
a serialised whodunnit revolving round a streetwise Glasgow
detective. McManus was given the scripts to gauge his interest
and, after having read them, asked producer Robert Love if he
could have the role. *Killer* went into production in the winter of
1983 with Detective Chief Inspector Jim Taggart making his
début to TV audiences. The show wasn't a huge ratings hit
immediately but it did achieve sufficient ratings for the ITV
network, who were more than impressed, to ask for more. Much
of the reasoning behind that request was the superb acting of
Killer's star in the role of the tough Glasgow cop Taggart.

It was all happening for Mark McManus now. That week the
first episode of *Killer* was screened, Mark was on stage at the
Theatre Royal with the Scottish Theatre Company's production
of *Jamie the Saxt* and during the day he was rehearsing for his
role in *Macbeth*, due at the same theatre the following week.

Within a few months, *Taggart* became firmly established on
the TV scene, blossoming into one of STV's biggest-ever projects.
The shows were major productions, requiring productions teams
in the region of 70 people, a million-pound investment and up to
six months' work for each three-part or one-off special. But it
was to be well worth it for the Glasgow-based TV company. Any
misgivings they might have had about the comprehension of the
star's up-a-close accent south of the border were quickly

dispelled with the performance of *Taggart* in the ratings, the show quickly rising into the UK's top ten programmes.

Taggart was a hit and McManus a star. That raw Glasgow accent, incidentally, while incorporated in the scripts, was to be more than emphasised by McManus himself, who had his own strong views on aspects of the man he was playing. Jim Taggart, according to the story, was the son of a Maryhill tram driver and had worked his way up the ranks of the force. Therefore McManus decreed that he should use the kind of speech a man like that would use – which was why he always called the police 'the polis', the neighbours were 'neeburs' and a noisy altercation was always 'a right stushie'. In other words, pure dead Glasgow. But the one thing he never did say was 'Naebody move!' despite the repeated use of the catchphrase by innumerable impersonators. It was a similar story to that of the legendary Humphrey Bogart, who never did precisely say, 'Play it again, Sam' in Casablanca. In Taggart's case, it was a very likely and believable expression for him to have used and was to become more identifiable with him than any other bywords he really did say. Irrespective, there were never any complaints from non-Scottish viewers about the stushies, the polis or the neeburs, just more enquiries as to when they would be likely to see the next series about the cop they had come to love.

Chief Inspector Taggart was a man with a puritan outlook on life, a bit like the Frost character played by David Jason. He seemed to be always feeling guilty about enjoying his own life if there was a rapist or a murderer out there to be caught. And whereas Frost might be somewhat sombre, Taggart was always downright dour. Glasgow dour. The kind of dour that put a whole new meaning into the word. When he made one of his clipped statements or observations, it was always with attitude. The dourest of attitudes. He could make the most cheerless of Glasgow football managers – and everyone knows who that was! – sound like Mr Happy Lad. And when Taggart asked a prime suspect a question, it came with a belligerent wrapper. No matter how simple and curt the question might be, the package in which it was delivered always had the inference, 'I don't like you, pal.'

The shows themselves, while being deservedly successful, had no magic formula and were more or less in the same genre as rival detective series. Being British, there were few car chases and never a bang-bang shoot-out. There would be the occasional explosion, though, gee-whizz spectacular flames and smithereens flying everywhere. The names of the episodes told much of the run of things: 'The Hit Man', 'Cold Blood', 'Knife Edge', 'Murder in Season', 'Death Without Dishonour', 'Death Comes Softly', 'Death Benefits' and 'Death Call'. You were always guaranteed death, sometimes of the most grisly kind. The ubiquitous murder came with a variety of suspects to give it a good whodunnit flavour, followed by Taggart successfully swimming his way round more red herring than you would get in a Moscow fish shop. We loved it here in Scotland because the characters were real and, like them or leave them, they were us. They loved it elsewhere because it was exotic.

McManus appreciated the clout that being the star bestowed on him and it gave him the leverage to make certain demands. While other macho TV cops were permitted and apparently enjoyed their dalliances, McManus insisted there would be no bedroom hanky-panky for his detective chief inspector and that was accepted. And despite the fact he was an inveterate smoker, there was also the insistence that for him, at least, there would be a strict no-smoking rule. This had come about as a result of a youngster on the London Underground who had recognised McManus when he had been in an episode of *Bullman*. 'Loved the way you held your cigarette,' the boy said. 'Real cool.' Mark said that the lad's comment had horrified him, as the last thing he ever wanted to do was encourage youngsters to smoke. Hence that rule of his.

Taggart was one of the biggest money-spinners ever created by Scottish Television. Viewers loved Mark's portrayal of the tough-talking Glasgow cop so much that they gave him their overwhelming vote as TV Actor of the Year in the prestigious Radio Industry Club of Scotland/Daily Record awards. In 1991 *Taggart* was voted Best Drama Series in the BAFTA Scotland awards and two years later won the 1993 Writers' Guild Award for Best Drama Series. It was to become the all-time longest-running police drama on British television, outlasting even such legendary shows as *Z Cars*, *The Bill* and *Morse*, and making bank-loads of money for the Glasgow-based TV company, now part of a media conglomerate.

Taggart and many of the rest of the regulars in the cast continued to be written by the series' originator, Glenn Chandler. Creating by request the role of a flinty Glasgow detective had been something of a challenge for the young writer. He was, after all, an Edinburgh public schoolboy whose knowledge of the real Glasgow must have been somewhat remote. He confessed that he did at times feel like an alien from another planet, particularly as he sat alone making mental notes in some of the city's less salubrious public bars.

For Mark McManus and the other regulars, having a role in *Taggart* was as good as being in a successful soap, the ambition of so many actors as it offers them a form of security that's rare in their most insecure of professions. In the case of McManus, though, having split from his first wife, the show was to bring him much-needed love too. It was while working at STV prior to landing the role that he had met and fallen in love with Marion Donald, the station's wardrobe mistress. Four and a half years later, after Mark was firmly established as the country's best-known TV cop, they married. Marion was to be, as Mark said himself, the love of his life. He often revealed to showbusiness journalists just how happy he was with her and how they shared everything together.

Life couldn't have been happier for Mark McManus. He had reached heights in his adopted profession he never imagined he would attain. There was the contentment of his marriage, even although he openly confessed to regular Friday night shouting matches, but then that's life. And, besides, they always made up. They had a beautiful home in Queen's Park and another two places in the country. They had their horses and went riding together. It was the life that so many dream about. But while Mark McManus might have wanted for nothing, neither was he spared the vicissitudes of fortune. They were to descend on him in a series of devastating blows, age and illness claiming the lives of his mother, then his two sisters, Mary and Helen, and his younger brother Danny, all in a period of just over a year. He then learned that his wife Marion was suffering from cancer. She died in 1993 after a three-year battle against the killer disease.

Mark McManus was 59 when he buried the love of his life in the little cemetery close by the Lanarkshire cottage near Biggar they had so lovingly restored together. He had by then been playing the role of Taggart for over 11 years. His appearance, though, made it look an awful lot longer, the youthful Jim Taggart of those first episodes metamorphosed into a face that told of the ravages of drink, the devastation of sadness. Critics had always written about him as the detective with the well-lived-in face. Not now. Now it was way beyond the stage of being well lived-in. 'I've worn out my black tie,' he said, confessing that life in those 14 months of terrible misfortune had become something of a hell on earth for him. He had worn out a lot more besides, his health taking a new down-turn through his increased drinking.

There was a series of incidents resulting in him being rushed to hospital with a 'mystery' illness. But Mark's only real mystery came in a clear vodka bottle. On one occasion he was even admitted to the same hospital where they were treating Marion. That too was reported as another one of his little medical mysteries. He had even twice been given that ultimate drinker's warning – one more and you're dead. Perhaps it was the news he wanted, particularly that second ultimatum, when his worse fears were confirmed on the news that there would be no recovery for his wife. Following Marion's death he was to confess to John Millar, the leading showbusiness writer and Hollywood correspondent, that he had stopped worrying about killing himself with drink: 'I've been at it so long and have done so many things, I should have been dead 20 years ago.'

Millar knew Mark McManus better than any other showbusiness correspondent and was to write innumerable news stories and features on him. They got along so well that Mark asked him to write a book about his life and they had gone over the collection of scrapbooks he kept of his newspaper and magazine cuttings, the earliest of them being from the years he had spent in Australia. Millar, however, was not surprised to learn about the dubiety of Mark's boxing claims, as he was aware the star did not like to disappoint newspaper people anxious to get some kind of story from him. 'At the same time, however, Mark was one of the most cleverly secretive people I have ever met,' Millar says. 'He did this by apparently speaking quite openly about himself, but when you analysed just what he had told you there was nothing really there that let you into the background of his life. That part of him was a closed shop. He might not have fought the champion boxers he said he did, but he genuinely was a well-known actor in Australia. He really was a star out there, and that's not a made-up story. And when he came back to Britain there were the major parts he had on TV in those other drama series before *Taggart*, and don't forget his serious stage performances in various Shakespearean productions. He didn't make any of these up, and really did have quite an accomplished CV in showbusiness.'

Having known him from the days in the early '80s when he first got his major parts on British TV, Millar remembers the fit and handsome, almost boyish, figure which he cut on screen. But all too soon it was a completely different visage which was showing – tired and haggard looking, he took on a grotesque, man-in-the-moon appearance. 'The drink, of course, became quite a factor in his life, particularly so after the death of

Marion,' recalls John Millar. 'Although he certainly did enjoy his drink before that sad event. I can remember one lunch I had with him and Don Henderson. Almost before the lunch got started they were knocking the whiskies back but it appeared to have no effect on either of them. Oh yes, Mark could hold his drink all right. But with the death of Marion, he really seemed to hit it. There was the time he missed out on an important lunch appointment in London because of it, and after that STV had one of their PRs act as minder for such appointments. Another time, when we were doing a photo-shoot, he turned up a bit worse for wear and spilled the coffee we gave him down his trousers and we had to disguise the pictures so that it wouldn't show. But unlike so many top actors I know, he never played the big-star bit. He was always co-operative and helpful in our meetings. I found him a real nice, easy-going kind of man who would never let you down for an interview and was always willing to help.'

However, the proposed book on his life story never got started due to Mark's untimely death. His drinking had been no secret at Scottish Television, although about the only thing that gave it away was the wan appearance and puffy face, the thickening of the lips, the weary eyes carrying their ever-increasing baggage. The TV people knew about his lunchtime habits, the lunches at which he consumed only liquid. But when the break was over, he could be as sharp as any of the rest of them, never missing a cue, his performance even having an extra edge to it.

Eventually, however, STV were forced to make provision for the likely further absence of their star policeman. Commercial considerations, as it were. A lot of money was invested in the series, a lot of jobs depended on it and the station decided to adopt a policy of giving him less to do. If, for instance, a storyline called for him to be out on location every day and he then fell ill, they would be faced with the problem of major rewrites and rescheduling of work. They therefore confined many of his scenes to the police station so that they could film them together. At the same time, the TV station retained considerable affection for the man who had done so much for them, appreciating both his own problems and the fact that he needed more time to be with his seriously ill wife. And following Marion's death, they even paid for him to have a long holiday in Australia in the hope that it might help him face up to a new life. But after his return from holiday, McManus was back in hospital once more, this time, it was said, suffering from exhaustion. Not many weeks later, he was back yet again, this time to undergo surgery for skin cancer.

Not many weeks later, James Macpherson, who had a major supporting role as Detective Inspector Mike Jardine in the series, called by Mark's flat in Queen's Park to find a rather pathetic figure sitting alone and looking terrible. He had never seen him looking so ill, the heavily lined and pallid face a ghastly yellow, yet he almost had to bully him to go to hospital for treatment. But it was too late for any more treatment for what Mark was suffering from and he was never to leave his hospital bed at the Victoria Infirmary. On Monday, 6 June 1994, just hours after coming out of intensive care in which he had been for 18 days suffering from pneumonia, Mark McManus took a sudden relapse and died. He was 60 years of age. And while his death certificate was to list various medical causes, close friends believe Mark had simply surrendered the will to live after the death of his wife Marion.

Mark McManus's death and funeral was front-page news, not only in the UK but in a variety of countries on the continent and overseas, particularly in Denmark, New Zealand and France, where he was a big TV favourite with a dedicated cult following. More than 2,000 mourners turned out to say a final farewell to their favourite TV star, his hearse being accompanied by police motorcycle outriders as a token of their respect for their best-known and best-loved cop. Co-star James Macpherson was to remember Mark with a fine tribute which evoked smiles of fond remembrance amidst the tears. They laughed when he told the mourners about the time when he was with Mark to open a cinema in Dundee. The new theatre's publicity officer had pulled Mark aside for the customary briefing about what he would like said when they got to the theatre, the message being perhaps slightly more complex than the norm. But, just like Taggart, Mark was a man of few words and on his arrival at the theatre his address to the big crowd of waiting fans was simply: 'Hello, Dundee. Let's go to the pictures!'

The congregation laughed even more when Macpherson told them about his first day working as an actor with Mark on an outside location for an episode of *Taggart*. The filming was taking place in a very muddy field and after shaking hands Mark had said to him, 'It's a bugger of a first day, Jim!' He said he was most proud to say he had worked with Mark McManus.

It was remarks like that which so aptly summed up the real character of McManus. *Taggart* creator, the writer Glenn Chandler, speaking more than six years after Mark's death, revealed to me that he was one of the most down-to-earth people he had ever met in the acting profession. 'When we were doing outside work anywhere in Glasgow, Mark would be the first to walk over and speak to the wee boys or the little old lady out doing her shopping. Always the friendly chat with them, as though he was an old pal. So many others in his position lock themselves away in the caravan accommodation provided for them on location. He used to live near me in Hertfordshire and do you know what? He hated it. "Nae books," he would always say after visiting any of the big houses he was invited to in the area, meaning quite simply they might be living in rather sumptuous houses, but they never appeared to read any books. And that always struck him as odd. As an actor, he really put everything into his role. He would work at getting the right facial expression, getting that little twist of one eye to make it look perfect. He confided in me too that he would not go on forever but that he hoped *Taggart* would continue long after him.'

Eight months after the funeral of Mark McManus, there was another funeral, this time of Detective Chief Inspector Jim

Taggart. It was the TV series' way of saying farewell to the man who had become Glasgow's best-known and best-loved cop. Significantly, the series continued to be made under the title that made it such a hit, *Taggart*. And perhaps no finer tribute has ever been paid to a TV actor than just that.

Chapter Seven

Cad, Casanova, Boozer, Brawler – Legend

The immediate descendants of those formidable people who first went out into the world to cross unknown deserts and polar wastes, penetrate savage jungles and climb the highest mountains, were those incredibly brave stalwarts who conquered the airways. Flying off in open cockpits in the flimsiest of machines relying on just one small engine, their skill as navigators combined with immeasurable courage. There would be a destination in mind, of course, but there would be no telling what lay between that point of take-off and journey's end. They flew the vast oceans, crossed the great continents and pioneered new and faster ways of reaching the furthest of destinations. They had – and had to have – the navigational skills of a Captain Cook, all the resourcefulness and enterprise of a frontiersman, and be able to cope with more adventures than an Indiana Jones.

One of the greatest of them was a man who grew up in a handsome red-sandstone tenement in the South Side of Glasgow in the days when those pilots were seen as the most heroic of adventurers. The dream of his life was that one day he would be one of them, but not even in the wildest of those dreams did he imagine that he would be one of the most talked-about men in the world for his incredible feats as a flying trailblazer. For Jim Mollison became one of the greatest aviators of all time. He smashed distance records in every part of the globe. He won the world's most coveted air trophies. They bestowed honours on him in South America and New York City gave him a Fifth Avenue ticker-tape reception and awarded him their coveted Gold Medal – twice. Texas made him an honorary lieutenant-colonel on the State Governor's staff, while Hollywood begged him to become a film star.

James Allan Mollison was born in the early afternoon of Wednesday, 19 April 1905, to Hector and Thomasina – they called her Tommy – at 33 Fotheringay Road, Pollokshields, which nearly a century on is still one of the most handsome and prestigious of tenement buildings in the city. Being Easter time and early spring, those Glaswegians of 1905 who could afford it were already thinking ahead for the summer holidays, mostly taken in the nearest resorts, and the first of the season's advertisements were in the newspapers that day, a typical one advertising houses to rent in Ayr at £7 – for the entire summer season. If you wanted to go further afield, there were cruises to Cork in Southern Ireland at £1 return, or a single fare by sea to New York at £5.75p.

The Mollisons of Fotheringay Road were delighted at the birth of their young son, who was to be their only child, and he would want for nothing. Hector was a consultant engineer and had come from a well-off Glasgow family, while Thomasina was the daughter of wealthy Greenock shipowners, some of whose financial skills had obviously been passed down to their daughter, as Thomasina insisted on a pre-nuptial contract to safeguard her personal finances before consenting to marry. Or did she even then have some doubts about behavioural aspects of her husband-to-be? Whatever the case, her precautions were justified, as their marriage disintegrated through Mollison's foul temper and drinking. Once, in a drunken rage, he even threatened to throw his young son from a window and when they split, it was on condition that he leave the country.

Thomasina later remarried, her new husband being Charles Bullmore, a lieutenant-commander in the Royal Navy Reserves, and they moved to Edinburgh for a time before returning to Glasgow to live at various addresses in the West End whilst Jim continued his education at Glasgow Academy. It was there that the young Mollison confided to one of his closest school pals that the great dream of his life would be to travel the world in the most romantic form he could imagine, by being an aviator. This was during the years of the First World War and schoolboys were fascinated by reports coming from the Western Front about the daring deeds of those heroic pilots of the Royal Flying Corps. Although he was on the opposing side, the legendary German ace, Baron von Richthofen, commander of the 11th Chasing Squadron, was to be a particular hero, being one of the most daring of this new breed of battling warriors and a man who claimed some 80 'kills' before he was shot down himself in 1918. The young Mollison had read every scrap he could about those skirmishes in the skies, but kept quiet about those dreams of his until that day at school. However, the reception accorded to that piece of adolescent revelation was not what Mollison expected. His friend laughed right in his face, at which point Mollison set about him and the pair ended up in the roughest of playground brawls, their fight only coming to an end when a school prefect intervened. And as Mollison modestly remembered, 'Just as well it ended that way, for my friend was much bigger than me.'

So the boy kept quiet about his ambitions after that and it wasn't till he was approaching 18 and at the breakfast table one morning that he was next to speak about it. This time, though, it wasn't just fantasising. He was calmly informing his mother and stepfather that he would be joining the Royal Air Force and that he was going to be a pilot. It was put to them as indifferently as he might have told them he would be late for evening dinner.

In 1923 pilots were about as commonplace as astronauts are today. It was less than 20 years after the American, Orville Wright, watched by his brother Wilbur, had taken that historic and very major step for man by coaxing his little 12 hp chain-driven plane called Flyer I off the ground at Kitty Hawk, in North Carolina, for the first-ever recorded, controlled and sustained flight. Going up there into the bright, blue yonder was the stuff of the most valiant of adventurers, and the youthful only child announcing the news that he wanted to emulate the likes of Wright and von Richthofen seemed to be reaching for the stars. Joining the RAF then was a far tougher proposition than it was to become in later years. It was the youngest service, having been formed just five years previously when the Royal Flying Corps merged with the Royal Naval Air Service, making it the biggest air force in the world. To enlist in it wasn't merely a case of going along to some recruiting office and volunteering one's services. It was more like joining some select gentlemen's group, more difficult even than getting membership of one of those exclusive golf clubs which were springing up in the wealthy outer suburbs of Glasgow at the time. You had to have influence, connections, or guarantors of distinction. So the services of the aspiring Jim Mollison's grandfather had to be enlisted. He was in his eighties at the time, but a healthy and alert old-school adventurer, spending much of his life at sea and eventually becoming a senior officer in the Turkish Navy. In later life he had become a senior bailie in Glasgow Corporation and, being on friendly terms with Lord Provost Sir Thomas Paxton, had enlisted his aid to nominate his grandson for a career with the RAF.

The patronage of Glasgow's No. 1 citizen vouchsafed the application of the young man from the West End and within a few short weeks Jim Mollison was one of a class of some 30 trainee pilot officers at the RAF's No. 2 Flying Training School at Duxford, near Cambridge. He was still just 18 when he qualified as a pilot, making him not only the youngest with his wings, but the luckiest. For it was at Duxford that Mollison was to reveal some of the non-flying aspects of his character which would get him in the news in later life.

Mollison had enjoyed the affluent life in Glasgow, frequenting the most exclusive of clubs, the best of restaurants, and saw no reason why that should stop just because he was now the young officer gentleman. Even as a trainee flying officer he earned good money, the rate at the time being 18 shillings – 90p – a day, but then that's the millennium-age equivalent of £50. It was enough for him to run a small sports car and head off for London as often as he could to frequent the clubs of Mayfair and the West End, or the nearby ones in Cambridge, one called the Cecil being a favourite. He smoked, liked spirits, loved company and adored the ladies. In Cambridge he had met one beautiful young girl, a pupil at that most famous of select young ladies' schools, Girton College. She had asked him if he really was a pilot. Of course he was, he assured her, even though he still hadn't qualified for his wings. But to prove he really was a pilot, he said he would fly his plane round her school one day.

Mollison thought he could get away with it during the regular solo practice lessons they were receiving at Duxford. These required them to fly out in groups and do wide circuits of the airfield. No one would notice, he thought, if he slipped away from the other fliers during such practice and headed across country for Girton, and he might never have been found out had it not been for losing his way on the flight back. He attempted a landing in order to ascertain where he was but crashed instead and was lucky to escape unhurt. He also miraculously escaped a court-martial for his deed, proceedings which would most certainly have terminated his career in the RAF.

In the early 1920s Britain, the supreme coloniser, had problems in various places with rebellious dissidents who didn't quite see life as the mandarins back in London would have liked them to see it. So the big stick had to be regularly waved at them, usually in the form of a Royal Navy gunboat, or the odd Highland regiment or two. Battleships, bayonets and bagpipes seemed a wonderfully easy solution to most such problems. But now there was an even more effective method – war planes from the RAF. And to that end, the newly graduated Flying Officer J. Mollison was dispatched from his base at Kenley, near Croydon, to India.

With some other young pilots he was sent first of all to Peshawar, at the eastern end of the Khyber Pass, where London's big stick was to be waved in the shape of their DH 9A bombers. Some rebellious Mahsud tribesmen had taken on the might of the British Army in Waziristan, that part of India bordering on Afghanistan, and their conflict had taken a nasty turn, the Mahsuds attacking neighbouring Hindus and taking some British officers hostage. So the British bombers were sent in and very soon another little war was over, men with swords and ancient flintlocks being no match for the warriors who descended from the skies with bombs and machine-gun bullets. It was patently obvious that Mollison would have preferred to have been doing another kind of flying, but as a loyal British officer he no doubt took the view that such duties had prevented further bloodshed. He was to remain in India for most of the five years he had signed on for as an officer-pilot in the service of His Majesty. It was to prove invaluable experience as an all-round flyer and he was trained to fly all of the latest planes being acquired by the fledgling Royal Air Force, even ending his career in the service as their youngest-ever test pilot.

Jim was also to note that being in the service had also rounded off some of his social skills. It had been while he was stationed in the old North-West Frontier of India that a commanding officer had asked him, 'What games do you play, Mr Mollison?' The CO had been somewhat shocked when the reply had been 'None', and immediately ordered him to be detached to a nearby cavalry regiment to undergo a crash course on horse riding until he became proficient enough to be a regular member of the squadron's polo team.

When his five years' service engagement came to an end,

Mollison resisted the promises of further promotion and headed for civvy street. He had loved the life of the pilot, it having fulfilled part of his boyhood dream about travelling the world as an aviator, but the action he experienced in Waziristan made him doubt his future lay in becoming another von Richthofen. But if he wasn't to be a famous wartime ace, there were still loads of adventures to be had as a civilian pilot, even if the chances of getting work weren't to be all that plentiful. The simple fact of life was that there weren't all that many planes flying, and so neither were there many pilots required. Having saved enough during his years in India to be self-sufficient for some time, though, he was in no immediate hurry for cash so there would be no better time, as he put it himself, to 'do a little pottering around the world'. Service life and the years in India had put him out of the social scene and he was by now a man who had a great hankering for life's pleasures.

Le Touquet, Aix-les-Bains, Nice, Venice and Gstaad were just some of the fashionable places where the high society of the day circulated and Mollison tried them all, and many others. He was there at the gaming tables in the best of casinos and he was there too in the fashionable restaurants, the appropriate clubs. Along the way on the first of these travels, there was an offer from a French firm to fly for them in Switzerland, which he accepted, moving on when another offer came from an Italian company to fly seaplanes. When the latter didn't work out, he decided to potter further afield.

Australia, it seemed, was the place for pilots, the word being they were taking to the new mode of travel in bigger numbers than most. But being in no hurry to get there, Mollison took a series of sea passages on the slowest ships of the day in order to experience en route some exotic places like Guadeloupe, Martinique, Panama, and then on to the islands in the South Pacific. Tahiti, as it does with most, bowled him over. He even went to live in the place they call Tusi-Tala, the Teller of Tales, named after its most famous resident, Robert Louis Stevenson.

There he met a rich American authoress and he became close friends with yet another arrival, Zane Grey, the famous author of western novels, who was fabulously wealthy from such bestsellers as *Riders of the Purple Sage* and who arrived at Tahiti on his huge yacht, *Fisherman*.

Then he moved on to Moorea, an even more remote island in the group. There, as he later was to write, 'I went native.' But Mollison could see the danger of becoming the South Pacific lotus-eater and after a month at Moorea he was searching the horizons for the next ship going anywhere. He said, 'Spend a month in Tahiti and you will take away a memory that will stay with you always. But if you stay longer, life is so easy it is demoralising.'

That next ship to come along was, as it happened, the very one he had wanted, it being bound for Australia. He had loved Tahiti but he was to like and enjoy Australia even more. He loved its way of life, its egalitarianism. It was where, he said, 'the parasite and the sycophant are almost unknown; where each man believes himself to be, and is, as good as his neighbour. It is probably the nearest approach to the true democracy that can be found today.' But if the parasite and sycophant were unknown, the Australian confidence trickster most certainly was not, and the one Mollison was to encounter took the guise of a prosperous businessman residing at the same hotel as him in Sydney. 'I heard you were looking for work as a pilot,' he had said one day to Mollison in the hotel dining room, going on to inquire about the extent of his experience in the air. When Mollison told him about some of his adventures with the British Royal Air Force, the man appeared more than impressed. 'Maybe I can help,' he said. He then went on to explain that he was in the process of setting up a major flying company. Everything was in place for his creation to go into business, except for one vital part. They needed a chief pilot. And from what he had already gathered, Mollison could be the very man. In fact, he might even offer him the job. They met again later and this time the businessman firmed up the offer of the post. But there was a condition. As it was such a big job, and to show that he really would have a stake in the venture, Mollison would be required to buy a number of shares in the company, perhaps even handing over his life savings, so good was the deal. But before long it got to the stage where the man was reduced to cajoling Mollison to hand over what money he had on him, and the sting was spotted. Mollison extricated himself from the situation and then found himself heading for Adelaide to take up a position as a flying instructor with a new airline there, this time as part of a genuine company which was putting money up front for his services without asking for any cash.

His spell in Adelaide was to give him some vital familiarisation with the kind of aircraft being flown in Australia at the time, as well as affording him time to become acquainted with the particular Aussie weather patterns, not all as pleasurable as might be imagined. It also helped him to meet the legendary Charles Kingsford-Smith, not only Australia's greatest-ever pilot and record-breaker – Sydney Airport is named after him – but a man held by many to be one of the greatest aviators ever. He held more records than anyone, not least that of being the first pilot to cross the Pacific. The pair got on well together and Kingsford-Smith offered him the job which was to lead directly to the first and greatest of his adventures.

Kingsford-Smith had been behind the formation of Australian National Airways, one of the first major airlines on the Down Under continent, and Mollison was invited to be one of their senior pilots, with no catches to the deal. Kingsford-Smith's company had pioneered the Sydney to Melbourne run, his small, three-engine planes carrying mail and a small number of passengers. Today it's a flight almost comparable to the London–Glasgow shuttle but in the early '30s it was one of the most fearful and dangerous flights in the world. After a number of fatalities it was considered so perilous that the Australian Federal Government ordered it to be halted until such time as planes could be fitted with radios. But to do that at the time would have involved the installation of ground-based relay beacons along the route, much of these in the mountains of the Great Dividing Range, a project way beyond the financial resources of any flying company then in existence. However, that Government decree on the route had not yet been made when pilots like Mollison took planes and passengers on that most hazardous of daily journeys.

Because of their limited fuel capacity, Kingsford-Smith's small passenger planes would take the shortest and most direct route between the two state capitals, which meant having to fly over the highest peaks of the Great Dividing Range. Australia is not renowned for its mountains, but the young Glasgow pilot was to have a number of the most nerve-wracking experiences of his life on the many regular flights he was to make on the route, not the least of them when he had been flying at 10,000 feet as he approached Mount Kosciusko and all three of his engines began losing power. Writing about it later, Mollison recounted how first of all he had become numb with the cold because of the height and the freezing conditions outside his tiny craft. Then to complicate matters, thick cloud which was too high to fly over, meant he had been flying blind for some time. Analysing his situation, he surmised that in all probability ice had frozen the spark-plug leads. That could have been easily corrected by dropping to a height below freezing level; but then directly beneath him was the huge mass of Mount Kosciusko, leaving only around 2,000 feet of leeway beneath his plane. It was a gamble but by losing height just to the point where he daren't get any lower, Mollison managed to manoeuvre his plane into a break in the clouds where he was met by brilliant, warm sunshine. Not only was he able to distinguish the peak of the big mountain below him, but his engines immediately picked up too, his diagnosis of the engine problem being correct.

Another time, in the same region and in the midst of the fiercest of gales, all his cockpit instruments froze, leaving him without the most vital of aids, including the altimeter and speedometer, as well as his turn-and-bank indicator, which meant he couldn't rely on his compass bearings. Again he was flying blind in thick cloud and, minus the aid of his instruments, could not ascertain whether he was banking, climbing or descending. Only the regular throbbing of the engines gave him some indication about the pattern of his flight and by the sound of them he appeared to be in a steep dive. Mollison pulled back on his controls, the engines responding with a more regular throb, and at the same time a clearance in the cloud showed him to be heading straight for the summit of a mountain, which he only avoided with the sharpest of turns. Eventually, though, after some more deaths, the Australian government issued the close-down order on the Sydney to Melbourne route and Mollison was looking for another job.

One of his regular passengers on those trips had been Cyril Westcott, a wealthy Australian businessman and representative in Australia of Lord Wakefield. Wakefield was a multi-millionaire English philanthropist, a patron of the arts and of numerous sports as well as being one of the greatest benefactors to those whose efforts were in the name of adventure and achievement. Mollison, ever on the move, needed something new, and so discussed his future with Cyril Westcott.

With the experience he now had – it was the early '30s – Mollison considered himself a good enough pilot for the utmost of challenges – record-breaking. Bold and audacious flying adventurers were pioneering new routes to various points across the world and they were being hailed as the greatest of heroes, the most outstanding men and women of their time, honoured and fêted wherever they went, each new record or feat producing yet another household name – Earhart, Kingsford-Smith, Lindbergh, Pangborn, Johnson. And very soon the name Jim Mollison would become one of the best known of all.

To appreciate just how immense were the exploits of these aerial pathfinders in the '20s and '30s, it helps to reflect on flying as it was known at the time. Planes were a rarity and if you saw or heard one, you stopped and stared. And wondered. Wondered at how people had the nerve to be airborne in these frail craft with their cloth-covered wooden frames, some of them so elemental in design they didn't even have bolted-down seats. Even the most sophisticated of them would only have a couple of instruments in an open cockpit. There was no Heathrow or JFK, Dulles or de Gaulle, O'Hare, Narita – or Abbotsinch. Airports were anywhere that had a grassy, level field the size of two football pitches and a wind socket on a pole at one end. No radar, no landing lights, no fire-fighters, no terminal halls. Flying then was much more dangerous than space travel is today – the casualties alone demonstrate that. And meeting anyone who had actually been up on a flight was like talking to someone just back from a walk on the moon.

An amazingly short space of time after that historic first flight by the Wright brothers – and remember, it was only a mere hop of some 120 feet – the first of the great pioneering flights were being planned and carried out. Within six years, Bleriot had crossed the English Channel. Ten years later there was the first crossing of the North Atlantic by an American crew refuelling in the Azores. Less than a month after that, the British team of Alcock and Brown made the first non-stop crossing. By the time Charles Lindbergh completed the first solo Atlantic flight in 1927 in his legendary Spirit of St Louis monoplane, he was the 79th man to have done the crossing by air. That flight, incidentally, from Long Island, New York, to Le Bourget, Paris, took some 33 and a half hours.

More and more record-breakers were coming forward. They were an even more daring breed of aviator, aiming to fly across continents where no one had ventured before. Distance seemed no object to them. Neither did living with danger. They were prepared, if necessary, to land on arid desert wastes, jungle clearings, or beside the remotest of native settlements whose inhabitants had never seen a white face, let alone an aeroplane.

For those who would be successful, there would be instant worldwide fame, as well as the chance to claim some of the huge prizes which were on offer.

But breaking long-distance world records was a costly business. Aircraft had to be specially prepared and arrangements made across the world for refuelling stops and spares. Only those who were either extremely wealthy or had sponsors with deep pockets could contemplate such ventures. When Jim Mollison had spoken so enthusiastically about trying such a challenging undertaking with Cyril Westcott, the latter immediately volunteered to take the idea to his own friend, Lord Wakefield who, he was convinced, would be more than willing to be a sponsor. And Westcott was right. Within days, the word came back from England that there would be sufficient funds for the necessary fuel and back-up services in order to try for the longest and most daring of air records – the solo flight from Australia to England. And not only would the noble English lord help with Mollison's funding, he would also present him with a specially prepared Gypsy Moth, one of the finest and most reliable light aircraft ever built.

The Moth was created and first built by the legendary aircraft pioneer Geoffrey de Havilland just six years after the first-ever powered flight. The small engine, the most famous light aero engine ever made, was known for its putt-putt sound and renowned for its reliability, the manufacturers recommending that it could run for 1,500 hours between major overhauls. The Moth became the most favoured plane of the early record-breakers.

Mollison immediately began making plans for the longest and toughest air record in existence. In the millennium years, the big jumbos do it daily in just under 30 hours. The record in 1931, which Mollison was determined to smash, stood at ten days and twenty-two hours. And in order to do it even in that time meant going much of the way without sleep. Undaunted at that prospect, as well as knowing he would have to fly solo over some of the world's greatest oceans, the densest and most fearsome of jungles, the remotest and most hostile of deserts, with not the slightest prospect of immediate rescue should he come down, Mollison, the man from Pollokshields, was confident he could break that ten-day record. It's the story of this flight more than any other which encompasses the life of the aviator record-breaker in this golden age of flight. Every hazard that faced these formidable adventurers was to be confronted in this amazing journey by Jim Mollison.

The adventure began in earnest when Lord Wakefield's organisation delivered to Mollison in Australia a specially prepared Gypsy Moth able to reach a maximum speed of 115 mph. The little all-black plane, with its big registration letters of VH-UFT, weighed only 1,750 lb, about three-quarters of a ton or the weight of a medium car. Normally it carried 20 gallons of petrol in a tank in the mid-section of the upper wing, but the main part of its modification was that it had a special steel tank fitted in the seats of the front cockpit. This boosted its fuel capacity from 20 to 119 gallons and contributed a weight equivalent of taking off with several extra passengers. And so, on a cool but sunny day in June, Mollison set out from Sydney for the first part of his hazardous 12,000-mile journey across the world. The first stage of the journey, across the vast Australian continent via Broken Hill and Alice Springs to Darwin, at the Top End, as Australians say, did not require a load of fuel, and from that most northerly of Australian towns he intended to make one of the longest non-stop stages of the trip, direct to the city of Batavia, now known as Jakarta, the present-day capital of Indonesia. This leg, however, was 800 miles away and would require his petrol tanks to be filled to the very brim, which they were. And that was to be his downfall. It was the first time he had attempted to take off with such a load of fuel on the little plane, and although the mechanic filling his tanks advised him to trim the load down a little, fearing he would not get off the ground, Mollison said a bigger danger would be not having enough petrol to survive the first 500 miles of the trip, which would be over ocean.

The little Moth never struggled with taking off, even with its tanks nearly full, and it would normally be airborne in around 150 yards. But that night, on the long and dusty airfield at Darwin, Mollison had gone some 300 yards yet could only manage to gain a height of around seven feet and no matter how much power he gave the four-cylinder engine and his cajoling of the controls, it was only rising by inches. There was also a light pole at the far side of the 550-yard runway, planes usually being well airborne long before they were even near that point – but Mollison's Gypsy Moth was heading straight for it. The plane then suddenly pitched down with an almighty jolt on the ground before bouncing again, shaking its pilot rigid. He was by then at maximum revs and the obstacle was right there, rushing unavoidably towards him with not the slightest chance of a reprieve. He later described the little plane as having folded up like a pack of cards after it had smashed headlong into the big wooden pole at the far end of the Darwin airfield. At the speed he had been going, Mollison was lucky to crawl out of the crumpled wreck unscathed to look with dismay at the heap of crushed wings and fuselage on which he had pinned his hopes. Now it lay in an irreparable heap before he had even begun the major part of the flight, his dreams of being a record-breaker shattered. Mollison didn't even consider how lucky he had been to climb from the wreck with hardly a scratch. His life had been saved because the plane had come down belly-flop fashion. Had it crashed nose first, the engine and the huge steel petrol tank would have been rammed back into his tiny cockpit and there would have been no chance of escaping with his life.

When he read the headline news of his crash in the papers, it seemed to him then that his great quest to achieve the paramount ambition of his life, to be a really great flyer, the Richthofen of his boyhood dreams, was over. 'This was probably the blackest day of my life,' he said several years later, when recalling the incident to a Glasgow newspaper. 'I saw all my hopes shattered and I imagined no one would ever give me a second chance.' However, despite what he called such 'cynical thoughts', he cabled Lord Wakefield giving him all the details of the crash. 'To my amazement, this brought an immediate reply stating that he would be providing another aeroplane for me. In effect, I was being given that rare thing – a second chance.'

Mollison returned to Sydney to make yet more preparations for that second-chance flight across the world, noting on his arrival at the New South Wales capital the absence of the huge crowd that had been there to see him off just days before. 'Failure is of no importance to the public,' he wryly noted. There would be better times, he assured himself.

Just over a month later a replica Gypsy Moth, again specially prepared with huge petrol tanks, was delivered to Mollison in Sydney and he had it shipped this time to Wyndham, one of the most northerly points in Western Australia, from where he would begin his second record attempt. He knew the airport facilities there – the usual shed at one end of the field, the wind socket at the other – and there were no obstructions at the furthest point of its long and bumpy runway of red soil, ensuring a much better chance for his little Gypsy Moth to take off.

It was just on midnight when he pulled down his flying goggles after powering the engine up to maximum revs, then he waved to a mechanic to pull away the restraining chocks from the wheels. A long line of oil lamps was the only indication of the direction of the runway and the Moth bumped and jolted on the rough surface as it roared its way in the direction of the furthest light. A final jolt from the slender undercarriage as it went over some rougher ground and it finally freed itself from terra firma. Mollison was airborne and on his way to Batavia in the Dutch East Indies.

The plan was to fly right through the night over the Timor Sea and the first chain of islands of the East Indies – Roti, Sumba, Sumbawa and Bali – which led to Java, at the top end of which would be his first destination. When writing about it later, he remembered his initial thoughts after take-off, reflecting on the importance of the engine, the sound of which dominated the thoughts of the long-distance solo flyer. They had no radios, no companions, no other distraction than that constant accompanying drone of the engine which drove them on. For hour after hour after hour, its hopefully perpetual rhythm was their sole lifeline. It was their one sound, their only sound. They would analyse every throb and beat like a heart surgeon examining a patient. They knew every vibration, every pulsation, quiver, twitch and tremble of the pistons and valves as they responded to the wonders of the combustion engine. 'The night had been very dark,' he wrote, 'and it was not long before the excitement of starting had been displaced by an overpowering sense of loneliness. I drove on into the blackness at 100 mph and as I cast my eyes below I seemed to see a faint opalescent light, reminding me of what would happen if my link shaft missed one single beat.'

He reflected too that this particular part of the Australia to England journey was perhaps the most difficult of any record-breaking flight. Going in the other direction, at least there was the vast continent of Australia to aim at after leaving the islands of the East Indies. But heading in the opposite direction, as he was, that Australian continent was being left behind and what he was aiming for instead was the tiny island of Roti at the far end of the Timor Sea. But he was proud of the navigation skills he had learned in the Royal Air Force, which he had put into practice over those remote villages and mountains in the North-West Frontier, and had it not been so good, he would never have successfully made those numerous journeys over the Australian Alps on those Sydney–Melbourne runs.

Daybreak came at around 5.30 and he realised for the first time the real scale of the venture he was undertaking, for there beneath him lay the vast expanse of the Timor Sea. He had been flying over it for hours by now, yet in every direction the horizon was that of even more water. Not long afterwards, however, he was sure he spotted land ahead. Was that it? Was that his target island of Roti? He continued peering ahead through his cockpit shield at the land formation he had seen, then some minutes later it disappeared. It had been a mirage. Another check with his compass and his flight chart. No, he wasn't off course. He strained into the horizon ahead again and once more saw the shape of land. But this time it was still there some minutes later and, as he flew on, its contours could be defined. He was right. It was Roti. It would be easier after that, the chain of islands which comprise that part of the East Indies would simplify his direction-finding, one leading on to the other, until he reached the far end of the Flores Sea and was north over Bali and its spectacular conical mountains towards Sourabaya.

It was by now mid-afternoon and flying in from the sea at just around 40 feet, having been airborne for nearly 15 hours, he located the town's small airfield, where they were expecting him. There was little time for anything other than taking on sufficient fuel to reach Batavia, where his schedule and advance arrangements expected him to be before nightfall, and just over 20 minutes later he was flying west once more, this time along the coast of Java to its most north-westerly point and its capital Batavia.

Mollison was amazed at how quickly the tropical twilight descended – with 'alarming suddenness', as he put it. Flying up the Javanese coast he realised there was no hope of reaching his destination before dark. And dark in such parts of the world, and especially in the early '30s, really meant just that. Light pollution was still a thing of the future, when the incandescent glow of tens of thousands of radiant fluorescent lights illuminating the night skies to thousands of feet can be seen from vast distances away. Cities in the East were still mainly lit by oil lamps and it wouldn't be until you were almost directly overhead that you knew a populous community lay beneath. It wasn't perhaps the perspective he held at the time, but he did say afterwards that 'the prospect of flying in darkness over a strange country and landing in an unknown aerodrome was not attractive'.

It was an hour after sundown when he eventually did reach Batavia and performed the customary circuit of the city to locate the aerodrome. But after one complete fly-over, there was nothing to be seen that resembled a landing field, which he had anticipated would have been identified with the customary parallel row of landing lamps lit for his arrival. It was obvious they had not received the wire telling them of his flight. At Sourabaya he had only taken on a few gallons of fuel, sufficient for him to reach Batavia, and this intensified his dilemma. He had to land somewhere – and soon. Of course, such predicaments were frequent companions of the record-breaking flyer, but they did have the advantage over the modern pilot whose planes can't cope with landing on anything other than a modern, asphalt airstrip. Little planes like the Gypsy Moth were aptly named, the skilful pilot being able to bring them in virtually like the creature after which they were named, almost hovering their lightweight frames on to the merest of landing areas. Which is what Mollison would have to do that night in Batavia. But where? He circled the city once more, the feeble lights from myriad oil lamps contributing virtually nothing to the dark skies. Taking a wider arc, he was about ten miles away from the centre of the city when he passed over a small native community well lit by fires and flares. From the light of these he could see a small stretch of what appeared to be reasonably level ground good enough for this resilient Moth. Down he went.

He reduced the revs of the small engine so as to keep the plane a fraction above a stall, and feathered it gently down to the clearing by the side of the bright fires. His observation of that clearing had been correct, there being sufficient room for a landing, but what he couldn't have ascertained from the air was the condition of its surface. The bumps and jolts the plane received when it made contact with the ground were among the most severe he had ever experienced and just before coming to a halt he heard the loudest of cracks, which he took to be coming from somewhere on one of the wings. When he jumped from the cockpit he couldn't believe the state of the ground on which he had just landed. It turned out to be a man-made clearing amongst forest scrubland, and there were big rocks and ugly tree stumps everywhere. Had he hit any one of them on his landing, he would have had another wrecked Gypsy Moth on his hands. As it was, when he examined the wings, two ribs of one were badly cracked and it would be impossible to even consider taking off again until they were repaired. Luckily, though, he was in one of the most helpful of regions and when the authorities at the airport heard of his arrival and plight they immediately organised experts to attend to the plane and enlisted the aid of hundreds of locals to clear the site enough for him to take off at daylight to fly the remaining few miles to Batavia where, he was assured, the airport was now expecting him. With his plane in trusted hands, and with mechanics making further checks on the repair and servicing his engine, Mollison was able to snatch a few hours of rest before continuing the next stage of his flight, another midnight departure for the crossing of the South China Sea to Singapore.

He could have flown north over the huge island of Sumatra, which would have afforded him the reassurance of being able to land somewhere should there be any problems, but instead he took the bolder course of the more direct route over water. This was to be his second long haul over a vast stretch of ocean, his only companionship as ever being the constant drone of the engine. He didn't enjoy the long flights at night over the ocean and the feelings they instilled in him, the loneliness of the long-distance flyer. Some hours out from Batavia he flew over a passenger ship. It was brilliantly lit and he thought about its passengers and the companionship they would be sharing on the voyage and for some bizarre reason, perhaps as if to share with them, even at a distance, a few minutes of contact, he flew alongside the ship, then circled it three times before severing his tenuous link with normal existence and continuing with his original flight route.

It wasn't all that long after leaving the ship behind that the moon disappeared and the night darkened menacingly. Although he didn't realise it at the time, he was heading for a monsoonal storm, a new and most frightening experience. All those hazardous journeys over Mount Kosciusko in Australia had taught him the terrors of manhandling a plane as it's buffeted in every direction but now, in the intensity of the storm, in this terrifying roller-coaster of a flight, he was undergoing something even worse than those Australian runs, although he did later admit that surviving what remained of that night had been due as much to good fortune as it had been to his skill as a pilot. When eventually there was a break in the heavy cloud formation, he observed more land but was unable to identify the contours with anything in his charts. This was his first landfall since flying out from Batavia and the more he studied the outline of the land, the more unsure he was as to precisely where he might be. He later put his hesitancy down to the lack of sleep, which was now telling on him and making it difficult to make a quick decision on what precise part of the world he was flying over.

Mollison knew it was wrong to trust in luck but it was all he was capable of doing at that precise moment. He kept flying in the direction which he was sure would take him direct to his final destination for that day, Alor Star in the north of the Malay Peninsula, but minutes later he was to reason with himself again, this time reaching the saner conclusion that it was indeed wrong to trust luck. Pilots put their trust in navigation, calculations and recognisable sightings, good fortune being only an occasional bonus. He prudently decided to look for a landing place so that he could ascertain his position. Beaches were usually a better bet than jungle clearings and when he saw one ahead, with some settlements nearby, he fluttered the Gypsy Moth down for a trouble-free landing. The man who then came out when he heard the plane and spotted him land turned out to be a Dutch colonial official who was able to show him on his charts exactly where he was. As it turned out, due to the buffeting he had received in the fierce squall, he was now miles off course and, had he continued, he would have ended up somewhere in the wilds of the wrong end of the Malay Peninsula. Now he was able to use his fresh bearings to work out a new route to take him on to Alor Star, less than two hours' flying time away and where, to his joy, they had received word of his impending arrival, the airport being open and mechanics ready to service and refuel his place when he landed just before midnight. Perhaps more important, though, was the fact that he wasn't scheduled to fly out until early the following morning so he was able to get his first decent sleep since leaving Australia.

Mollison was well aware of the adventures and ordeals of the long-distance flyer but no pilot he had ever read about had had to undergo such a series of unexpected trials and tribulations in their efforts to cross the world. His journey seemed to be one testing misfortune after another, each of them having to be confronted and overcome on his own resources. When Kingsford-Smith had made his record-breaking flights he had been accompanied by a crew of three. But on this flight so far, Mollison had already undergone more than most. And much more was to come.

Although there would still be some stretches of sea to cross, the greatest of these watery expanses were now behind Mollison and much of the journey ahead would be over land, for which he was most truly thankful. Again, it must be borne in mind that such flights were undertaken without satellite-assisted distress signals, helicopters, high-speed coastguards and long-distance radio equipment. If you were in trouble over the oceans, then that would be the last of it. At least over land there was the very good chance of being able to put those little planes down somewhere.

From Alor Star he would be heading north over the dense rain forests of Northern Malaya, then Thailand and out over some sea stretches of the Gulf of Martaban before striking land again on the Irrawaddy Delta at Rangoon, in southern Burma. There he was due to refuel before continuing north to complete that leg of the journey at Akyab on the Bay of Bengal in north-west Burma.

He was only an hour into the journey when he noted the first of a series of irregularities coming from the engine. It seemed to be misfiring and every other detail of the flight was instantly wiped from his mind as he concentrated on the plane's heartbeat. There was a definite miss in the constancy of the ignition and the prospect of what the trouble might be terrified him. Then it corrected itself and he concentrated once more on other details, such as the constant checking with his compass readings. But then that was interrupted when the sound of the misfiring resumed, only to correct itself once again. In the midst of this problem, he was to hit yet another monsoonal squall, not nearly as vicious as the one the day before and yet for some reason he seemed to get more wet. Despite his weather shield, he remembered how the intensity of the rain hitting him as it lashed back from the propeller had felt like he was being 'peppered with bullets'. In his open cockpit he was soaked through within minutes, though that problem didn't concern him half as much as that missing beat from the engine. And yet perhaps it was that tropical downpour which ultimately helped him to diagnose the problem he was experiencing with the engine. He remembered there hadn't been the slightest trace of a misbeat before he had filled his tanks at Alor Star and that there had been lots of water around on the sodden field where the fuel he had taken on was stored. His conclusion was that some of that ground water had probably got into the petrol and it was this which was causing the difficulty. After a while, the periods of misfiring decreased and eventually disappeared. His conclusion had been correct and after landing on the racecourse at Rangoon – it doubled as the capital's airport! – there was no recurrence of the problem.

It was almost like being home in a way, as his flight went into its fifth day and he was flying over India, heading for Karachi. It was here, after all, that he had got his early flying experience, making regular patrols and being shot at by warring tribesmen. Well, at least there would be no shots this time. India was to come and go without a hitch, the refuelling stops being ready and waiting for him, mechanics servicing his trusty engine. After Karachi the flight continued along the coast of the Persian Gulf to Bandar Abbas for a scheduled refuel. But away from the Dutch and British colonialists, he was now in the hands of others who didn't view flights such as this in quite the same light.

The officer who questioned him at Bandar Abbas in Persia (today's Iran) was perhaps one of the scruffiest he had come across, which rendered ironic the demands he was making of the stranger who had landed in his country. 'Where is your bill of health?' he demanded. Mollison, of course, had no such document. He had a passport and his flying licence, and that was it. But rather than reveal that he didn't have a bill of health, whatever that was, he tried bluffing his way round the situation. The officer would have none of it. 'You must have a bill of health,' he demanded. Mollison tried a number of other tactics. He explained he was a record-breaker. He was flying across the world. Time was important. The help of the officer would be much appreciated to get him on his way. He would be truly thanked for any assistance he gave him. And more. But still the demand came: 'Your bill of health!' He knew at the end of the day bribery would be the only answer and eventually a sum was mentioned. The officer said he could arrange the vital document but it would cost Mollison 100 crowns – a mere £1. Desperate to get away, he promptly handed over the sum and the officer began writing out the certificate to prove that 'Mr J. Mollison is free of any disease and is mentally sane'. He was now at liberty to leave Persia, that first visit giving him absolutely no desire to ever land there again. But he was in fact to do just that not many hours later. His route took him from Bandar Abbas up to Basra at the head of the Persian Gulf. Before he could reach the Iraqi port, however, he noted with alarm a drop in his engine oil pressure. Assuming he had a leaking pipe and keen to fix it before it could create further problems, he decided to land once more in Persia, at the port of Bushire. And this time, he thought, there should be no problems. He had no diseases, was mentally sane and had a certificate to prove it.

A crowd of officials surrounded him as he taxied up to the little building which served as the airport office. Mollison ignored them as he set to work on finding the source of the oil problem and attending to it, the long-distance flyer being pilot, navigator, engineer and mechanic too. Then the one who appeared to be the most senior of the officials pushed his way through to demand who had given him permission to land. Mollison tried to explain much as he had done earlier at Bandar Abbas . . . he was on a record-breaking flight, in a great hurry, would appreciate their help, etc., etc. But no. The official demanded again. Who had given him permission to land? Mollison explained about the oil problem and that it was a case of either landing where he was or crashing somewhere and getting himself killed. That was no good either. He still had to have permission to land and where was it, the official persisted. There seemed little point in arguing after that and, not getting the reply he had wanted, the official said he would have to be fined for landing without permission in Persia. Fortunately, however, the fine was cheaper than his bill of health, it being only 50 crown – about 50p. He promptly paid up and got ready for another take-off.

The delay caused by repairing the oil leak and those various arguments with officials was compounded when Mollison eventually crossed the border into Iraq and his destination that night, Basra. The city was in the midst of a raging desert storm, making it impossible to sight the airfield. Luckily he had enough fuel on board to circle the town until the storm had subsided and he was able to view the landing area. By the time he did touch down, however, the various delays had cost him the time he had scheduled for a decent sleep and he had to make do with a short nap.

Basra was on the route taken by small passenger planes then doing scheduled flights from England to India under the flag of Imperial Airways, the forerunner of British Airways. That meant he was able to get some expert flight mechanics to give his plane a thorough check, including reinforcing his own repair to the oil leak. This gave him some comforting reassurance that his little aircraft was ready for anything that might lie ahead. And on such ventures that could be anything.

The dust storm at Basra wasn't to be the last. To get from there to Aleppo in northern Syria meant going over the northern end of the great Arabian desert, and there he flew straight into a raging sandstorm. It was of such dimensions that when it eventually cleared he found he had completely lost his bearings. He needed something to coincide with his compass direction in order to get back on his route again and there was only one way of doing that – by making another landing. There was little point in landing on the lonely desert and he flew on till he was able to locate a small encampment below at a point where the dunes had levelled and there appeared to be a suitable landing area.

Within seconds of the little Gypsy Moth coming to a halt, Mollison was immediately surrounded by wild-looking nomadic tribesmen, none of whom had the appearance of anyone likely to say, 'Can I help?' One appeared to be the sheikh and Mollison singled him out to greet with a friendly shake of the hand. Despite their menacing appearance, though, there was no hostility from any of the party, just a severe language problem, and it was some time before he could decipher from what the sheikh was saying the direction in which he should be going. More problems ensued when he had to persuade the sheikh to be the one to spin his propeller in order to get his engine started again. Planes of that vintage, like cars of the day, had no electrical starters and required some physical assistance to spark their engines into life. In the case of the Gypsy Moth, that meant someone rotating the propeller half a turn at a time till it built up sufficient cylinder pressure for the necessary kick-start. Eventually, after what seemed an age, Mollison was able to make the sheikh understand precisely what he wanted him to do, and at the same time convince him he would come to no harm in the process. Minutes later he was waving a grateful farewell to the bemused tribesmen and trusting that their directions had been the ones he had wanted. They were.

He was well inside the northern hemisphere by now, the monsoons and their fierce storms all behind, and so too were those incredible desert storms in which the very desert itself could be blown into the heavens. After Aleppo, the destination in northern Syria which the desert tribesmen had helped him find, there were no more grasping airfield officials, no more monsoon squalls, sandstorms or unlit airports closed for the night. And for the next two days there were the joys of being the low-flying adventurer as he headed out over the serene waters of the eastern Mediterranean, a mere 40 feet above the gentle waves so that he almost felt as much a part of the sea as he did the air. Over on his left he could see the northern tip of Cyprus before making another landfall, that of the south-western shoulder of Turkey, and beyond that there was more sea again, this time the Aegean and the islands of the Dodecanese.

After what he had come through, the journey on to Athens was idyllic, and thereafter on to Rome where, after a week with neither a wash nor a shave, he took time to do both. 'I had to make some effort to clean up,' he recalled, and with his schedule still in place there was the luxury of the time to do just that.

It would have been so nice for Jim Mollison to have ended his mammoth flight by flying in from the continent over the Channel and clocking in at Croydon, near London, the main airport of the time, to stake his claim to the new record for the solo flight, Australia to England. But the English weather doesn't work that way, even in summer time. The flight across those last few miles in France had been uneventful, but as he headed out over the

Channel he could see what lay ahead – huge banks of dark grey cumulus clouds. He was in for a rough and wet welcome. The storm broke before he reached the coast and was to become so fierce, the cloud cover so dense, that he had to abandon his plan of flying direct to Croydon. When he reached the Sussex coast at Pevensey Bay, between Eastbourne and Bexhill, he immediately looked around for an emergency landing site.

Of course, it didn't really matter whether or not he reached Croydon there and then: the time for the record was clocked at the point where he landed. And on Tuesday, 4 August 1931, precisely eight days, nineteen hours and twenty-five minutes after leaving Australia, Jim Mollison, the man from Pollokshields, Glasgow, touched down on that beach in southern England to smash the existing record by two days and three hours. He nearly smashed the little Gypsy Moth in the process, however, the beach on which he landed being soft shingle which broke the plane's landing and brought it to a sudden halt as its wheels sank into the gravel. The aircraft then flipped forward in a most undignified fashion on its nose.

Nearby villagers who had heard the plane circling rushed down to rescue its pilot as he sat, trapped vertically in the cramped cockpit. When they eventually released him, they were nonplussed as to why the weary-looking, oil-stained and weather-beaten pilot began waving a paper and imploring them for their signatures. They were vital, he said, as his impartial witnesses to verify his time of arrival and his claim to the record. The villagers then escorted him to the nearest telephone where he was told by Flying Club officials that if his plane was all right he could carry on with his flight to Croydon. Luckily the Moth was as hardy as its exhausted and dishevelled pilot and together they took off again for the remaining 70 miles to Croydon.

Word had quickly got around about his anticipated arrival and there was a huge crowd there to greet him. The reporters' first questions were about what his immediate plans might be.

When they insisted with that line of questioning, he said they reminded him of a favourite Scots expression: 'Here's your hat – what's your hurry?' He did go on to say, however, that he was in no hurry to make any more distance records and first of all he wanted to get up to Glasgow. He also told the pressmen how exhausted he was and how it had really hurt to climb back into the plane at Pevensey and fly those last few miles to Croydon. Only the refreshing cup of tea the villagers had given him had helped him make it.

Mollison was fêted as the hero of a nation. There was an instant message of congratulations from the King, while the Prince of Wales made immediate arrangements to meet him. Other great heroes like Sir Malcolm Campbell and Sir Alan Cobham, the legendary land-speed record-breakers, Kaye Don, the great motor-racing and speedboat champion, and Amy Johnson, the greatest ever British woman pilot, were all to be seen with him. Glasgow, of course, was ecstatic as the news went around the world about the amazing achievement of one of its sons. The city is sadly not noted for acknowledging its heroic offspring – it even refused a civic dinner for the boxer Benny Lynch when he became Scotland's first-ever world champ – but decided in Mollison's case to hail him with a civic reception held in all the splendour of the Satinwood Salon of the City Chambers. And Lewis's in Argyle Street, then the city's biggest store, quickly secured his record-breaking Gypsy Moth for a public display which was to attract thousands.

Mollison had the world at his feet. He only had to mention another record attempt and the backers and sponsors would queue up, each challenge generating huge sums. Flying's golden age had its golden flyer and the records came tumbling one after another – England to Capetown, the first by the west-coast route; first solo westward flight over the North Atlantic; first solo westward flight over the South Atlantic; first England to South America; first United Kingdom to USA together with Amy Johnson (who was to become his wife); the England to India record, again with Amy Johnson; New York to London; England to Capetown by the eastern route.

Then there were the honours, the ticker-tape receptions, the awards. Warner Brothers, the Hollywood movie production company, were making a film about heroic pilots, the cast to be headed by Bette Davis and Douglas Fairbanks Jnr, and when they heard about the exploits of the handsomely rugged Scotsman, they immediately dispatched Fairbanks to meet him in New York and talk it over. They wanted as a star in that movie the greatest flying hero of the hour, the guy with the hottest name in town. But Mollison didn't need Hollywood to make him a star. He already was one. He was playing a role more dazzling than that of any film star because he was doing it for real, not for celluloid. As a result, the talks he had with Fairbanks were to prove negative, no specific reason being mentioned, although it was accepted by many that he had declined the film offer due to that streak of diffidence in his character. But that diffidence was just one layer in the complicated strata that made up the Mollison persona. He was also labelled a bounder, a rotter, a lout, a churl, an alcoholic, a Casanova and a brawler. None of which deterred Amy Johnson, who was the greatest heroine of her day for her own flying exploits, not the least of which was being the first woman to fly solo to Australia, also in a Gypsy Moth and subject to similar trials and challenges as Mollison's. Lost over India, she had even landed on the barracks square of an army regiment while a parade was in progress, scattering soldiers and officers in all directions.

Amy Johnson was the daughter of a wealthy Hull fish merchant and had taken flying lessons as a hobby while working as a shorthand typist in London. She began solo flying after 16 hours of tuition and, in an echo of Mollison, had got lost on her first solo cross-country flight in England. Undaunted, she then took off in a Gypsy Moth for that first-ever female solo flight to Australia. Other records followed, making her the most outstanding woman of her day. But, like Mollison, while she was undoubtedly a fearless and most courageous pioneering solo flyer, there was also the other side. At times moody, rebellious and haughty, she suffered from nervous anxiety, was unstable and lived in a constant state of tension, often near or at emotional breaking-point. Indeed she had suffered more than one nervous breakdown and she was being courted by a man labelled, among so many other things, as an alcoholic, a brawler and a Casanova. It was the perfect recipe for a disastrous marriage. A human cocktail of nuclear fissionable material.

To marry Johnson, Mollison performed one of those exploits which had won him some of those derisory titles, dramatically terminating a much-publicised love affair and engagement with the young English beauty, Lady Diana Wellesley, a great-granddaughter of the Duke of Wellington. That done, the marriage to Amy went ahead and the pair immediately became the darlings of the 'in' crowd, the star attraction of the top end of the social whirl. They called Mollison and Johnson the 'Flying Sweethearts' as the pair of them created more and more world air records, some together, some separately. But Mollison's drinking got worse and, perhaps in some perverse form of revenge, Amy also took to alcohol. After one particularly boozy party she was chased and stopped by police in Miami, at which point the bold Yorkshire lass proceeded to take a swipe at one of the cops. And there were other similar incidents. Predictably, the marriage did not last and Mollison was next seen in the company of the wealthy socialite Phyllis Hussey – but his continued heavy drinking and a string of affairs with other women brought that union to an end after a few months, much as it did his next liaison, with the Dutch widow Maria Kamphuis.

Mollison's drinking exploits and succession of marriages were sadly to tarnish his name, for this was in the days when people would take a step back at the news of one divorce, never mind three. And as for fisticuffs in public! Goodness sakes, that just wasn't on. So the huge rancher he decked in Sydney because he sniggered at his accent, the nightclubber in Bermuda he thumped for not standing to attention at the national anthem, and the property owner he whacked in Bayswater when waiting for a taxi did not go down well. In today's Britain he would have been seen in a very much different light, but in the Britain of that age, such a lifestyle really wasn't the best of news.

By the outbreak of the Second World War the name Jim Mollison was much in the past. He was rejected for service in the RAF but, being the kind of man he was, was determined to help in the war effort in some way and enlisted in the Air Transport Auxiliary, the invaluable service which flew new planes from factories, both here and America, to the airfields of the bomber and fighter squadrons. He made over 1,000 such deliveries. His former wife Amy also enlisted in the ATA and was the first person in the service to be killed, her plane crashing into the Thames Estuary.

Mollison's drinking then became so bad, and so publicised, that in the post-war years the Civil Aviation Authority revoked his pilot's licence and the world heard very little about Jim Mollison after that. He spent his remaining years in comparative poverty in the company of his mistress, a lady called Molly Jermey, as the owner of a small hotel in an outer London suburb, slowly losing his grasp on reality to the affliction of alcoholism.

By his early fifties he was crippled as a result of alcoholic neuritis and admitted to a Surrey nursing home where he died on Friday, 30 October 1959, at the age of 54. When told about his death, his third wife Mary spoke of how fond she had been of him. They had been separated for 18 months after eight years of marriage 'but I couldn't live with a genius like Jim', she said.

His mistress Molly, who ran the small hotel he owned, had insisted that the premises had no bar. 'He would have stood drinks for so many friends we would have been out of business in no time,' she said, going on to comment that if only he had married her things might have been different. 'Jim's mistakes had been in marrying wealthy women and because of that he didn't have to work and had no other interests – only his memories.'

But no one was more aware of the frailties of his character than Mollison was himself. In writing about these he made the point that, despite all his weaknesses, he was the sort of person who was kind to animals, had never robbed a blind person, had an immediate capacity for falling in love, could weep when he heard music that appealed to him and was indifferent to death. Perhaps it's best to remember Jim Mollison, the great flying adventurer, in that vein.

Chapter Eight

The Day Glasgow Went Broke

The day a Glasgow bank went broke was one of the most sensational stories of the century. For the bank was the biggest of its kind in the country. There were branches in every sizeable Scottish town as well as in many centres throughout England, and it was the main bank used by small businesses in the Isle of Man. Thousands faced the prospect of losing their savings, hundreds of firms were to close, countless numbers faced redundancy and hundreds of investors were not only to lose their deposits, but were to forfeit everything they possessed by being burdened with a share of the bank's colossal debts. When the shock news hit London, the stock market had one of its gloomiest-ever trading sessions and there were emergency questions asked in Parliament.

And yet such were the times back then that on the morning when Scotland's biggest-ever banking disaster was first made known, you would hardly have noticed anything had occurred by what appeared in the latest newspapers. It was in the days before the turn of the last century and you had to be the most patient of newspaper readers if you wanted to find out just what was news. All our morning and evening papers at the time had a dreary similarity, their front pages being crammed with column after column of advertisements. And when you eventually did get to the pages with news stories, there were no captivating headlines to draw your attention to something you might want to read. And often as not, there was some kind of news information hidden in a paid advertisement in those front-page columns – but first you had to plough through them. Here's a typical selection from a page one of the day:

> Reid and Co., Crossmyloof bakers. Trilby pies, from the celebrated recipe of the famous cook of Charles II. One penny each. These pies will be greatly improved if they are heated before being used . . . J. & T. Sawers, West Howard St. Visit our new oyster bar . . . The Glasgow Apothecaries, Virginia Street; Drunkenness, or the liquor habit positively cured with a powder to put in a glass of beer with the knowledge of the patient. It is absolutely harmless but will offer a permanent and speedy cure, whether the patient is a moderate drinker or an alcohol wreck. It never fails . . . Royal Lochnagar Balmoral, The Queen's Whisky. The finest all-round whisky in the kingdom. Sandringham Stores, Great Western Road. Price 42 shillings per dozen bottle case . . . Rheumatism, Sciatica, Bronchitis, Asthma, Consumption, Rickets, St Vitus Dance, Debility, Indigestion, Anaemia. Take Dr Walton's Pink Pills for Pale People. No other remedy ever discovered has effected so many wonderful cures.

And so they went on. At least they provided some light relief, but on the morning of Wednesday, 2 October 1878, one of these paid advertisements was to convey information the like of which few had come across before. Information about one of the most well-known and patronised of Glasgow business institutions. Information which was to rock the entire country.

In today's terms the announcement in that classified advert would warrant the biggest of headlines: the City of Glasgow Bank, the biggest of its kind in the country, would not be opening its doors the following morning and would immediately cease the issue of any further banknotes. In other words, the bank was broke. And so too were thousands of prudent Scottish savers. It was to be the biggest financial scandal of the day and failures in more recent times, such as those at Barings and BCCI, bear no little resemblance to what happened right here in Glasgow all those years ago.

The City of Glasgow Bank began trading at its foundation in 1839 with a paid-up capital of £1,000,000, which was huge money in its day. The bank's head office was in Hanover Street, the main branch in Virginia Street, and it soon proved itself one of the most popular and successful banks of the day. There were nine active Scottish banks trading at the time, such as the Royal Bank of Scotland and the Bank of Scotland, each with the name of the nation somewhere in its title except for the City of Glasgow. And yet the Glasgow bank's popularity was to outstrip all its rivals in the number of branches it had throughout the country.

Whatever asides others may make about Scots and their prudence, our forebears most certainly did like their banks and in fact had them before most. The Bank of Scotland opened up for business as long ago as 1695, and by the mid-19th century we had one for every 4,000 of the population, whereas in England and Wales it was one for every 12,000. In Ireland it was one for every 14,000.

But the City of Glasgow had branches in almost every county, ever major city and town. It was the latest bank, the bank with new and modern ways, the bank for progressive people, the bank that was best suited to service the phenomenal commercial growth taking place in the city at the time. It also found more modern methods and attitudes, with less stuffiness from staff, particularly popular with small shopkeepers and traders who apparently appreciated its services and the availability of local branches. There were 133 of these ranging from Oban to Aberdeen, from Inverness to the Isle of Man, where indeed much of that island's wealth was transacted through its four local branches. They were scattered right across the Highlands and Islands, too, but it was in Glasgow and the West of Scotland that the bank had the most depositors, as well as shareholders and investors, with 25 branches in the city, 21 in Lanarkshire and another six in Renfrewshire. It was those small investors, merchants and business people who were to bear the brunt of the disastrous financial news, hundreds of them having to cease trading and thousands suffering untold hardship as a result. In the days before unemployment or hardship benefit money, with no national health service, no sickness or disability provisions, if you couldn't help yourself, you starved. And that was the prospect now facing countless families throughout the country.

While no new City of Glasgow banknotes were to be released, the other Scottish banks had an emergency meeting just prior to the release of the news and were to offer the only comforting words of the day, that they would for the time being continue to accept City of Glasgow banknotes. That item of welcome information was to be included in the shellshock advertisement about the Glasgow bank's closure and, as a result, banks throughout the country were inundated the following morning with thousands wanting to immediately exchange their City of Glasgow notes for more reliable cash and before any announcement that they were completely worthless. Thousands too turned up at the offices in Hanover and Virginia Streets wanting to know about their investments. But they were to be told nothing further, police guarding the locked doors while, inside the building, staff who had turned up for work as usual were set to tasks such as returning all City of Glasgow cheques sent to them by traders and merchants and preparing new balances. Managers then agreed to admit some of the hundreds of anxious and angry customers waiting outside, but only on a one-at-a-time basis, each being given the same cruel news. Any monies they had in the bank would be frozen. And, even worse, they were also informed: 'Sorry, we can't tell you when you will be able to get access to your account. If ever!'

There had been rumours, of course, that something was happening at the City of Glasgow Bank. But what? About a month before there had even been a story in one of the Glasgow papers that 'a certain Scottish bank' was having financial difficulties. But with no other paper following up whatever lay behind the whispered revelations, or even trying to pinpoint the bank in question, the story had apparently not been taken too seriously. Inevitably the gossip was to reach London banking circles in the weeks preceding the announcement but when the rumours were put to the managers of the major joint-stock banks, their answers were that they were 'absurd and unfounded'. It was the work of unprincipled speculators on the Stock Exchange, they said. But then that's the kind of thing they would have said, it being in none of the industry's interests for one of them to go under, the shockwaves of such events being incalculable.

So the whisperers had whispered on. And, as if to substantiate their lack of specifics, they would lard their stories with such innuendo as 'and remember what happened to the City of Glasgow Bank before'. That was a reference to the time when more than 20 years before, yet another bank, the Western Bank of Scotland, had failed, and in its wake the City of Glasgow had been forced to suspend its activities for a month. The failure of the Western had dealt a major blow to the theory that Scottish banking was an unassailable establishment. At the same time, however, the main banking institutions were to show their faith in the City of Glasgow Bank's future and reserves of gold held in London were released to them. Trading continued and that hiccup had been forgotten, except by those with a pessimistic outlook in the final days before the bombshell announcement.

In view of the stories, other banks had insisted on a summary audit by an independent Edinburgh auditor and his report was made known to them on Saturday, 28 September 1878. The result was a collective turning of backs on the City of Glasgow Bank. There were to be no piles of gold ready for them this time, for when you hit the kind of financial waters the Glasgow Bank was now in, there are no lifeboats on hand. The Edinburgh auditor's findings confirmed those initial stories about the bank's involvement with overseas companies, and just three days later the directors held an emergency meeting which decided that for them and the City of Glasgow Bank the game was up. The wording of the advertisement for the newspapers was drawn up and instructions given that telegrams be dispatched to each of the 133 branches informing them they must not open for trading the following day. The telegram was the quickest method of communication at the time, the telephone only having been invented two years previously and not yet in general use, but in some cases there were to be even faster ways of news dissemination – by word of mouth. And it was to be to the great advantage of some of the bank's customers in the rescue of their precious savings accounts. At the main Inverness branch, for instance, the manager had received no word on the morning of 2 October about the closure and his office opened for business as usual. But if he hadn't heard, others in the town certainly had. No wildfire had ever moved as fast as this piece of news and his branch was to be inundated that morning with unprecedented requests by account-holders who had somehow got the word from Glasgow to withdraw their entire savings. Concerned at the huge amount of money the bank was paying out – somewhere in the region of £15,000 – he contacted the head office for instructions, getting a prompt return message ordering him to close immediately, which the bank did at 12.40 p.m.

It was the same story at the Motherwell branch, and in Islay there was a strange report of a woman said to have had a dream the night before about having no money in her purse and walking many miles the following morning to lift what little savings she had from the branch in Port Ellen. Others in Glasgow who had paid attention to the whispers had promptly withdrawn their savings the day before the announcement.

So what had gone wrong? The bank's immediate difficulties had come about because of the amount of advances given to firms trading in the East Indies and Australia which, in turn, had been caught up with financial problems of their own. The advances to these overseas merchants had been for enormous sums, something in the order of between £5 million and £6 million, equivalent today to about £230 million and £276 million. The City of Glasgow Bank had turned to other banks for some backing because of these difficulties, but when these banks had looked at the City bank's books, they shied off, for their accounts revealed they were in an even more parlous state than initially expected. In fact, they were millions in the red. They could no longer be supported.

It must be borne in mind this was in the days long before there were computers, calculators or any form of mechanical or technical aid in solving complicated accountancy situations and problems. It was teams of bookkeepers on tall stools with ledgers on sloping tables using pen and ink who performed such tasks, and they worked with incredible efficiency and haste in discovering the true nature of the bank's plight. On Friday, 18 October, just over a fortnight after the first public news of the failure, the investigating auditors issued their first report (today's equivalent sums are given in brackets).

We regret deeply to have to state that a more melancholy picture of wreck and ruin has never before been given to the public. It far exceeds even the worst anticipation that had been formed and we stand appalled before the revelations it makes of management, not merely frightful in its recklessness, but bristling with transactions of the most dubious character.

When we ventured to assume £5,000,000 (£230,000,000) as the probable loss, we were condemned as alarmists. The actual state of the case is now disclosed. By the course of trading the bank pursued, over £5,000,000 (£230,000,000) has been lost in addition to the capital of £1,000,000 (£46,000,000) with which it started. The shareholders have not a penny of the money they invested and they will have to make good five times as much (as they had invested). There appears to be £7,250,000 (£333,500,000) of bad debts and the securities held against these are valued at £1,750,000 (£80,500,000). But these securities are of a rather speculative character and which will no doubt require very great care and caution, perhaps even great delay, to realise them without adding to the extent of the disaster.

The dealings of the directors have been of the most varied character – New Zealand and Australian land, American railways, property in Karachi and Rangoon, buildings at home and the colonies, shipping, life policies, and even produce, all figure in the securities, showing how far the bank had travelled from ordinary fields of legitimate business.

By a systematic cooking of the accounts every year since 1873, the shareholders were led to believe that the bank had lent thousands less than it really had and the more they went through the books the more they were to find many other examples of the books being cooked.

There is not within the four corners of the report a single point which can dispel gloom or inspire hope. One reads its details with mingled feelings of shame for the country, compassion for the unhappy shareholders and bringing indignation against those who had brought this calamity on both. We deeply regret we don't have a word of comfort to give the shareholders. The actual extent of their suffering is far beyond the most serious calculations. A great deal of them appear to be people of what may be called 'limited means' and there is no doubt their all will be swept away.

Trade has received a severe shock by the failing of the bank. Credit has been impaired and a spirit of suspicion is around. The City Bank fell from a combination of things which we hope and believe for the honour of our country and the safety of our commerce was confined to itself.

The police were among the first to see the report, promptly picking up on the expression 'cooking the books'. As what had obviously been happening at the City of Glasgow Bank had been deliberate fraud, they now had to find out just who the perpetrators were. The miscreants didn't take much hunting, though, for when the Crown Office had gone into the details of the auditors' findings, it was more than clear just who the main culprits were – the principal members of the board of directors of the City of Glasgow Bank, together with their two chief executives. The six directors were named as Henry Inglis, WS, a 72-year-old lawyer of Great Stuart Street, Edinburgh, and Torrance, near Glasgow; William Taylor, a 66-year-old merchant of Langbank, Newton Mearns; Lewis Potter, a 71-year-old shipowner of Claremont Terrace, Kelvingrove, Glasgow; John Innes Wright, a 68-year-old merchant, of Queen's Terrace, Woodlands; Robert Salmond, a 74-year-old company director of

Rankinston, Ayrshire; John Stewart, a 61-year-old wine merchant of Moray Place, Edinburgh; and the two executives, Robert Stronach, 52, the bank's manager, of Crown Gardens, Dowanhill; and Charles Leresche, of Blythswood Square, Glasgow, the company secretary. Leresche was to be later released after questioning, being required as one of the chief prosecution witnesses.

The seven men detained were the *crème de la crème*, as it were, of the Glasgow business community, the kind who would think themselves and who would want to be thought of as the very pillars of society, the most distinguished and honourable of professional gentlemen, men of integrity, honesty and principle. They were certainly not the parcel of rogues expected to be arraigned for a financial scandal of proportions such as Scotland had never seen before – or since. One of them owned the main shipping line carrying migrants to Melbourne and Sydney, another was a leading grain merchant, another a wealthy wine merchant, a highly esteemed lawyer and Writer to the Signet. Several of them were prominent Freemasons and held various positions in the respected echelons of Glasgow establishment, one a president of the YMCA, another a regular representative at the General Assembly of the Church of Scotland. Yet another was a substitute Grand Master of the Freemasons, some were elders of the Church of Scotland and others board members of the most prominent schools. Their homes included a prestigious country estate, a collection of mansions and the finest town houses in Glasgow and Edinburgh. Just imagine the talk, the sensation it would be in today's society if such a collection were hauled in and kept in custody. Accordingly, when the order went out to the arresting policemen that morning of 21 October 1878, that on no account were their families to be put in any state of alarm when they were being arrested, it was merely put to them that their presence was 'required in town'. The niceties would be over soon, though, as en route to the city they were told that this would be no joyride and in fact they were being arrested on the most serious of charges and would be detained in custody.

When the six men – two others being arrested and detained in Edinburgh – arrived at the Central Police Station in St Andrew's Street, just behind Glasgow Cross, it was discovered that all the holding cells of the division in nearby Turnbull Street were full. Well, it was, after all, a Monday morning and it had obviously been a good old-fashioned Glasgow weekend. The men had to be detained, however, and as there were no cells – or was it because of their being such estimable prisoners? – it was decided to hold them in the private rooms of the Chief Constable and magistrates at the Central Police Station. Each was kept alone under the charge of a police officer and they were forbidden to communicate with one another.

The charges against the men were to be the most serious of their kind ever heard in a financial case. The indictment accused each of them of falsehood, fraud and wilful imposition in connection with the issuing of a false balance sheet relating to the bank's affairs. And as if to emphasise just how serious the authorities were in this case, the charges went on to allege the 'wicked and felonious fabrication of balance sheets, using them with intent to defraud; theft, breach of trust and embezzlement, intent to defraud the company and the public and that they concocted and fabricated balance sheets'. As the saying goes, they were getting the book thrown at them. Commenting on the apprehension of the bank's directors and executives, the *Glasgow News*, one of the city's main newspapers at the time, in their main story of the day – to be found as usual buried somewhere inside the paper – said that 'the news spread around Glasgow and was met with great excitement'.

As soon as they were known to be in custody, the press let fly at the suspects with not the slightest trace of restraint. Details of the Edinburgh auditor's initial report on the bank had obviously leaked and the first comments on the case were based on these early findings. The *Glasgow News* loudly proclaimed that 'the law has at last got hold of the men whose unredeemed villainy has brought ruin upon thousands of innocent people and imperilled the stately fabric of Scotch credit and commerce'. The writer did go on to observe, somewhat condescendingly, that 'of course, they are entitled to the presumption of innocence. But looking at the revelations . . . it would be idle to conceal the conviction which must have been forced on every mind. Falsehood, fraud and wilful imposition are words which go straight to the mark. It may well be that they don't share the guilt to an equal degree – some may be knaves, others fools. But they will deservedly stand together in the dock as one of the most audacious bands of swindlers that every preyed on a confiding country.'

With the publication in full detail of the investigators' report some days later, however, the newspapers were to become even more scathing and venomous in their reports. In these uncompromising and untrammelled accounts, nowhere will you find the word 'alleged' in reference to the deeds said to have been committed. Nothing is left to the imagination and none of the investigators' report was in any way censored on the grounds that it might prejudice the prosecution case against the accused, the papers in all apparent freedom revealing every precise detail of what had been going on at the City of Glasgow Bank. It was fraud and those involved were the fraudsters, was the consensus. *The Scotsman*, in a long feature on the investigators' report, was to ask: 'How has this been brought about? By what means have these millions been squandered and the losses concealed till now?' Having asked the vital questions, they then offered their conclusions, the foremost being that 'in the record of commercial frauds there is not to be found a blacker case than that of the City of Glasgow Bank'. The paper then went on to give details from the report which would undoubtedly be the basis of the Crown's case. 'The revelations in the report are startling because of the criminality which they disclose,' said the Edinburgh paper.

'The investigators say that they had repeatedly to ask questions "seriously affecting the course of management", and "in most instances we were told that the explanations we invited related to points which were as new and as startling to the parties interrogated as to ourselves".'

Before long it had to be known who they were that answered thus. If some directors were kept in ignorance, logic dictated that the manager could not be and, indeed, neither could all the directors. The nature of the fraud ruled out such a supposition, the accounts were cooked in the most imaginative ways. By a system of cross and false entries, the shareholders were led to believe that they had lent on foreign and colonial credit £937,000 less than was the fact. Then, out of £149,000 of bills handed to the bank for collection, £54,595 had been discounted in London or pledged. In addition, more than a million in doubtful securities were made to figure as if they were either government securities owned by the bank or cash in its coffers. There cannot be a shadow of doubt about the intention with which this was done. The draft balance sheet of the accounts for 1878 was recovered and showed the alterations made. The effect was to induce the shareholders to believe that the bank had less lent upon credit and more in good assets. Still another instance of the falsification of the balance sheet may be given. A sum of £280,000 was entered as an asset under the heading of 'Suspense Account' which the investigators rejected altogether; and another sum of £36,000 entered as an asset under the heading 'Credit Account' shared the same fate because it 'is made up of balances so hopelessly bad that, as we are informed, they were specially removed under this heading to prevent the possibility of interest being calculated on them from year to year'. The report went on: 'It would seem that deliberate fraud on the shareholders could not go much further. Yet there is even a lower depth in which, moreover, the public as well as the shareholders are touched. It is in the manipulation of the account of gold held against notes.

The story of the report is clear enough. Every week the amount of the notes in circulation was entered in the circulation ledger. Against this was put, in the usual-sized figures, the actual amount of gold held, while the amount necessary to make the gold tally with the notes was added in smaller figures.' After going on to reveal some of the more technical details of the financial finagling that had been going on in the Glasgow bank, *The Scotsman* turned some of its invective on the seven accused.

> But what is to be done with the men who have been guilty of this fraud? The fact that penalties are exigible from the bank because of their act does not free them from responsibility to the criminal law; and there is no vindictiveness, nothing but a regard for common justice, in hoping that they will be placed at a criminal bar before many days are over . . . Recklessness in management could not be carried much further. But recklessness led to difficulties, and difficulties led to fraud in order that the true state of matters might be kept from the shareholders and the public . . . One evil step led to another . . . Recklessness leading to fraud caused the downfall of the City Bank.

The *Glasgow News* was to thunder on in a similar vein, revealing more details of how the accounts were altered and faked.

> There is no sin against the rules of sound banking, of honest bookkeeping, or of common good faith which the men who managed the City Bank have not committed . . . They have done this for ends which deepen and blacken the enormity of the means and with results whose wide-reaching mischief the imagination fails to grasp. They have lied to the Government, defied the law, defrauded the public, and ruined hundreds of helpless men and women

whose sole crime was that they would not believe their directors to be knaves; and they have done all this that they might carry on speculations for their own profit or the enrichment of their friends . . . The City Bank has not been smashed by one or two indiscretions, nor have its directors been stained with only one or two sins. On the contrary, one offence has been heaped upon another, with a wanton superfluity of wickedness which almost seems to have revelled in boundless defiance of every principle of honour and honesty.

So there! The press had spoken. And having done so it was now the turn of the cartoonists, with their lampoons on the sensational financial shenanigans at the City Bank. Their wicked caricatures of the accused parodied them in a fashion which would today have both cartoonist and editor jailed for contempt of court. One depicted four of the bank's directors sitting at a table piled high with money and the bank's manager telling them, 'Help yourselves, gentlemen. There's plenty more where that came from.' And looking on at the cash capers of the directors is Robert the Bruce and John Knox, the valiant Scottish king commenting, 'Has Scotland come to this after all our struggles?' with Knox reassuring him, 'Fear not, my friend. The Lord will judge them!' Another, with the caption 'The Pursuit of Gain', shows a director who absconded grabbing a pile of money saying it would be enough to pay his fare to Spain.

After an appearance before the magistrate at the Central Police Court, the seven accused were ordered to be held in custody at Duke Street Prison. They were the most unusual group to have appeared in court, a collective of mainly elderly men, each dressed in the expensively tailored business suits of the day, gold watch chains and bejewelled fobs glinting in the pale autumnal sunshine filtering through the tall windows of the court. Only Taylor and Stronach, the two youngest, were clean shaven, the others having copious grey beards or whiskers. All, however, were in a state of utter dejection, nervy and anxious looking, and even the youngest of them appeared much older than his years.

Bail was refused and they were ordered to be held in the East Wing for untried prisoners at Duke Street Prison, now the site of a housing estate in the shadow of Glasgow Cathedral. No more pleasant rooms with comfortable armchairs for their period in custody. Duke Street was prison with all the harshness and deprivations that meant in Victorian Glasgow. Each was held in a solitary cell whose bare furnishings consisted of a chair, a small table and a wooden bunk. The only exercise permitted was that of the daily 'airing', this being a half-hour walking period in an outdoor area known as the cage, so called because it had the appearance of one and was divided into small pens so that prisoners had no contact with one another. One newspaper was to report, however, that an inside contact had informed them the men from the bank were getting food of a 'finer quality' and were being supplied with small amounts of liquor, books and daily newspapers.

In today's Scotland it would be many months before the accused in such a case would stand trial, but just as quick as the police had been in making their investigations and arrests were the authorities in bringing the seven directors of the City of Glasgow Bank to trial, that being set down for the High Court in Edinburgh on 20 January 1879, just three and a half months after the initial sensational news of the bank's demise.

It was during the compilation of the case against the accused by the office of the Lord Advocate that yet another hammer blow was to be announced for the bank's shareholders. Still reeling in shock at the probable loss of all they had invested, they were now informed by the investigating auditors that all those who held capital stock in the bank would be called on to make payments amounting to 500 per cent on their holdings. It was the most devastating of news and was to instigate a wave of bankruptcies throughout Scotland, with businesses collapsing by the score and their workers made unemployed.

As the trial date neared, newspapers described it as 'the most important trial ever held in Scotland in the estimation of the layman, if not the lawyer'. It was, of course, given enormous coverage, although because of those universal page-one advertisements of the day it was never to be front-page news. The Crown called 156 witnesses and the productions – that is, the items to be shown in court as proof, such as books, accounts and other documents – were to come, as one paper described it, 'by the wagon load'.

Despite the gravity of the charges and the impact the case had upon thousands throughout Scotland, it was not the most exciting of trials. For a start, the Crown withdrew some of the severest of the charges against the accused, those of theft and embezzlement, and most of the debate was based on accountancy, bookkeeping and financial arrangements, little of which was compelling and all of which was taxing to the 15 members of the all-male jury, comprising in part of two innkeepers, an outfitter, a builder, an iron company manager, an ironmonger, a chairmaker, a draughtsman and a jeweller, all from Edinburgh and Leith, with the exception of one from Peebles. Women, who still did not have the vote, were barred from serving and not granted that right until 1919 under the terms of the Sex Disqualification Removal Act.

The seven accused, still visibly shaken and downcast by events, were to be given the sharpest of reminders of the severity and consequences of their disastrous role in the bank's affairs in the opening remarks of the Lord Advocate, Mr W. Watson, MP, the supreme law officer of Scotland. He was to speak of how the accused 'had abused the confidence reposed in them, how by insidious substantiation converted a once sound and prosperous banking concern into a mere machine for the abstraction of the hard-won savings of small and all-too-confiding investors, only to throw them into the lap of wealthy and unscrupulous speculators, and how while posing as pillars of commercial integrity they were in reality the rotten props of a decaying and worthless concern'.

Much of the case put by the counsels for the defence had rested in trying to persuade the jury that men of such stature, such respectability, and with such position in society would never be involved in the kind of allegations being made about them by the prosecution, and this was a course to which the Lord Advocate took the greatest of exceptions. They had, he said, repeatedly referred to the outstanding character of each of the accused although he did stress he was not inferring they should not have raised the matter of character. But he regretted having to say that 'to press that evidence to the length which has been done by witness after witness is the most preposterous thing I have ever heard in court'. If that evidence was true, he argued, not one of the directors was capable of committing such an offence and nobody did it. The evidence of character had amounted to nothing.

In his address to the jury, the main judge, Lord Moncrieff, the Lord Justice Clerk, said the trial had been without precedent in Scotland and he made reference to the vast amount of documents, accounts, figures, balances and results which had been shown in court. As a result of what had happened, he said, the country was suffering under a great calamity. Hundreds had been reduced from affluence to poverty, and although the accused were persons who had held high position and enjoyed the respect and confidence of their friends and the community, it all boiled down to whether or not the balance sheets were false, whether the persons knew they were false and whether they did what they did with the balance sheets with the intention of deceiving the shareholders and public. His summary, however, was not tinged with any form of rebuke, reprehension or condemnatory remarks, and by comparison with the tones of the press long before any evidence had been heard, he was surprisingly compassionate in his charge to the jury. On the bank manager Stronach he was to comment that there had been no doubt that the 'weight of this blow' had fallen very heavily on him: 'His position unquestionably was a very painful and a difficult one; but that will not, as I have said more than once, in any degree remove the consequences of the truth of such a charge from his shoulders.' He was also to note, somewhat favourably, that Salmond, the largest shareholder of the directors, as well as Stronach and Taylor, had held his shares till the end. He continued:

> And indeed there is nothing in the conduct of the prisoners at the bar to indicate that they were making ready to quit a falling house, or that they were making preparations for a catastrophe that they thought was at hand. Mr Stronach had quite means enough to meet any advances that he had received and, indeed, it was proved that he has been able to pay the first call [for money] now due upon his shares.
>
> Gentlemen, I have now discharged the very painful duty that has been imposed upon me and which has now occupied our time and attention for so many days. I have never, since I had a seat on the bench, experienced so much feeling of pain, of regret – I had almost said of mortification. The circumstances that we have been inquiring into have a large significance outside these walls. I need not allude to them again. But I have only in conclusion to say, as I said at the beginning, that we have nothing but an ordinary duty to perform here, which is to weigh the evidence that has been led and come to the conclusion that right, and justice, and conscience dictate. You will give the prisoners the benefit of every reasonable doubt, as all prisoners are entitled to have. You will take into view their character, as you would take into view the

character of any prisoner accused of a crime at this bar. But if you shall be satisfied that the prosecutor has established his charge, then you will deliver the verdict which your conscience may dictate; and whether your verdict be to convict or to acquit, it will be enough for you, doubtless, that your own conscience approve; but I think I may safely say that, be it what it may, it will carry with it the respect and approbation of the country.

The jury did not let the complexities of the case delay their decision. On Friday, 31 January 1879, after listening for 11 days to complicated evidence crammed with reams of financial technicalities, the jury returned just two hours after retiring. Their unanimous findings were that the accused Potter and Stronach had been guilty of the first three charges, that is the more serious ones, and the five others only guilty of the charges in relation to the bank's balance sheets. Sentences were deferred until the following day, Saturday, 1 February.

A huge crowd ringed the High Court in the centre of Edinburgh's Old Town in anticipation of the sentences, most of them expecting to hear long periods of imprisonment being handed down to the seven accused. They were to be sorely disappointed. The judge had little to say, despite having specifically referred to the gravity of the charges, and commented that Potter and Stronach, the two men who had been found guilty of the more serious charges, had not acted for their personal gain but for the advantage of the bank. 'That does not remove it from the category of crime – very far from it – but it does remove from the crime of which you have been convicted the element, as I have said, of corrupt personal motive for personal ends. That consideration has weighed with the court in the sentences, being one short of penal servitude [hard labour].' In other words, he was being sparing. Potter and Stronach were sentenced to 18 months. Of the others he was merely to say that, having considered their case and the crime of which they had been convicted, and also the fact that they had been in custody since the previous October, their sentence should be one of eight months.

The leniency of the sentencing caused a furore throughout the country, and the newspapers unanimously reflected those feelings in their own comments. Said the *Glasgow Herald*: 'When they have dreed their doom [endured their sentence], the places that knew them before will know them no more forever. They will have to end their days that remain for them in poverty and seclusion, shunned and despised by those who formerly held them in respect. This is part of the punishment following their conviction and, in whatever light we view their conduct, it is so severe that a touch of pity might arise on their behalf.' The *Herald* went on, though, to make the point that they had concealed the facts from the proprietors of the bank and led them, by paying huge dividends, to believe that their property was in the most flourishing condition. They also questioned if any of the directors could be completely ignorant of all the bank's indebtedness: 'The directors might not all know everything about the accounts, they must have known that they were hanging like a millstone round the neck of those concerned, yet nevertheless went on issuing balance sheets which lied to the shareholders and entirely misrepresented the affairs of the bank. It had been doubtlessly on such plain commonsense grounds as these that the jury had founded their verdict.'

The Scotsman made great play of the 'absurdly lenient sentences', saying they had been so light it had to be questioned if they would act as a deterrent. The *Mail* asked: 'If the chief perpetrators got so little, why have the others got so much?'

Because of the widespread ramifications of the bank's downfall, the English papers also gave the trial major coverage and reflected at great length on the verdict and sentences. The *London Times* observed: 'A commercial fraud of the first magnitude and with consequences so distressing that the imagination fails to follow them and they get punishment no greater than an ordinary case of shoplifting.' They would have been glad, they said, had the judge even declared he was genuinely convinced it had been proper to withdraw the more serious charges of theft and embezzlement against the men. The *Daily Telegraph* rounded on the defence counsel, pointing out that the plea of ignorance on their behalf and the 'witnesses of character' argument could not be admitted for a moment.

> As the Lord Advocate hinted, it would have been a good thing for both shareholders and depositors if the directors had been men of very doubtful character. Then they could have done little harm, because the public would not have trusted them.
>
> It was the excellent repute of the men, as established by the infallible Scotch tests of church communion, family worship and liberal subscriptions to all pious objects, that aggravated the offence by aggravating the danger. Who could distrust a pillar of the local kirk, a ruling elder, a lay representative to the General Assembly, and a man who was so consistent a professor as to discharge his butler for refusing to attend family prayers? No one; but their counsel seemed to forget that to put forward such a defence was only to heap up reasons for the gravest responsibility . . . In their anxiety to prove the accused absolute nullities, dummies and fools in their directorial capacity, the eloquent advocates irresistibly provided the question: 'Of what use, then, are bank directors? Are they mere decoys to attract depositors and is that the sole consideration they give for the enjoyment of salaries, honour and prestige?'

The *Daily News* asserted that the very minutes of the board showed that the directors were not passive in the hands of the manager, but that they knew the real nature of the accounts. They had excluded the bank secretary from the boardroom when discussing them and when they had been asking assistance from the other banks had refused to show them the accounts. The *Echo* also commended the verdict, saying that some of the directors had been simple knaves, others had been not quite so knavish because they weren't so close to the action, while a few were legally rogues on account of their own stupidity, want of business capacity and their credulity in the manager and more active directors.

The Economist, the London-based financial magazine, remarked that all fears that some legal difficulties might stand in the way of prompt punishment being inflicted upon the perpetrators of the greatest banking fraud of modern times were now set at rest with their conviction: 'It would certainly have been lamentable had the arm of the law been found too short to reach such gross offenders.' The *Leeds Mercury*, meanwhile, intoned that the verdict asserted in the most emphatic manner the sound principle that fraud shall not escape exposure and retribution merely because it is carried out on a colossal scale. And the *Newcastle Chronicle* noted that there had been no doubt that Scotland had been deceived and thousands ruined: 'If the result of this trial leads Glasgow to have less confidence in pompous mediocrity,' the paper said, 'then the terrible lesson which the fall of the City Bank has taught Scotland may yet prove a blessing in disguise.'

The charitable sentences imposed were not, however, well received by the seven men, observers describing them as all being 'deeply affected' at the judge's pronouncements. The face of Stronach, who had been the bank's manager and who was sentenced to 18 months, was described as having an appearance of hopelessness before he broke down and cried bitterly. Potter, who received a similar sentence, was said to be showing 'nervous anxiety' and looking 'extremely agitated', perhaps not even fully comprehending what the sentence passed on him really was. Several of them were described as having 'tottering steps' as they shuffled from the dock to descend down the stairs to the cells below.

Outside in Parliament Square, the crowd had swelled in the expectation of seeing the removal of the prisoners to the Calton jail. The police debated with the prison authorities how the men should be transported from the High Court, suggesting at first they be taken to the prison in private cabs so that they might be hidden from the crowds. It was decreed by a police superintendent, however, that this might be misconstrued as some sort of special treatment and it was decided in the end that they should go in the normal prison van. This allowed the crowds what they wanted, a good view of the seven bank officials and directors. People surged forward when the old men, some of them most unsteady on their feet, emerged from the court building to walk to the van. They were booed and shouted at by spectators described by the newspapers as 'principally, to all appearances, young lads or worthless characters'. There was also a crowd waiting for them at the prison, as well as at Waverley Station, where five of them were put on the train under escort for Glasgow. Potter, the shipping company owner, and Stronach did not accompany the party, being sent instead to Perth Prison, where they would serve their 18 months.

Enterprising reporters naturally accompanied the five on the trip to Glasgow, noting that by then most of them had recovered their composure and were even seen to be laughing and joking with their escorts, who seemed to enjoy their company. The compartments in which they travelled were heated with warming pans but one of the prisoners could be heard saying they should have got a better standard of seating. Another was heard to ask permission to buy a pint bottle of brandy for the trip on the grounds that under medical advice he was to be provided with stimulants. His plea was refused, however. One of them then produced a box of cigars, which most of them seemed to enjoy for the rest of the journey.

On their arrival in Glasgow, three of the party – Taylor, Wright and Stewart – were taken to Duke Street Prison, where they had been in custody on remand. Salmond and Inglis, on the other hand, both in their seventies and under medical care, were allowed to serve their sentences in Ayr, spending much of the time in the prison hospital.

Follow-up stories about the men's time in prison regularly appeared in the newspapers, undoubtedly bringing an element of satisfaction to some of those enduring the woeful consequences of the bank's failure. The harsh rigours of life in the Duke Street jail were described in detail: unbleached cotton shirts, moleskin trousers, serge underwear and canvas shoes, the routine of the 5.45 a.m. reveille, the 6.45 a.m. breakfast of porridge and a pint of sour milk, the 12 o'clock dinner of scones and soup, and the five o'clock supper of more porridge and sour milk; the passing of each day in the long-since banished and dreaded compulsory labour of picking oakum. If ever there was a cruelly tedious form of prison labour/punishment it was this wearisome and painful work. Each morning the prisoners would be issued with a length of ship's rope, tarred because it had to be made waterproof for use at sea, making the rope firm and rigid. The prisoner would then have to reduce their piece of stiff rope by picking at its fibres till it was transformed into a pile of fluffy material. This was the substance they called oakum and which would then be sold to shipyards, whose tradesmen (known as caulkers) would ram it between the wooden decking on ships before tarring it to create the perfect seal. At Duke Street the daily ration of rope issued to each prisoner would be 2½ lb, a fair length of rope, and it had to be reduced to the oakum fluff by four o'clock each afternoon; if not completed by then, the prisoner would be put on governor's orders, as often as not a specified time on a bread-and-water diet. It was the most soul-destroying and tedious of work, the countless thousands of fibres having to be picked individually from the stiff and unyielding rope, the process breaking the pickers' nails and tearing the flesh from their finger-ends. 'We tore the tarry rope to shreds, with blunt and bleeding nails,' as Oscar Wilde had described it from his experience in Reading gaol some 16 years earlier.

The seven prisoners duly served their sentences, though, and virtually nothing was heard of them again, except that most of them were declared bankrupt and the lawyer Inglis was struck from the register of Writers to the Signet. The City of Glasgow Bank was never reconstituted, the strait-laced principles and the older and more prudent methods of handling money of the other banks doubtlessly preserving the otherwise good and unsullied reputation of Scottish banking institutions.

The great financial calamity had come and gone, the men who had perpetrated the biggest bank scandal the country had ever known dealt with, albeit in an all-too-lenient fashion. But what of the victims? They were to be found in all walks of life but mainly, as the initial auditors' investigation had observed, were people of 'limited means'. Letters pages of all the newspapers were inundated with harrowing tales of hardship and suffering, some writing poems about their own and others' plight. Some of those who held shares stood to lose everything, as these most plaintive lines written to the *Glasgow Herald* were sadly to convey:

> Pity us, God, must all our things go?
> All, even our mother's things, cherished with care!
> Must we leave the old home, the one home that we know?
> But not for the Poorhouse – surely not there!
> But to leave the old house, where old memories throng,
> For the Poorhouse! Oh, rather the peace of the grave,
> Pity us. Pity Oh God!

That was from a family of elderly spinsters whose only income had been from shares left them by their father. Many expressed their wrath and utter disgust at the officials of the bank, while others were to extend a Christian hand in deepest sympathy. This letter writer expressed their feelings in a short poem entitled 'Words of Comfort for Desponding Shareholders':

> Sufferers! Do not grieve so sadly
> God is King, God is love
> Trusted men have acted badly
> Some will rage and curse them madly
> Wail not, rail not – look Above!

Another, writing to the *Edinburgh Courant* newspaper, was not only to show their sympathy – they were willing to do something to help those who had lost their money too:

> At the present time, when every eye is moistened and every heart throbbing with mingled feelings of righteous indignation at the way in which shareholders and others have been betrayed, and the most profound sympathy goes out to the many helpless sufferers who are the innocent victims of this unparalleled and gigantic fraud, is it not befitting that all who have escaped the widespread calamity bestir themselves and do something as far as they can to lighten the suffering and gladden the hearts of the many who have been unwittingly more than deprived of their all?

The writer went on to explain that they lived in a tenement property with six other families and there were 40 other similar properties in the street; they intended to raise money from every other family who lived there – 240 of them in all. The writer concluded with the suggestion that the Glasgow Lord Provost call a meeting for the purpose of starting a national fund to alleviate the suffering of those who had lost their savings. There already had been considerable activity in the Glasgow City Chambers, however, about what steps might be taken in that direction. And all credit to the city council of the day, for they were to react with the same zeal and effort that had been put into that first auditors' report. Exactly a month after the devastating news that the bank had closed, Lord Provost William Collins, as a result of a meeting of the city council, convened a public meeting in the Merchants' Hall. Its purpose was 'to consider the best steps we can take to relieve the distress occasioned to the shareholders by the failure of the City of Glasgow Bank'. Provost Collins read out a long list, featuring the names of many prominent business people, as well as the provosts of cities and towns throughout Scotland, all willing to help with a relief fund. Many had already contributed, mostly with sums of around £1,000 (about £46,000 today). Perhaps even more impressive, though, is the fact that, by the time that meeting had been called, a total of some £50,000 (the present-day equivalent of £2,300,000) had already been raised, which says something very praiseworthy about the philanthropic character of the 19th-century Scot.

It was also to say something about the prevalence of Scots throughout the world at that time who, when they heard the news, immediately offered help. Donations poured in from expatriates in Montreal and Moscow, Shanghai and Sydney, from India, South Africa, Switzerland, New Zealand, France and the remote outback regions of Australia. In Scotland itself, most of the money raised was from citizens of Glasgow, who responded magnificently with some £162,224. Again it must be emphasised that this is an absolutely staggering sum, today's equivalent being £7,462,304. Edinburgh and Leith contributed almost £100,000 (£4,600,000) and towns and villages throughout the country responded with similar generosity. It had been speculated when the relief fund was initially launched that around £250,000 (£11,500,500) might be raised. In all some £389,892 was to be received (in today's terms a colossal £17,935, 032).

There had been more than 1,660 shareholders of the bank and between them they had surrendered to the liquidator an incredible £3,250,000 (£149,950,000) of the £5,190,983 (£240,000,000) demanded of them, enabling him to pay out six shillings and eight pence (34p) in the £1 of all claims made prior to December 1878. These were to total around 13,000 claims. The call on the shareholders was made because the bank was not a limited liability company, the onus for any debts falling on those holding its stock. Each was given a demand by the liquidator of £500 (£23,000) for every £100 (£4,600) held by them. The money could be recovered from them by all the customary debt processes (seizure of property, warrant sales, etc.) and it was having to pay this money to the liquidator which had placed so many in need of aid.

Studying the list of those receiving the liquidator's demand makes sorry reading. Many of them lived in inner suburb areas such as Bridgeton and Gorbals, their most meagre incomes supplemented by their small investment. Included were 84 widows, many with young families, and 143 spinsters, 87 of them over the age of 70. One small syndicate was made up of a husband and wife and friends with addresses in Gorbals and Crossmyloof. The rest were a cross-section of the workforce of the day who had put their savings into investments with the bank. Each is listed with his trade or profession, most of them in the type of occupation long since gone from the Glasgow scene: corn factor and portioner, bleacher and coalmaster, candle merchant and measurer, soapmaker and farmer. A total of 1,039 of the shareholders made an application to the relief fund for help, and the fund itself remained active for the next ten years, dispersing the huge sum it had raised and rescuing hundreds (through loans or annuities) from abject poverty and the misery of the poorhouse.

Such was the value of the assistance the loans provided, within ten years some £110,000 (£5,060,000) of the borrowed money had been fully repaid And such was the efficacy with which it was dispersed, not one complaint was received about its distribution. There was no finer demonstration of the administration's efficiency than in its management costs – less than 2 per cent of the total amount received. 'This is a peculiarly bright feature in the record which today ends the story of one of the most painful disasters in the commercial life of Scotland,' commented the *Glasgow Herald* on the flawless management of the fund on the day it was eventually wound up on 3 November 1888.

The closure of the fund brought to an end one of the most exceptional episodes in Scottish life. The painful and humiliating spectacle of the City of Glasgow Bank's collapse had somehow led to a display of unstinting benevolence never before witnessed in the country, and probably never equalled since. As the *Herald* put it: 'Future historians of Glasgow will have few more remarkable events to chronicle than those associated with the history of the City Bank Relief Fund . . .' The disastrous and spectacular failure of the City of Glasgow Bank had seen a few grasping and careless Scots at their very worst. The overwhelming response to the relief fund and the generosity of its donors was to see many, many Scots at their consummate and absolute best.

Selected Bibliography

Miracle, Des Hickey and Gus Smith (Hodder and Stoughton)

The Winning Counter, George Pottinger (Hutchinson)

Encyclopaedia of British Cars, Tony Holmes (Bison Books Ltd)

Death Cometh Soon or Late, J. Mollison (Hutchinson)

Mollison: The Flying Scotsman, David Luff (Scott and Black)

The Tiger Moth Story, Alan Bramson and Neville Birch (Cassell)

Women of the Air, Judy Lomax (John Murray Publishers)

The Scottish Nation, T.M. Devine (The Penguin Press)

Scotland: A Concise History, P. Hume Brown (Longman Group)

Glasgow 1858: Midnight Scenes, John F. McCaffrey (University of Glasgow Press)

The Making of Urban Scotland, Ian H. Adams (McGill-Queens University Press)

History of Banking in Scotland, Andrew William Kerr (A. & C. Black)

The Trial of the Directors of the City of Glasgow Bank, William Wallace (William Hodge & Co.)

City of Glasgow Bank Publications: Special Report of the Trial and Newspaper Cuttings, Mitchell Library Collection

City of Glasgow Bank: Report of the Trial, Charles Tennant Couper, Advocate (Edinburgh Publishing Company)

Prisons and Punishment in Scotland, Joy Cameron (Canongate)

Night Train, The Sonny Liston Story, Nick Tosches (Hamish Hamilton)

Taggart Casebook, Geoff Tibballs (Scottish Television Enterprises)

Taggart's Glasgow, Mark McManus and Glenn Chandler (Lennard Publishing)

L'Osservatore Romano, Catholic Directory

Scotland, Journal of the Chamber of Commerce

Scottish Field

Daily Record
Sunday Mail
Daily Express
Glasgow Herald
Evening Times